Ask the Animals

Ask the Animals

A Vet's-Eye View of Pets and the People They Love

Bruce R. Coston

THOMAS DUNNE BOOKS
ST. MARTIN'S PRESS NEW YORK

THOMAS DUNNE BOOKS.
An imprint of St. Martin's Press.

Printed in the United States of America. For information, address St. Martin's Press, 175 Fifth Avenue, New York, N.Y. 10010.

www.thomasdunnebooks.com
www.stmartins.com

Library of Congress Cataloging-in-Publication Data

Coston, Bruce R.
Ask the animals : a vet's-eye view of pets and the people they love / Bruce R. Coston.—1st ed.
p. cm.
ISBN 978-0-312-38295-7
1. Pets—Anecdotes. 2. Pet owners—Anecdotes 3. Veterinary medicine—Anecdotes. 4. Coston, Bruce R. I. Title.
SF411.5.C67 2009
636.089092—dc22
[B]
2009013472

First Edition: September 2009

10 9 8 7 6 5 4 3 2 1

This book is lovingly dedicated to my wife, Cynthia, and our two boys, Jace and Tucker. I am much indebted to them for their patience with my obsessive devotion to it over the years and for their forbearance at being its unwitting subjects. You are its inspiration. I love you all!

Contents

Acknowledgments

There are innumerable people to be thanked for their assistance in bringing this book to you. Attempting to list them makes certain the reality of missing many whose names should be included here. To those people, I extend equally my apologies for this oversight and my gratitude.

The first ones whose aid cannot be ignored are the pets who are the skeletons of these stories and the people who put flesh on those skeletons. They have provided me unlimited material, characters galore, and such rich examples of the love shared between animals and humans that I continue to be inspired by their devotion and challenged both professionally and personally.

I am deeply indebted to those who saw merit in these stories. To Bobby and Leslie Myers, the original publishers of the *Bryce Mountain Courier*, and to Bernie and Peggy Boston, who later took over its publication, I offer a nod of appreciation for giving these stories room to grow and develop and encouraging me to seek broader audiences for them. Because Bernie is a Pulitzer Prize–winning photographer and journalist, his endorsement came with clarity and credibility. When Art Linkletter, the ageless entertainer, publisher, lecturer, and author of one of the all-time bestselling books (*Kids Say the Darnedest Things*) became enthusiastic about the manuscript, I began to think publication might actually be possible. Thanks to him for encouraging me and agreeing to back this project with his name. Thanks also are due to Joe Wheeler, anthologist and author, whose ringing endorsement of the manuscript came by way of a phone call that crossed two time zones to reach me sometime after midnight, and jerked me awake to the possibility of success. It was also Joe who introduced me to his agent, Greg Johnson of WordServe Literary, who agreed to represent me. Greg and his team have been tireless in their efforts on my behalf.

Without Dr. John Killinger, this manuscript would have ended feet-up in the cage bottom. It was John who took a special interest in the project and introduced the manuscript to his editor; hosted me in New York City at the Marble Collegiate Church where he was pastoring; and risked his literary reputation by personally introducing me to the staff at Thomas Dunne Books. Not that the reputation of someone with as many published titles behind him as John has was ever really at risk. At a time when I thought all hopes for publication had died, John administered the CPR that brought the book back to life.

The wonderful people at Thomas Dunne Books are to be credited for seeing in my work a veiled sculpture in the bare rock. The enthusiasm and vision of Thomas Dunne shaped the direction and development of *Ask the Animals* through several revisions. His exuberant support kept me motivated to continue improving the manuscript. With the skilled application of her editorial hammer and chisel (which sometimes felt like surgery without anesthesia), Ruth Cavin sculpted the raw material to its current form. I am appreciative of her insight, experience, kind words, and encouragement. Ruth's assistant, Toni Plummer, has been a fountain of information and insight into the editorial process and has kept me on task throughout the endeavor. From the copy editors to the publicists and those in the art department, everyone at Thomas Dunne Books has made the process of publication seamless. I am grateful to each professional who worked on this book.

Finally, a big thank-you to my wife, my kids, my parents and in-laws, brother, friends, and members of my staff who continued to believe that *Ask the Animals* would become a reality, despite the overwhelming odds against it. Your support and belief in these simple stories never waned.

Introduction

This book began as monthly newspaper articles in the *Bryce Mountain Courier*, a small, regional newspaper whose founding editor was a client. I began by writing short informational pieces about such compelling topics as flea control, heartworm disease, and the benefits of surgical sterilization that I shamelessly hoped would highlight the services I could provide in my office. They were unbearably dull, but my client dutifully printed them anyway—probably because he didn't quite know how to fire me.

One month, after monotonously writing about most of the quickly identifiable pet health care topics I could think of, I found myself up against a deadline. Out of sheer panic, I wrote a quick story about practice life, planning to correct my literary lapse with the next issue. To my surprise, the response from my clients was amazing. For weeks people told me how much they had enjoyed the story. From that point on, my informational pieces gave way to the more human side of my work, the part that makes my job so rewarding. Since then, there has been no shortage of material.

The stories included in this book are true—pretty much. One of my favorite authors, when asked if his stories were true, responded by saying that he never let the truth get in the way of a good story. I can certainly agree. Though all the events certainly occurred, in places I have changed names and have taken the liberty to rearrange details, invent dialogue, exaggerate personalities, and embellish descriptions. In some cases, I have combined fragments of separate stories to make a cohesive whole. The object of these changes has been to improve the telling of the story, not to belittle or chagrin the subjects. But the medical situations and the outcomes are real and actually occurred in my practice life.

In some ways, I tremble at having people read these stories, especially my colleagues. I certainly hope my veterinary skills will not be judged by the contents of this book. I have recorded the medical cases pretty much as they occurred. They were my best efforts at veterinary care, utilizing the knowledge and equipment available to me at the time, hopefully delivered with compassion for the animals and sensitivity for the client. Some of the patients recovered fully; others did not. Please note that I am not, nor do I claim to be, a specialist in any way. Every day I do my best. And every day I learn things that enable me to perform as a veterinarian better than I did the day before. I guess that's why they call our professional activities practice.

I have sometimes shared the stories in this book with the people involved. Their reactions often surprise me. Some folks just get it and are touched. Others, even those who are portrayed in a positive light, seem a bit put off, not understanding the writer's liberty I have taken with the turn of each story. If you recognize yourself in any of these stories, please forgive me. It just means I have been careless in disguising the events or their participants. My interest is in the story and its telling, and less so for the exact duplication of fact.

I hope you enjoy these stories as much as I have enjoyed recording them. They are the pith and marrow of my life.

Prologue
Within the Fragile Circle

> We who choose to surround ourselves with lives even more temporary than our own live within a fragile circle, easily and often breached. Unable to accept its awful gaps, we still would live no other way. We cherish memory as the only certain immortality, never fully understanding the necessary plan.
>
> —Irving Townsend, *The Once Again Prince*

I could tell Mr. O'Reilly had once been a large man. When he stood up fully straight he looked down on my six-foot-one-inch frame. But Mr. O'Reilly seldom stood up straight anymore. His once muscular and powerful upper body had long since melted here and sagged there until it had transformed itself into an ample and soft midline. Brooding and sad gray eyes hid furtively behind large, horn-rimmed glasses that perched precariously near the tip of his nose. Repeated bouts of barely controlled heart disease were evident in his pale, sallow cheeks and the short-winded, puffing breaths as he walked with stiff-legged and choppy arthritic steps from the waiting room into the examination room. Once there he collapsed with little ceremony onto the corner bench, knotted hands gripping his knees, elbows bowed out, head down, and rocking noticeably with each breath he drew.

I was concerned for him. I could see myself administering cardiopulmonary resuscitation to him on the exam room floor. "Are you all right, Mr. O'Reilly?" I asked.

Between heaving respirations Mr. O'Reilly replied in an apologetic, trembling voice. "I'm not here to get treatment for myself, Doctor." He paused to catch his breath. I certainly hoped he was going somewhere to get treatment for himself. "I'm worried about Cephus."

So absorbed had I been watching his owner's slow progress into the room, I had all but forgotten about my patient, Cephus, who also showed advanced signs of age. He was a ninety pound, mixed-breed, black-and-tan hound of the type seen on old country music television programs. Cephus, like his owner, sported a gray-peppered beard, muzzle, and sideburns. Like his owner, he too panted and wheezed with the effort of navigating the stairs into the hospital and making his way into the exam room.

A quiet cough came from the corner of the room where Cephus and Mr. O'Reilly were sharing, about equally, the corner bench. I had to look closely to tell from which of the two old gentlemen the cough had originated. As I did, though, Cephus hung his head, stretched out his neck, and heaved another quiet, moist cough.

"What's going on with Cephus?" I asked.

Now that Mr. O'Reilly had had a moment to catch his breath he wasn't tugging quite so much for each one, and his conversation was a little less strained. "Hear that cough? That's why I brought him in to see you. He's got the same thing I do, I'm afraid."

I tried to conceal a grimace. That was just what I most feared. "Oh, yeah?" I replied. "What has your doctor found in you, Mr. O'Reilly?"

"Well, they say I have congestive heart failure. I'm on fluid pills now and on some other heart pills that I'm not quite sure what they're for—except to strain my budget." He chuckled a little at this witticism, necessitating a little coughing spell of his own.

"And has all that medicine helped?" I asked hopefully.

Mr. O'Reilly dismissed my question out of hand. "I think what would relieve me the most would be knowing Cephus was going to be okay. Please don't be offended, Dr. Coston, but I already have a doctor. Cephus is the one that needs one right now."

"Of course he is, Mr. O'Reilly," I responded, adequately chastised. "How long has he been coughing like that?"

"Oh, it's been getting worse and worse over the last two or three weeks. It's worse at night when he's just resting. He doesn't mean to, but he's been keeping me up at night and that frustrates my lady friend."

Altogether too quickly I snapped my head up from making notes in the record. Mr. O'Reilly hadn't struck me as the playboy type, but there it was. The thought that immediately ran through my mind was, "You devil!" But I was able to quash my impulse to say it. Noticing my amusement, he hastened to clarify.

"No, no, Doctor! It's not what you think!" He chuckled again, a little embarrassed. "When I don't get my rest, I tend to nod off while she's talking to me. For some reason that seems to annoy her."

"Oh, I see." I laughed. "Is Cephus as active as usual now?"

"Heavens, no. He just lays around and pants. And when he does try to come on a walk, he tires out even before we make it to the mailbox."

"Let's take a look at the old fella, Mr. O'Reilly." I crouched down to Cephus's level.

He turned his attention to Cephus who responded with a distracted wag of his tail. "Come here, old boy," he said affectionately. "Dr. Coston wants to look at you."

I lifted Cephus onto the examination table with effort, knowing full well my weak back shouldn't be called on to lift that much. Even with this minimal stress, Cephus's panting worsened dramatically, mouth open and eyes staring ahead anxiously. I lifted his lip and noted his pale, grayish blue gums. He barely reacted to my hands in his mouth, concentrating instead on the wall in front of him and the effort of the next breath. I pointed his nose at the ceiling and looked at his neck. His jugular veins stood out prominently on both sides like supporting pillars, and with each heartbeat a pulsating wave climbed them from bottom to top, not a good sign.

I placed my stethoscope against the great chest and listened intently. The heart rate was racing at about two hundred beats per minute. Even more ominous was the rhythm. Instead of the even, steady rhythm of the normal heart, I heard a random cacophony of independent beats, like a hundred people applauding slowly without organization or purpose. I suspected an abnormality of heart rhythm called atrial fibrillation that, in the dog, is usually an indicator that heart disease is approaching its end stages. It was a grim finding and I drew in a deep sigh.

The remainder of the examination was anticlimactic. Everything was consistent with the diagnosis of congestive heart failure and functional deterioration of the heart. The pulses were weak and thready. Fluid was building up in the lungs. And the decreased circulation to the limbs was causing a swelling of the lower legs. Cephus had apparently read all the textbooks. With resignation I stood up and faced Mr. O'Reilly. He had already read my face.

"It's not good, is it?" he said simply.

"Unfortunately it isn't," I replied, not wanting to encourage any false hopes. "Cephus has fairly advanced heart disease. There is quite a lot of fluid leakage into his lungs. That's one of the reasons he's tugging so hard to breathe. He also has a dramatically abnormal heart rhythm. I need to do an electrocardiogram to determine exactly how bad the abnormal rhythm is. We also need to do chest X-rays to look at the heart and the lungs. Then—"

Mr. O'Reilly interrupted me abruptly. "Doctor, I know you need all that information. But I don't think I can afford to do all that. I wasn't kidding about how expensive my medications are." He put his head in his hands and was quiet for a moment. Then, eyes red and swimming, he looked up at me with anguish etched on his face. "Do you think we should just let him go?"

And there it was. The nemesis of all veterinarians had interjected itself into my professional passion once again. Every day in veterinary hospitals across the country decisions turn, not on the basis of prognosis or intractable animal suffering, but on financial factors. These decisions result in the loss of dear and treasured friends, leave families with tattered emotions, and present a professional and personal dilemma to caring and capable veterinarians. Every vet knows well the heartache of edging a pet into eternity fully aware that with their knowledge and skill the animal could be successfully treated and returned to the family that loves it.

For a few owners the decision is obviously one of simple convenience. When given the option of treating the pet or spending the weekend at the ski resort, they have no hesitancy to put their adoring companion to death, justifying their decision by asserting loudly that it would be unfair to the pet to put it through any more discomfort. Most, however, are caring and committed to their pet and suffer untold pain and guilt when honest financial constraints prevent them from providing lifesaving care. In Mr. O'Reilly's case, it was obvious that he was experiencing this quandary.

In an ideal universe, veterinarians could provide care to all animals regardless of the owner's ability to pay. How much would it take, after all, to snap some X-rays of this patient or repair a fractured leg on that one? But given the realities of practice life—the economics of stocking the shelves, paying the staff, keeping the lights and water on, while at the same time trying to keep costs down as much as possible—altruism unfortunately cannot be routinely indulged.

Even so, I know of few vets who can completely resist charity work. But if that were the norm, we would be forced to close our doors. With no social safety net for animals, it is simply impossible for veterinary practitioners to assume the entire burden of care for these cases. For veterinarians, who almost universally have entered the profession with lofty and selfless motivation, this lesson is a difficult one to learn, and harder still to practice. But learn it we must.

"If it's at all possible for you, will you at least let me do an electrocardiogram? Honestly, we may not be able to do much, but I won't know until I get a little bit more information."

"Well, Doctor, you know that I want to try if it's at all possible. But you know I may not be able to pay it all at once. Is that okay?" Mr. O'Reilly plied me with a questioning look that nearly broke my heart.

"That's not a problem. I'm sure we can work out something." I lifted Cephus down from the table and led him slowly into the treatment room. There I hooked him up to my electrocardiographic monitor and held my breath as I looked at the screen. The pattern that I saw made my stomach lurch.

Leaving Cephus in the care of the technicians, I returned to the examination room where Mr. O'Reilly was pacing nervously. As I entered he was wringing his hands with anxiety, his face the picture of internal torment. He caught sight of my expression and sank into the corner bench again.

"It isn't good, is it?"

"No, I'm afraid it isn't. As I suspected, the heart is in an abnormal rhythm pattern called atrial fibrillation. It is a symptom of severe heart disease and usually indicates disease that is fairly well progressed." I watched his face carefully for how he was taking the news. "We can try medications to normalize the heart rhythm, but we would still need to figure out what the underlying heart problem is. That would require X-rays, an ultrasound of the heart, and most likely some blood work."

"That's expensive, isn't it?"

"Unfortunately it is."

He agonized for a moment. "But, Dr. Coston, if you could tell me that it would make him better, I'd find a way to pay for the tests somehow. Will it make him better?"

"I can't promise you that. Overall I think the chances for good response to medications is fairly guarded. Chances are that the heart is just too badly damaged already."

I watched the glint of hope in Mr. O'Reilly's eyes vanish, his face given over now entirely to clouds of grief. He was quiet for a while. Then his head sunk down again on his hands and his shoulders began to quiver. I went over to him and placed an arm around his shoulders, my own eyes filling. Both of us needed a tissue from the box that I slid across the table to him.

"He's been such a great friend to me, Doctor. I'm going to miss him a great deal," he offered between quiet sobs.

"I know how much you loved him, Mr. O'Reilly." It was blatantly obvious to me. "You gave him a great life. I know this is difficult for you."

He turned tear-streaked cheeks up to me with an earnest question in his red eyes. "Am I doing the right thing for Cephus, Dr. Coston?"

Sometimes the most important thing I can do for a client is to validate an incredibly difficult decision. In this case, even though diagnostics and treatments were theoretically available, the likelihood that they would provide a successful outcome was very low. "I think, if he could, Cephus would thank you for easing his passing, Mr. O'Reilly."

He took a deep, courageous breath and let it out slowly, not quite hiding the catches in it as it escaped him. "Then will you please do it right away?"

"Yes, of course."

"He's been with me through some pretty tough times. If you don't mind, I would like to be there for him during this one. It's the least I can do for him."

"That would be just fine. I'll go get everything prepared. My technician will bring him in and you can spend a little time with him." I turned and left to fill a syringe with the solution that would finally let Cephus sleep peacefully. But before I could get the door closed behind me, I heard Mr. O'Reilly quietly call my name. I turned to face him again.

"Thank you so much for what you've done."

I couldn't respond. Closing the door, I headed down the hallway to the treatment room, fighting unsuccessfully the large lump that was forming and rolling around slowly in my throat.

My sadness was not for Cephus. Soon he would be resting

and comfortable after a long fight for each breath. No, my sadness was for the kind, softhearted gentleman in that room roiling with overwhelming grief at the decision he was making. Though he had three or four other dogs and a cat or two at home, these friends comprised his whole world. The absence of one of them would be a heavy blow to the makeup of his home. It would take a long time for him to recover from this loss.

As Mr. O'Reilly, tears streaming unbridled down his cheeks, cradled Cephus's big head in his arms, I slipped the needle into the vein in a front leg. Cephus continued to tug and struggle for each breath until the effects of the drug began to ease his tension. Gently the eyes closed and, almost with relief, he sighed deeply and drifted into a peaceful sleep. Mr. O'Reilly pressed his forehead against Cephus's noble one and moaned quietly. The loss was palpable in the room and my tears joined his.

It was the ultimate picture of bonding. It represented years of constant devotion, an unequaled depth of understanding borne of countless hours together. It evoked images of long winter evenings spent with aged fingers endlessly tracing the lines of a graceful face that rested lovingly on a lap. It was reminiscent of many a fall afternoon when the two of them, accompanied by the rest of the canine crew, explored the wildness of the woods around Mr. O'Reilly's secluded house. It encapsulated all the daily partings and reunions of a lifetime of sharing. It was indeed the essence of what it is that makes our pets so important to us.

Irving Townsend in his book *The Once Again Prince* had it just right. We do indeed live within a fragile circle. And what an all-encompassing circle it is! A circle woven from the very fibers of the bond I witnessed that day between Mr. O'Reilly and his grand and noble dog, Cephus. It is my pride and passion to be the mender of those gossamer fibers; to patch soul and sinew with science and sensitivity the fraying strands of the web. No other calling for me could equal this mission. For it affords me the awesome privilege and responsibility of spending my days within the fragile circle.

I've Not Forgotten

The morning dawned clear and bright, unusual for the first day in May in southern Tennessee where steamy rain is so common. Somehow it seemed appropriate for the day to be as bright as my spirits, which were riding high in anticipation of a day for which I had worked so long. I was graduating from college. And I was going out in style! I had recently received, at the annual awards ceremony, the outstanding senior award from the biology department, a great honor from my biology professors. The speech I had written and rehearsed, which it was my honor to give as senior class president, was ready for the ceremony. My proud parents, who had attended this very college not quite two decades previously, had arrived for graduation weekend, the first time they had been on campus since I had started school four years earlier. I had managed, through grit, determination, and hard work where natural ability had not sufficed, to pull down grades good enough to earn a cum laude sash that would ornament my graduation regalia. Nothing could make this day better!

Well, that wasn't quite true, if I was honest with myself. Two pieces of business seemed unfinished for me that day. Both, in my mind, were huge, life-defining issues that I had not yet nailed down. And try as I might, they still clouded just a bit the celebration of the day.

First was the little issue of my career. For me, the goal of becoming a veterinarian had not been what it so often is for many young people: an impulsive, poorly understood, and naïve phase of passing fancy. Not at all! Sure, it started that way when I was seven or eight. I felt certain still that my career path had been ordained at birth. But I had spent a great deal of time and energy in developing that interest. I had spent a couple of years working for a veterinarian in high school. I had devoted many summers at summer camps working with horses, my first love. Knowing the difficulty of gaining admittance into veterinary school, I had committed myself to my studies in both high school and college, earning very respectable grades. I had studied for, and done well in, both the Veterinary Aptitude Test and the Graduate Record Exam, tests that would figure prominently in whether or not my application would be given serious consideration by the admissions committee. I had left no stone unturned. I've since discovered that for most of us veterinarians, the realization of our future vocation is less a decision than it is an acceptance of a calling, a calling that to pursue demands a great deal of such sacrifices.

Getting into veterinary school is extremely difficult. This is so because, with so few veterinary schools in the country, the competition for each spot in each class is keen, and schools have the luxury of being extremely discriminating about whom they admit. Many states that don't have a veterinary school enter into formal agreements with states that do to admit a certain number of their resident students. If your state does have a school, the chances of being accepted into another state's school are quite low. Nonetheless, many astute applicants hedge their bets by applying to several veterinary schools. Apparently, I was not an astute applicant. I had placed no such hedge bets and applied only to the University of Minnesota College of Veterinary Medicine, my resident state school.

And now here it was graduation day in May, and despite my

good grades, excellent test results, awards and accolades, I had still not received my letter of acceptance. This was a problem for me because the notion that I may not be accepted into veterinary school had never entered my mind until the week before graduation. To be clear, it was not that I was so arrogant as to assume my acceptance was assured. Far from it. I knew the difficulty. It was just that I had never allowed any negative thoughts to dampen my aspirations. But in so doing, I had also failed to plan any alternative should that acceptance letter not arrive. What does one do with a degree in biology to earn a living after college anyway? For me, my degree had always been just a necessary step in my plan. It had never been an end in itself. At least not until about the last week or so of school when each day failed to bring a letter from the University of Minnesota College of Veterinary Medicine. But in that last week, I noted a rising level of discomfort about my insecure future that crescendoed into sheer panic by about Thursday.

What would I do if I didn't make it into school? I had no idea, no plan. Even then I knew I would not desert my goal of being a veterinarian. I would step back, take stock, and do some specific things to make myself more competitive for my next application. Perhaps I would go on and get a master's degree. I knew that as many as a third or more of most classes had advanced degrees. I could do that too. But I had not applied to graduate school either; never thought I'd need to. Maybe I could get a temporary, one-year stint at some job to pass the time for a while.

With these scary thoughts swirling in my head during my last college test week, my ears perked up when, at the cafeteria on that Thursday, one of my classmates mentioned that his father, the principal of a school in California, was in dire need of a science teacher. It had to be dire for him to consider me, with no training at all in education, no student teaching, no licensing. Yet, strangely, these thoughts did nothing to dissuade me from considering this option. That might work, I thought. I could spend a year at the front of a classroom instead of behind a desk while I formulated my next move. So, with a good recommendation from his son, the principal and I had set up an interview in his son's dorm room for two o'clock on the afternoon of graduation day. It was an appointment I could generate little enthusiasm for, to be sure, but at least I had a backup plan and that went far in relieving some of my uneasiness heading into graduation weekend.

The other issue was more complicated. I had been so focused in college on setting the stage for my lifework that I had put off thoughts of a life partner. Not that I didn't have prospects. I just didn't allow such things to distract me from my primary goal of getting good enough grades to get into school.

But there was Cynthia! Cynthia was a young woman who had first caught my eye during my sophomore year. I remember well the first time I saw her. One of my distractions from my studies during college was singing in a male chorus, Die Meistersinger. Few things can produce such rich, interlocking harmonies as the perfectly blended voices of thirty men. During my sophomore year, as the Christmas concert approached, Die Meistersinger held a rehearsal in the venue where the concert would be staged. As rehearsal began, I noticed a beautiful girl with auburn hair, a ready smile, and dancing eyes struggling to remove from the stage an ornate harp that towered over her short frame. Surely, our director, Dr. Roberts, suggested, there was, among thirty men, a gentleman or two that would be willing to help this poor girl move her heavy harp. Little did I know at the time, that the damsel in distress was his niece, a senior at the local high school, who lived in his house.

I was one of three men that came to her aid. But I was not the first one to reach her. In fact, two other men nearly vaulted over chairs to be the first one there. Both of them, rather bumbling and overbearing, were clearly vying for her attention. I was quite amused by their obvious fawning over her as the two of them awkwardly fumbled in tandem to accomplish a one-man job. Though my assistance was not really needed, I went along anyway to watch with amusement the two of them display to her, like preening birds of paradise. I was certainly not doing the same thing, you understand. Though she was undeniably gorgeous, I gave little thought to her beyond my amusement with the exhibitions of the other guys. She was too young for me, anyway. She was just in high school, after all. I was halfway through college. It was not until later that I learned Cynthia had gone back to her uncle's house that night and announced that she was going to marry Bruce Coston and have blond, curly-haired babies.

Early the next semester, Dr. Roberts, mentioned casually while standing at the urinal next to me, that he knew of a girl that might like to get to know me. And that's when Cynthia really came up on my radar screen. The next year, we went out for the first time to a banquet at which my male quartet sang and she played her harp. This required me to once again move her harp, a job that has been mine since the first time I saw her. I had a good time during the date, but was too focused on my studies to recognize that this girl had her eye on me.

That summer, though, things took a decidedly different turn. The male chorus was scheduled to tour Russia and Romania, quite a thrill for my young American heart in 1982 during the height of the cold war. Cynthia was invited by Dr. Roberts to come along as the female vocal soloist. During that two-week trip, Cynthia and I spent all of our time together. I have many memories of the amazing things we saw in Moscow, Leningrad (now Saint Petersburg), Riga, and Bucharest, but my most enduring memories of that trip are the times when Cynthia and I were huddled down in our seats on the bus engaged in deep and earnest conversations or laughing uproariously at some inside joke.

She had such an amazing giggle that just seemed to bubble out of her toes, enticing in its honesty and spontaneity. And her eyes. They just seemed to look right into me. And what she saw there, surprisingly, did not deter her. In fact, those incredible eyes reflected back the most amazing trust and confidence and warmth. I loved that music was important to her. Her musical talents far outshone my own, of course. She was a skilled harpist, pianist, tympanist, and vocalist; I merely sang. But our music was a touchstone that we could share forever. Her wit was keen, edged with an uncommon combination of innocence and cynicism. Not to mention that she thought I was funny too—and what's more irresistible than that? Both of us were serious about and committed to our religious heritage and spiritual journeys, which provided us a foundation of understanding that grounds us still. I fell in love with Cynthia in Russia. Our first kiss was in Bucharest in the stairwell of the Hotel Internationale.

I remember in the plane on the way back across the Atlantic, we spoke of the future, of how we envisioned our lives would unfold. It seemed idyllic. Cynthia's major was office administration so she could support her music hobby, and that fit perfectly with my vision of one day owning and operating my own hospital. We would make music together. I would carry her harp. We would have blond, curly-haired babies.

Upon our return, I immediately headed west for the summer camp in Alberta, Canada, where I was in charge of the horsemanship program. Cynthia returned home to Georgia where she faithfully wrote me a letter several times a week. I immersed myself in the activities of camp. I loved getting Cynthia's letters, but must admit to writing no more than three or four letters back the entire summer.

When school started in the fall, I was pleased to discover that Cynthia would be the pianist for both Die Meistersinger and the Southernaires Quartet in which I was the baritone. This meant that we would be on tour at least two or three weekends of every month—more time to spend together. As the fall semester progressed, however, and I once again dove into the all-consuming work of continuing my academic pursuits toward veterinary school, an alarming realization began to dawn on me. I began to see in Cynthia's eyes a reality that was becoming more clear for her each day. Cynthia loved me, and she loved me for the long term. This should have come as no surprise for me. I loved her too. But the weight of knowing that she might really be *the* one generated in me an alarming sense of finality that is common to the male psyche.

And, though I am not proud of it now, I did what many a red-blooded American college man does when he realizes that a beautiful girl has long-term plans for him. I fled. Just a few weeks into the year, I broke up with Cynthia while sitting on the brick wall in the promenade late one Friday evening. I remember with regret the feeling as her hand went limp and cold in mine as the intent of my conversation struck her. I remember the set of the jaw and the fierce control of her features as we parted that night. The effect of my self-centered fears on her tender heart remains one of the deepest regrets of my life to this day. The scars of that night still haunt and still bite. It wasn't because I didn't love her; I did. And if I could explain on behalf of all men the fear that thoughts of forever somehow evoke in our hearts, it would still not excuse the pain I brought her that night; nor would it erase the memories of a broken heart.

Still, with our commitments to Die Meistersinger and Southernaires Quartet, we spent a great deal of time together during my senior year in college. Though we weren't officially dating, our friendship and understanding of each other deepened. We still often engaged in deep and personal conversations of great significance to both of us. We shared fun times and inside jokes. Throughout the remainder of the year my heart still skipped a few beats when I would hear her laugh in just that certain way or see the unmistakable message in her transparent eyes. Somehow, despite the trauma I had inflicted upon her, she still allowed me close enough to maintain an emotional intimacy that unnerved me. In an effort to keep her at arm's length, I started dating Lucy; whose laugh annoyed everyone in the quartet (including me) so much that they were relieved when I would take her to the back of the van and keep her mouth otherwise occupied. But truly, my heart just wasn't in it, and it lasted only a few weeks. Cynthia and I remained such close friends throughout my senior year that most of the men at school who wanted to ask her out assumed she was taken and didn't. This, frankly, suited me just fine.

So entering into graduation weekend there remained this tension of unfinished business with Cynthia. Immediately after graduation weekend, my plan was to spend two weeks in the Boundary Waters Canoe Area Wilderness in northern Minnesota with Tim, one of my best friends. From there, I was headed back to Alberta, Canada, and another summer in the horse barn at camp. Cynthia's plan was to move to Atlanta and find work there. Graduation weekend was shaping up to be our final good-bye. The angst this generated in my heart took me off guard.

The graduation ceremony was truly a high point in my life. As the president of the class, I marched into the auditorium first and turned to face my classmates as they marched down the aisle. As each of my friends came past, my mind relived the good times we had shared in school. It was a bit awkward as Lucy came by in her nursing regalia, though we did manage a smile and a mutual good luck wish. But as Cynthia came down the aisle, I was transfixed. I watched her the whole way, mouth alive with her four-lane smile as she acknowledged her family and connected with friends. Then our eyes met and held, hers with such resolute conviction of feeling, mine with emotions that I still couldn't sort out. And then she was past me, possibly forever out of reach. I gave a perfunctory speech with little to distinguish it. And then we graduates were out on the lawn, throwing our caps, extending and receiving congratulations, and saying our good-byes.

Afterward, still flush with accomplishment, I made my way to the dorm to change for a meal with my family and a few friends. As I passed the front desk, I noticed some envelopes in my mailbox. I dialed in my combination and pulled out three envelopes, sorting through them as I walked to my room. Two were junk mail, of course. But the third was rather thick and bore the logo of the University of Minnesota College of Veterinary Medicine in the return address corner. I stopped in my tracks, sucking in an apprehensive gulp of air. I was too afraid to open it immediately, setting it instead on the dresser in my room where, like an unexploded grenade, it occupied a huge place in my consciousness as I changed. Finally, I stuck it unopened in my pocket and went to meet my family at the restaurant.

After we ate, those around the table began handing me cards and gifts for graduation. I opened them one by one and extended my thanks to each person. But my mind kept coming back to the envelope burning a hole in my pocket. After all the cards were opened, I pulled it from my pocket.

"I have one more graduation card that came in the mail just today," I said. "This one is from the University of Minnesota."

With trembling fingers I tore the envelope open and took the folded papers from inside. I closed my eyes and unfolded the letter, sending a prayer up as I did so. Starting at the very top, I read the letter aloud. "Dear Bruce, We are pleased to inform you . . ."

Immediately a raucous cheer rose from everyone at the table, interrupting the diners around us who looked up with a mixture of curiosity and annoyance. My mother proudly announced to them, "It's a big day for him. Today he graduated from college and has just been accepted into veterinary school."

The whole restaurant erupted in applause. I could hardly hear them. My head was buzzing. I tried to look down at the letter again, but my eyes were blurring. I just couldn't believe it!

Back at the dorm, I raced up to my friend's room where I was to interview with his father for the teaching job in California. The principal was waiting for me there, a little sternly it seemed since I was fifteen minutes late. With excessive exuberance I informed him that I wouldn't be needing the teaching job since I had just gotten my acceptance letter into veterinary school. He was very gracious.

I wanted to tell Dr. Carter next. He had been my favorite professor in the biology department and we had developed quite a close friendship. He had the ability to challenge me academically, mentor me in my scientific development, and still connect with me on a personal level too. He would be excited for me, I knew.

I jumped into my car to try and find him. Driving my car in college was something I did only in the most serious of necessities. In a unique strategy designed to limit excessive dating, my parents had purchased a car for me that was guaranteed to minimize the number of girls who would agree to go out in it. It was a lovely three-toned beauty, sporting green, black, and rust (the oxidation, not the color). A 1970 model Oldsmobile Delta 88 with a landau vinyl roof and no muffler, it could be heard long before it could be seen. I had become accustomed to driving onto campus as the center of attention in my chick-magnet land yacht.

It truly was a great car for college. It was so large, with two five-foot bench seats, that it could comfortably fit almost all of my friends and their dates. On one particular Saturday night, two friends and I drove it around the campus and, one by one, stopped random students, some of them completely unknown to us, lured them to the car and pulled them in through the open windows. We were able to capture fourteen people that way, cramming them in sarcophaguslike until a girl I did not know at the bottom of the pile became claustrophobic and began to scream and fuss. No charges were filed.

The Delta 88 was also completely reliable. The only time it did not run was once immediately after I tried to tune it up, a circumstance that confirmed the fact that I was not equipped to make my living as a mechanic. I was pulling for a new car as my graduation gift.

I drove to the biology building and walked the halls. Dr. Carter wasn't there. I drove to the cemetery where the graveside service for a retired professor was just concluding. My approach to the cemetery, complete with the low frequency rumble of my car, was not exactly welcomed or appropriate, earning me dirty glares from many in the funeral party. Though Dr. Carter was not among them, several of my other professors were there. But it seemed an incongruous, and now an unwelcome, place to celebrate my news. As I drove around the back side of campus again, Dr. Carter passed me in his car going the opposite direction, casting fearful glances around for the source of the tugboatlike sounds that he was sure was placing him in mortal danger. It was my Delta 88. I honked, yanked the steering wheel, performed a perfect three-point U-turn, and chased him down, lights flashing. He pulled over and I flew at him like someone bent on revenge. He was thrilled at my news, though I think he was a little disappointed that I would not be following his suggestion that I pursue a doctorate in paleontology.

By five o'clock that evening, my mind had begun to calm a little and get used to the reality that I would be entering vet school in the fall. I still had one more person to share my news with. Cynthia and I had an appointment to meet in the music building at that time. I had agreed to sing at the wedding of one of my friends the next day and had asked Cynthia to accompany me. With all the activities of the weekend we had not yet been able to rehearse the song, so we had set up this appointment to practice. I entered the music building with an odd blend of emotions. There are few times when a university building feels so empty as the afternoon of graduation day. There were no professors present; no students blowing horns in the practice rooms. There were not even any secretaries tapping away at typewriters in the office; no phones ringing. I was alone in this quiet building where I had spent so much time rehearsing with the male chorus and with Southernaires Quartet. It contained a great many nostalgic memories for me as I walked the empty halls looking for Cynthia and thinking through the four years in this building and the events of the day.

Well, I was not quite alone. I knew Cynthia was in the building. Though I could neither see nor hear her, the wonderful aroma of her signature perfume hung powerfully in the air. It didn't seem right, though, to call out to her in these hallowed halls. It seemed somehow irreverent to break the silence, so I continued to turn down empty hallways following Cynthia's fragrance. She must have been doing the same, because we both turned a corner at the same time and found ourselves at opposite ends of a long hallway. She saw me and immediately began to run toward me, launching herself into my arms when we met; me twirling her around with her feet off the floor and her cheek on my shoulder. We embraced there in that quiet hallway for a long time. Nothing seemed more natural or appropriate.

With unbridled excitement I shared my news with her. She was appropriately happy for me. She had wonderful news as well. Her parents had given her a car for graduation, a red Toyota Corolla five-door hatchback with white striping on the sides highlighting its sporty lines. I, on the other hand, had gotten a used TRS-80 computer with an amazing 512 kilobytes of random access memory, which I could use only by hooking it up to a black-and-white television set. This I considered a true necessity for me since I had just completed a computer class where I had learned to write astonishingly useful computer programs in bASIC with which I could make the simple task of balancing my checkbook considerably longer and more complicated. But at least I could conveniently save my data by using a tabletop cassette tape player.

The next evening after the wedding, Cynthia and I sat in her new car in the parking lot of the church. Surprisingly, she had not wanted to take my car. The stars were bright, the moon full. All the wedding party and guests had long since left for the reception. But Cynthia and I couldn't seem to leave. After tonight, I would be going north to Canada and Minnesota; she south to Atlanta. It all came down to this night in this parking lot. I was at a loss for words, still conflicted.

She turned to me, her face lit in the moonlight, but shadowed by deep emotion. Handing me a gift bag, she said, "Bruce, I have something for you."

I removed two gracious brass bookends from the bag and looked back at Cynthia. Tears were welling in her eyes.

"I want you to remember me next year while you study. More than that, I want you to remember me all the time; while you eat breakfast, and between classes; when you play racquetball; when you go to church. I want you to remember my smile and our talks. Don't forget what we've shared. You've been my best friend. You know you have my heart, don't you? So don't forget." Her head nodded and she swallowed hard. But she didn't wipe the tears that were now making wet trails down her cheeks.

My heart was Jell-O, conflicted no more. I lifted her chin with my hand. Her eyes searched mine. I kissed her gently. Her lips were soft and pouting. I felt the wetness of her tears on my lips. How is it possible for the bucket seats of a manual transmission Corolla in the empty parking lot of a church to be romantic? But that night, that car, those cries for me to remember, that kiss—it all remains the most romantic moment of my life. For in those few minutes, I realized that I would not forget—not ever—this moment, this moonlight on her face. And I knew that I would never allow Cynthia to slip from my life.

The next day was May 3, Cynthia's birthday. As I drove out of town, my parents following me in their car, I impulsively turned into the parking lot of a florist whose sign had caught my eye. Inside I handed them a twenty-dollar bill, the only money in my wallet, and asked them to send as many red roses to Cynthia as twenty dollars would buy. On the card for those five red roses, I wrote three simple words that I knew she would understand. Even now, on birthdays, anniversaries, or just on some random day, I will send Cynthia five red roses. The note is always the same. "I've not forgotten." And I still haven't.

Myself the More

Mine, and mine the more.
But still yourself.
And I, new and yet the same,
Am myself the more.
You and I. We became us; became me.
We still ourselves remain; but one the same

And when alone I face my world,
Two times the strength I feel, twice the purpose.
Your smile and mine, the two entwine
Quiet on my lips and kiss.
And they, the one smile, are mine.
Ah yes, mine and mine the more.

—*Bruce Coston*

We drove north out of Tennessee on the Tuesday afternoon after graduation; me in my Delta 88 and my parents following in their maroon Peugeot, both loaded down with the contents of my dorm room. I drove with my windows down since my old car was not equipped with air-conditioning, letting the rush of the warm May air blow the confusion from my mind. The radio was on, but I didn't really hear it. I was replaying the events of the previous weekend: graduation, the letter of acceptance to vet school, my evening with Cynthia. Each event required my full attention to thoroughly process. It was a good thing that the drive lasted many hours.

I was a bit too distracted with my mental meanderings, perhaps, because somewhere in southern Virginia, while navigating a sharp right-hand turn on a two-lane road, I crossed the yellow line and veered into oncoming traffic. My mind snapped to in just enough time to narrowly avoid a full head-on collision. The resulting contact with the car was so slight that I heard the staccato crunch of metal, but felt no impact. The bumper of the oncoming car had connected with the back side of my front wheel well, which peeled the metal from there back to the door panel in an intricate scroll of rusty green metal, like a chiseled filigree, which remained as a reminder of that mental lapse until the day I gave the car away two or three years later. I drove more carefully after that and we arrived back home safely, though not without increased insurance rates.

One of the things I was looking forward to when I got back home was seeing my dog, PC, again. I had gotten PC during the winter of my junior year in high school. He had been so small, and the Minnesota winter had been so brutal, that house-training him brought with it unique challenges. Unable to simply let him outside to relieve himself for fear he would freeze solid in the yard with his little leg raised against a post, I would instead place him on the front porch for the thirty seconds it would take him to pee or poop. Even with that limited exposure, his little five-pound frame would be shivering compulsively before I scooped him up and brought him back inside. This method of house-training, as you can imagine, was very inefficient and produced less than stellar results. Thus the origin of the name PC. It has often been assumed this moniker meant politically correct. But in reality, beside the fact that the term had not yet been coined, there was absolutely nothing politically correct about PC. It really stood for partly cloudy since there was always at least a 60 percent chance of precipitation in the house.

PC holds a special place of honor or infamy (depending on your perspective) in the family lore. I loved him dearly and we shared a deep and special bond. My parents, on the other hand, despised him. He was of the Arctic persuasion as far as breeds go, though no one would confuse him with a purebred. He had the coat of a malamute, the coloration of a mutt, the curled tail of a chow, and the sharp nose of a husky. I thought he was beautiful. He displayed intelligence that was unusual for a dog; an intellect that required significant and constant stimulation in order to prevent it from manifesting itself as destructive or compulsive behavior.

At the time I got PC, I worked part time for a mixed animal veterinarian named Dr. Virgil Boyd. As a fringe benefit for me, Dr. Boyd offered to perform PC's neuter free of charge. I would have none of it. I often find this to be true of my male clients with their male dogs; an illogical, emotional gut reaction to the thought of surgically removing their dog's testicles. Women generally do not have the slightest hesitancy about the procedure. But men frequently behave as if they would personally experience every physical sensation and psychological trauma their dog might undergo if the surgery was performed, as if they shared their dog's testicles. I know this to be true, because that was my initial instinct. The upshot of this thinking, however, ended up to be not in PC's best interest. Because he was not neutered before his hormonally controlled behaviors had become habitual, those behaviors were not curbed when I finally agreed to have him neutered when he was about a year and a half old.

He was, for instance, a roamer. If not tied up, he would leave our home, which was about a mile outside of town, and wander into our little hamlet of Hutchinson. He knew the rounds, where all the cute girlie dogs were and when they would be in heat. And he followed his nose and his instincts in completing his rounds on a regular basis. Apparently he had had enough interactions with the police and with the animal control officers to know that they were to be avoided at all costs. It became fairly routine for me to receive a call from an officer telling me that PC was wandering the streets again and that if I didn't go pick him up in the vicinity of Cherry and Fourth Avenue, I would be issued a citation. I would drive to the area and invariably find him trotting along, often trailing a portion of the rope that should have kept him tied. He was always ecstatic to see me, wagging his entire south end from the shoulders back and greeting me with enthusiasm as if to say, "Oh, I'm so glad you decided to come along with me today. Let's go! I know where there's a really hot little number." He never hesitated to jump into my car; never resented the trip home. But neither did he show the slightest remorse, despite many a heartfelt discussion between us about the dangers of cars, the risk of capture at the hands of the dog wardens, or the extent to which such behavior would force my hand at developing more successful means of future confinement.

Because he was so committed to wanderlust, I tried virtually everything I could think of to prevent it. He became a master at thwarting my every effort. If I chained him to the wooden doghouse I had constructed out of the odd pieces of lumber left over from the construction of our new house, he would get free either by slipping out of the collar, detaching the snap that connected the chain to his collar, or, by unhooking the chain from the doghouse and dragging its entire length on his roustabouts. I took to confining him in our garage, but found that he either managed somehow to activate the automatic garage door opener or scratch violently at the door into the house. On more than one occasion, he destroyed the wooden door frame, chewing at it until it was splintered and ruined, behaviors that did nothing to bolster his standing with my parents. Outdoor kennels were inadequate to hold him for a single morning. He would either dig out of them or scale them like a rock climber.

Once he was fully house-trained, I would as often as possible leave him in the house. This bored him to distraction and resulted in any number of acts of malfeasance. My schedule for my junior and senior years in high school was that I would work from seven till eleven every morning. I would then come home, shower and change for my afternoon classes. At that time, my father sported a toupee that he was very particular about. One morning I returned from work at eleven fifteen to find my father storming around the house, grousing in no uncertain terms about the egregious behavior of the dog. PC was pleased to see me, of course. But I quickly noticed that he steered clear of my father, who continued to stomp angrily around. I thought it strange that Dad was still at the house at this hour, still not completely dressed, and without his hair in place.

"If you don't do something about that stupid dog, he's gonna have to go. This can't happen again."

"What's wrong, Dad? Why are you so steamed?"

"That stupid puppy has taken my hair and I can't find it," he virtually screamed at me. "I've already missed two appointments. You know I can't leave the house without my hair."

Prior to getting PC, my dad had developed a protocol for washing his hair. He would shampoo it in the sink, then, like tanning a hide, would drape it over a head-shaped bowl before placing it in front of one of the heat registers to dry. Apparently that fateful morning, PC in his boredom had come upon this irresistible prey, had stalked it carefully, and taken the kill off to share with his pack. When I returned he led me, with obvious pride and delight, into my closet where he had buried the kill under a pile of dirty clothes. Dad was apoplectic. His hair now smelled like a locker room and he had to wash it again before he could leave the house. PC was confused and angry and kept circling Dad as if to take back what was rightfully his. If Dad wanted one, he should have gone out and killed his own.

PC extended his kleptomaniacal tendencies to his entire territory, which consisted of our yard and the eight or ten houses that made up our small neighborhood. Our neighbors were extremely long-suffering, but eventually PC became the target of a neighborhood watch sting operation. This was necessary because PC found it irresistible to peruse the contents of any space rendered accessible by open doors. Not only did he scope out those spaces, but he also considered it his responsibility to bring whatever items he found to his liking back to our house. It was not unusual for a neighbor to stop in at odd hours requesting us to check on the whereabouts of items that had forsaken the climes of their garages or outbuildings. We would invariably find the damning evidence of PC's capers in his doghouse or in our garage covered with slobber and tooth marks. Over the course of the six or seven years we lived in that neighborhood, PC escorted innumerable things to our garage. Among the things he pilfered were shoes, shovels, handsaws, garden gloves, a full bag of charcoal briquettes, and plastic bottles of motor oil. The crowning glory of his thievery, though, was the successful heist of a complete children's tin toy oven set that belonged to a set of four-year-old twins who lived four houses down. They had been horribly violated by watching PC struggle with the effort of dragging their favorite toy out of their garage and down the street.

I was sitting in the kitchen eating a sandwich one day when two young boys of about nine or ten years of age came hesitantly up our driveway and made their way to our front door where I could see them clearly and hear them speaking through the open window. A discussion between the two ensued over which one was going to ring the doorbell and who was going to be the spokesman once the doorbell was answered. Both were fearful of what the people with the thieving dog would do to them. The argument was finally settled when one of them played the trump card.

"You ring the doorbell," he said. "It's your shoe."

Despite his numerous escapades, PC was a wonderful companion for me. We had an amazing bond that transcended the things that separated us. He would do anything I asked of him, usually immediately upon my asking him politely in full sentences. He quickly mastered the most mundane tricks and behaviors that I taught him. He would hold a treat undisturbed on his nose for several minutes awaiting my cue that it was okay for him to flip it up in the air and deftly catch it in his mouth in one quick move. My parents, however, were not equally enamored with him. His adventures proved too much for their patience, and when I left for college, I was instructed to find a new home for PC, which I did with one of the teachers at my high school.

So upon my return home after college graduation, I was eager to go see PC. However, when I made my way to the teacher's house, I learned that PC no longer lived with them. His mischievous nature had not meshed well with their lives either, and they had placed him with a farmer in the country. Try as I might, I was unable to find PC even though I followed the trail of ever-increasing numbers of places at which he had worn out his welcome. Although I never saw him again, he lives still in my heart and my memory. My parents are unaware of the degree of anger I still feel whenever PC comes up in conversation and the stories of his misadventures begin to flow. I tell the stories with nostalgia and humor. But my parents tell them with a level of residual ire and frustration that to this day irks me.

My friend Tim met me a few days later at my home in Hutchinson, sixty miles west of the Twin Cities, where we planned the logistics for our two-week camping and canoeing trip. We put in our canoe in Ely, Minnesota, and entered into Quetico, on the Canadian side of the Boundary Waters Canoe Area Wilderness, on the first day the park opened in the spring. The ranger issued stern warnings that the ice had been off the lakes for only a week or so and the water would be so cold that a person only had a few minutes in the water before succumbing to hypothermia.

The time was spent enjoying the beauty of the wild places, dodging bears and moose, narrowly escaping the loss of our canoe, and seeing virtually no other people. But for me, regardless of what else was happening, my mind was swirling with thoughts of Cynthia. Not only had I not forgotten her, but, thanks to her soliloquy in the car, I simply could not shake her from my mind. While I was out in the wilds of southern Canada, she was probably looking for a job in Atlanta.

By the time we arrived back in Hutchinson, I had come to the conclusion that I did not want Cynthia working in Atlanta. I called her on my first evening home, not quite sure how to broach the subject. I did not exactly have a great deal of capital with her as a result of how careless I had been with her emotions. After telling her of my escapades on the water, I asked how her job search was going in Atlanta. I was a little afraid to hear her answer.

"Well, so far, not so good," she replied. "I've had a couple of interviews, but so far no one has called me back yet." I breathed a sigh of relief.

"You could come get a job in Saint Paul," I said quietly, with no emphasis and as little drama as possible.

"I've got two more interviews set up for later this week," she continued. "One of them I'm pretty excited about." Either she hadn't heard me, or was not going to place herself in a position to be emotionally thrashed again. I couldn't blame her.

"Would you consider moving to Minnesota and getting a job here?" I tried again.

"The one that I'm most excited about is at a finance company. They need an executive secretary."

"Cynthia, did you not hear me?"

"No, I heard you. I'm just not sure what I'm supposed to do with that information," she replied. "You've said it twice now. If you say it again, I'm afraid I'm going to start thinking you might really mean it."

"I've been thinking about it a lot," I said. "I think you should get a job up here."

"You think I should, or you want me to?" It was a fair question.

"I would really like it if you were here with me."

"Are you sure?"

"I know you have every reason to doubt it. But, yes, I'm sure."

Three days later I was picking her up at the airport. We went first to the veterinary school where a junior student with whom I had become acquainted gave us a tour around the halls that I would soon know well. As we walked the polished halls, Cynthia reached for my hand. It sent a thrill of happiness and terror through me.

Within one week, Cynthia had landed a job as a receptionist at the corporate headquarters of a large company located on the eleventh floor of the American National Bank Building in downtown Saint Paul. She would start in two weeks. She was excited by the opportunity, unsure how in the world she was going to be able to spend all of the twelve thousand dollar a year salary they had offered her. I put her on a plane back to Georgia where she and her parents packed everything she owned, including her harp, into the back of her Toyota Corolla and hauled her across the country to the hinterlands of the frozen tundra of Minnesota. Cynthia and her parents found a two-room apartment, rented some inexpensive furniture for her, and got her unpacked.

For my part, I headed across the plains of Saskatchewan in my Delta 88 back to camp in Alberta for another summer with the horses, a commitment that I now wished I could back out of. The night before Cynthia's folks left to drive back to Georgia, while sleeping on the floor of the living room of Cynthia's new apartment, policemen raided the apartment next door, complete with a battering down of the door and the removal of an accused felon in handcuffs. Cynthia, able to sleep through a Kansas tornado, never woke up. But although her mom and dad each heard the whole thing, both feigned sleep, never speaking of it until years later, convinced they were each allaying the fears of the other. The next morning they drove away, leaving their daughter alone in a strange city, thousands of miles away from the man who had invited her to move there three weeks previously. The same man who, just a few months before, had broken her heart.

Even so, that was a good summer for us. I did better about writing her letters, though I was still a rank amateur compared to her faithful posts. We also talked frequently on the phone. My absence provided her the opportunity to concentrate, undistracted by me, on settling into a job that she grew to like very much. And she spent the weekends with my parents in Hutchinson, developing a comfortable friendship. She developed some good friendships too with people at her office. In general, she got along quite nicely without me.

When I returned, there was a brief period of time when my gender-related fear of commitment sent a jolt of panic through me and a rush of regret through Cynthia. But I quickly came to grips with my ridiculous concerns and was soon entirely contented to find things as they were. What more could I ask for, after all? I had entered veterinary school as a freshman, had found a room to let only two blocks from the school, and had the love and adoration of a beautiful girl whom I loved. Life was good!

The first two years of basic sciences in veterinary school are a slog. As students, we had few options as to the curriculum. We simply had to follow the prescribed path through the general medical course work: pathology, parasitology, biochemistry, pharmacology, physiology, and other courses designed with equal part boredom and challenge. During those first two years, we hardly ever had the opportunity to touch live animals. The closest we came to them was touring the animal wards of the veterinary hospital during our lunch breaks.

If we wanted to tie some of the things we were learning to clinical cases, our best hope was to observe gross pathology rounds, which were presented during the lunch hour. But frankly, these were rather gruesome events during which the organs of animals that had not survived their diseases and had been autopsied were displayed with their attendant pathologic changes. These rounds were presented by senior students who were completing their gross pathology rotations and attended by sandwich-toting freshmen and sophomores standing in the small amphitheater. It always struck me oddly that the professor responsible for overseeing the dissection of diseased patients, who should have been intimately familiar with the consequences of toxic substances on the body, chewed tobacco nonstop during the rounds. While holding up a lung lobe with a gray, nodular tumor invading the pink tissue, his lower lip would bulge grotesquely with a thick wad of tobacco that muffled and slowed his speech, punctuating it with pauses for spitting into a soda bottle.

There were two places where the vast majority of my time as a first-year vet student was spent. The first was the histology lab, the student equivalent of office cubicles. We spent perhaps fifteen hours a week with our red eyes pressed against the eyepieces of our seven-hundred-dollar microscopes learning the magnified intricacies of the gastrointestinal tract, the kidney, the heart, or the lungs of the seven basic species we studied. Each of us was issued a wooden storage box at the beginning of the semester that contained microscope slides with extremely thin sections of all of these organs and more, and dyed with the histology stains, hemotoxylin and eosin. We knew these slides intimately and personally from long hours of study in which we learned to distinguish the cow's abomasum from a dog's stomach, or the muscle of the heart from the other muscles in the body. The histology lab was set up with many aisles, each with several cubicles side by side. These carrels housed all eighty of the people in my class and, with places to store our personal belongings, became our home away from home. We became very close friends with the classmates who resided in the carrels next to us, but were only distantly familiar with those in the other corners of the room.

The other place where we spent a great deal of time was the anatomy lab, which was nothing if not ghoulish. By necessity, the entire lab reeked with the caustic and infiltrating odor of formaldehyde that insinuated itself into your clothes, your sinuses, your dreams. The effect was intensified by the constant and pervasive chill of the room. It was bad enough in the first half of the semester when we dissected dogs and cats. The second half of the semester, however, brought new meaning to the term *morbid*. The necessity of learning the entire anatomy of large animals like horses and cows required two things: a system of refrigeration for such mammoth cadavers and a way to move them in and out of the cooler. The first problem was solved by means of a huge walk-in refrigerator that maintained temperatures of about forty degrees. The second required an elaborate system of ceiling tracks with trolleys that rolled on these rails from which were suspended the study subjects.

It was an incredibly eerie task to spend a Saturday night studying anatomy. It meant going into the dimly lit cooler, finding your own specimen among the twenty or more cadavers hanging in rows from the ceiling like some macabre merry-go-round, carousel creatures without skin, then navigating it out of the cooler by a series of train-yardlike maneuvers to single your specific cow or horse from the herd. Suffice it to say that there were many Saturday nights spent this way during anatomy class, Cynthia quizzing me on specific body parts while the two of us shared a pizza and sipped a soda. I'm not sure I should admit to becoming accustomed to it, but actually, both Cynthia and I did. I doubt that she could identify all those muscles and nerves still today (I know I couldn't), but at the time I suspect she could have passed those exams with very respectable scores.

As that first year in veterinary school progressed, I became more and more certain that my decision to become a veterinarian was exactly the right one for me. True, at that time, I had visions of plying my trade strictly on horses. When asked if I had interest in small animal medicine, I would shake my head and decry the onerous task of being cramped in an office all day working on some little old lady's little old poodle with pink-painted nails and ridiculous bows attached to the ears. No, that was not for me! I wanted to work with real animals; animals that required some skill to handle; animals whose size and temperaments demanded your respect and necessitated your constant attention.

But there was at that time no wishy-washy floundering about whether or not I would enjoy my work. In fact, I would swell with pride and accomplishment whenever I was asked what I did; a pride that was rewarded when the person responded with awe and appreciation. I was in veterinary school and would soon be a vet. This enthusiasm persisted despite the arduous task that being in vet school was. And Cynthia was beside me all the way.

Here we were, partway through my freshman year in veterinary school. She had become such an integral part of every aspect of my life. I studied until all hours of the night at her apartment. Since my rented room did not include kitchen privileges, she prepared most of my meals. She helped me study. She encouraged me when the demands of school seemed overwhelming. We went to church together. She even washed my clothes so I could devote that time to my studies. There was nothing that I did that did not involve, did not revolve around Cynthia.

It was somewhat of a surprise to my male mind that, given my history with Cynthia, I did not find these circumstances to be oppressive, even stifling. But they were not. On the contrary, I could not imagine what my veterinary school experience, what my existence would be without her. In fact, the thought had began to play around the edges of my mind that I would really like Cynthia to become a permanent part of my life. I had not yet actually articulated this in concrete terms to myself, and certainly not to Cynthia, but I could not deny that the specter of that notion was beginning to develop like an embryo in my mind. As freshman year progressed, so did this notion, growing stronger all the while.

I'd like to describe here the intricately designed, flawlessly executed, and remarkably romantic manner in which I proposed to Cynthia a few weeks later. Heaven knows she deserved it. But this is not a book of fiction so I must instead tell you how it really happened. One evening, just before I headed reluctantly back to my apartment, I nonchalantly threw out a comment something like, "What about next summer?" That's the smooth line I came up with. In my mind it was really just an opener to a discussion about our future. I was not actually fully prepared at that moment to follow through with a formal proposal. I had not even purchased a ring yet. But my intentions were transparent and I was not wavering. And this time I didn't have to repeat it.

"Next summer? Do you mean it?"

I've since teased Cynthia that what I really meant to suggest was a picnic, not a wedding; that she had grossly misunderstood my intentions. But that's not true at all. The truth is, I couldn't wait to have Cynthia as my wife. So we began to make plans for a wedding the following July. Man, did we make plans!

Basically a shy person who does not particularly enjoy crowds, my idea for a wedding was a few close friends standing with us in a quaint country church in the mountains. Cynthia's idea, on the other hand, included an elaborate affair with hundreds of guests in a large church with battalions of musicians and forests of candles and flowers. My role in the planning stages of our wedding as the groom was to enthusiastically agree to all the things my fiancée wanted. Weddings, after all, have little to do with the groom. Once the question is popped, however awkwardly, the groom's responsibilities are over. This is as it should be. Left to me, our wedding would have been equally binding, but boring and unmemorable beyond measure.

As it was, our wedding was absolutely stunning; a fittingly graceful and elegant beginning to our lives together. On the front of our wedding program was printed the poem that came to me one Saturday night when I should have been studying biochemistry, "Myself the More." Cynthia and I had wanted to perform a vocal duet at the ceremony, but knew that our nerves and emotions would be overwhelming with a high risk of our voices thinning as a result to unseemly wavering and unsteady buzzing. Instead, we recorded a six-part Gaelic blessing, Cynthia and I singing each part, which we played as a prayer. Our fathers, both clergymen, shared the duties of officiating at the wedding, providing an added level of emotion and meaning. Handbells, brass instruments, violins, and our vocal number provided musical highlights to the service, and a thundering pipe organ accompanied us as we walked proudly down the aisle after the service, husband and wife.

All of these details I recall more from watching the video of the ceremony than from memory. The actual event in my mind is a blur. I do clearly remember standing at the top of the stairs in that sanctuary filled with five hundred people as my bride, escorted by her father, walked down the aisle. Instead of being nervous, I was overtaken with a calm sense of correctness, an inescapable assurance that this was right and meant to be. I remember locking eyes with Cynthia and feeling so confident, so resolute about the future, and thoroughly infused with gratitude that this beautiful woman would be my life's companion. It was a powerful feeling, more substantial than emotion. It was sentimental, to be sure, but surpassed that by far to a level of certainty, of purpose. It embodied an acceptance of responsibility and a contentment for the future that made all of my early misgivings trite and senseless.

Our honeymoon, strapped as we were for cash, consisted of an extended road trip from Tennessee, where the wedding had been held, back home to Minnesota. Our first night we stayed in the Chattanooga Choo Choo Hotel where a cloud-bursting thunderstorm, breaking only a few minutes after the outdoor reception had concluded, flooded the elevators and threatened the power in the rooms. Along the way home, we drove the Blue Ridge Parkway, stopping off at the Peaks of Otter Lodge in Virginia. We rode horseback to a hidden waterfall in the Blue Ridge Mountains that I had discovered while working at a camp there. We enjoyed the Fourth of July fireworks on the Mall in Washington, D.C., with five hundred thousand of our closest friends, stayed in the historic Shoreham Hotel within walking distance of the National Zoo where we passed a pleasant afternoon. We raised a toast to each other as the sun set over Catawba Island on the shores of Lake Erie. We spent Saturday night in Toledo, Ohio, just to say we had. And five or six days later, we arrived back in Saint Paul to start my sophomore year in veterinary school, and our new lives together as husband and wife.

Ralston and Squirt

As a veterinary student, the impulse to have a pet is strong. But as an apartment dweller, your options are limited. The rules of the apartment complex were very clear: no dogs; no cats; no ferrets; no rabbits; no exceptions. But they didn't say anything about parakeets.

In my home growing up, the rules had been similar. My parents were not big fans of having animals in the house. They weren't really big on having animals at all, truth be told. Despite the clear preferences of my parents, I had managed, with the help of my aunt Jan who bred Shetland sheepdogs, to procure an oversized sheltie who had sustained a broken leg as a pup. The hollow sounds of his cast on hardwood floors and the cadence of his hobbled gait had earned him the name Thumper, short for Captain Thumper Blaze, and had left him with a barely noticeable limp. Both his size and his gait had precluded a successful career in the show ring, so Aunt Jan had offered Thumper to us. Mom and Dad did their level best to refuse, but had the combined forces of their three boys and a sister exerting intense pressure to which they finally caved. I had also finagled a hamster by promising to keep the cage extra clean, which I did faithfully, and assuring them that they would never have to touch or hold it. Having two pets in my parents home was a confounding coup for me in second grade; an accomplishment that, even at that age, I understood to be beyond belief given the lack of interest or commitment to pet ownership that my parents felt.

To this incredible menagerie was added, quite surprisingly, a parakeet. One of my father's parishioners bred and raised budgies in an outdoor aviary in her southern Florida backyard. We called her Aunt Ada because, although she was no relation to our family, she seemed like she should have been. An Aunt Bea–like figure, she was large and soft and always laughing, and would envelop you in a bear hug at the slightest provocation, which would literally bury you in her ample middle and compress you like a plant in a press. A hug from Aunt Ada was a wonderful thing, nurturing and comfortable and refreshing like a quick nap on a soft feather mattress. I don't remember how old Aunt Ada was. From my second grade perspective, I judged her to be in her fifties, but she could have been older. She could also have been younger, though.

She certainly didn't act like any fifty-year-old I had ever known. Once when she babysat for my brothers and me, she turned all the lights off in the house and lured us into a game of hide-and-seek in our cavernous four-bedroom home. The bleak darkness already had me scared out of my wits, hiding behind the bed in my parents' room listening to Aunt Ada's heavy footfalls as she lumbered around on the terrazzo floors. But when the footsteps stopped at the door of the bedroom and I heard her fingers drumming on the doorpost, I involuntarily sucked in my breath out of excitement and terror. When she let out a moan worthy of a Stephen King novel from the door of the bedroom, low and unending like a hungry slobbering fiend, I was up and over the bed and into her arms before the echoes died down in the room.

I loved Aunt Ada and would often ride my bike over sandy dirt roads the mile or so to her house where she would press me into service helping her care for her parakeets, her lazy dogs, and the steer she was raising in the back lot. She took notice of my affinity for the array of animals under her care and, quite unknown to me, approached my parents with an offer of a young parakeet and a cage. My folks could hardly refuse; so I had my third pet.

He was a wonderful addition to my world. I named him Tweetie. I kept Tweetie's cage in my room and went to sleep by his quiet, constant chortle of pillow talk each night in the cage under a towel. He became very tame and loved to accompany me about the house on my shoulder as I played with cars or built things out of LEGOs. Tweetie loved Thumper and would follow him around the house whenever possible. It was from Thumper, I suspect, that Tweetie picked up the funny habit of walking. As a member of the avian world, you would expect his means of transportation to be on the wing. Not Tweetie! He walked instead. It was as if he didn't realize that flying was anything other than a method of getting from his cage to the floor and back, because he would walk around the house on the floor after us or tag along behind Thumper. You had to be extra careful not to step on him as you moved around the house.

Tweetie's favorite game was to find Thumper while he was asleep on the floor and hop onto the tip of his tail where he would bury his head deep into Thumper's sheltie hair and run along his back toward the shoulders with his head down. It was a funny thing for everyone but Thumper. Tweetie was so deeply buried in the long fur that he was completely invisible at the surface, but you could clearly follow his progress as a furrow developed in the coat that rapidly moved forward, inducing spasms of ticklishness on the dog's back. Thumper despised the feel of the bird on his back, a fact that only seemed to make Tweetie increase his speed. When we first saw this game we were concerned that Thumper might seek revenge through violent means, but violence was just not in him. He suffered this abuse regularly and his only defense was to walk slowly under a low chair rubbing his back along its supports vainly trying to scrape the annoying bird from his back. This ingenious use of tools, though, did not work as planned. It only pushed Tweetie down his back again to the tail where he would be in perfect position to repeat the onslaught like a little avian plow.

In the end, it was Tweetie's love for people that did him in. We became so accustomed to his flying to our shoulders that we quite often didn't notice him there. That was a good thing, of course, except in certain critical situations. Suffice it to say that a bird on your shoulder is not a good idea while applying heavy doses of hair spray. To this day my mom claims to have felt bad about it.

I remembered Tweetie as Cynthia and I pondered the thought of a pet. He had taught me that a parakeet can be quite a good pet if given enough attention. So I suggested to Cynthia that we get a budgie. While a parakeet wasn't our first choice, we both came to the conclusion that a bird might be our only option.

At the pet store we selected a cage with plenty of room, a cuttlebone, and some birdseed. Then we went to the window that looked into the budgie cage. We wanted a young male because Aunt Ada had always said that males bonded better with people and had a better chance of learning to talk and the younger you got them, the better pets they would be. Who was I to argue with Aunt Ada? She had also taught me to judge the age by the stripes of color on their heads. The younger they are, the further the stripes come over the tops of their heads. The youngest birds have foreheads that are striped all the way down to the beak. As they get older, the stripes give way to solid color. The further over the forehead the solid color extends, the older they are. The same thing has occurred on my forehead with age. The hair has given way to a solid color, skin color, which extends my forehead almost to my shoulders.

The gender of a budgie is identified by the color of the cere, the beaklike area where the nostrils are located. Male budgies have a blue cere. Females have a cere that is the same color as the beak. So our search centered on male birds.

Among the greens and yellows which accounted for the vast majority of the birds were a few budgies with blue feathers. We found ourselves especially drawn to them. We cornered several of them and held them carefully in our hands. They struggled and bit ferociously trying to free themselves from our grasp. One blue male in particular caught our eye. His blue, rather than being the gentle, pastel blue of a little boy's baby blanket, was a much deeper hue, the color of a cloudless sky on a perfectly clear day at high altitude. When he was caught and carried away from his cohorts, he did not struggle and fight quite so much as the others, and though he did nibble at our fingers a bit, it was not with the same unconcealed venom as many of the other birds had displayed. We purchased him and carried him into the cold Minnesota night air in a miniature cardboard carrier, his nails tapping on the bottom of the box as we made our way to our car.

We named him Ralston. Cynthia wanted something regal and dignified for a bird of his beauty and personality. I sarcastically extended the name to Ralston Purina Cat Chow, but Cynthia did not appreciate my connecting the obvious dots. Ralston tamed up very quickly. He loved being with us and soon preferred us to the mirror in his cage. He would jump to my finger and I would nuzzle my nose along his deep sky blue belly. He would respond by nibbling at my eyelashes and the frames of my glasses, issuing all the while a satisfied little murmur of contentment. Ralston's cage door was always left open so he could choose the safety and comfort of his cage or the camaraderie of our company, depending upon his various moods. This pleased him greatly.

I discovered that, despite his diminutive stature, he loved to wrestle. His favorite game was to fly to our bed and challenge me to a duel of finger wrestling. For Ralston, this game was a deadly serious matching of wits and wills in which he invested a great deal of strategic planning. The rules of engagement were simple; I would tap my index finger on the bed. This was his cue that war had been declared and, being hawkish, he would invariably engage. From wherever he happened to be, he would immediately fly over, F-15-like, and land a few inches from my finger. Then he would advance and attack, pecking at my finger ferociously while doing a strange little hopping dance with head bobbing, feigning and dodging like a boxer: jab, jab, then ducking and coming in from the side with an uppercut. I would also spar, coming at him with my finger pointed at his blue chest or over the top, pinning a tail feather to the bed or tapping at his beak with my fingernail. He would respond to each foray by fluffing the feathers on his neck in a bold threat posture or suddenly squawking a loud complaint as if to the judges that I had hit below the belt. His naked aggression was unmistakable, but the constant and contented chortle that always accompanied these fights belied his real feelings. He was just having fun, and this game was his passion.

He enjoyed it so much that he would always come from wherever he was to the tapping of my finger. If I wanted him to fly to my shoulder, all I had to do was tap my finger on my shoulder. He would fly there instantly, head bobbing and feathers fluffed, ready for action.

I made a little perch out of wood with a mirror on one side that Ralston loved. I would set it on my desk while I studied so Ralston could sit with me, admiring himself proudly and wolf whistling at what he saw. If I had a glass of soda or juice with me on the desk, he would eye me jealously as I drank it, complaining loudly that I did not provide a glass for him too. When I set it down, he would hop over to the rim of the glass and drink, eyeing me belligerently between sips, daring me to object. He especially loved root beer. This system worked well for him until, between the two of us, we had drained the cup below the halfway mark in the glass. Things got dicey for him after that because it forced him to lean way down, stretching to reach the liquid. I don't know how many times his feet lost their grip on the slippery rim of the glass, sending him face-first into the drink. I can still picture his surprised face through the glass, eyes wide, his tail still poking from the top of the glass, his neck bent double against one side of the glass to keep his head out of the drink, his feet scratching helplessly at the other—a little blue parakeet root beer float. I would reach in with my hand and pull him out, leaving little parakeet down feathers floating on the surface of my root beer. He would fly away, dripping and sticky, squawking angrily at me and casting accusing looks over his shoulder as he flew, as if I were the one who had dunked him into the carbonation.

Ralston challenged the wisdom and knowledge of my veterinary professors in one trivial detail learned in anatomy class. During one lecture, they had taught us that birds, by virtue of their comparatively small olfactory lobe, don't have a good sense of smell. Based on Ralston's responses, however, I wondered how true this really was. His response to Dorito breath argued powerfully against this notion. I discovered this quite by accident, but with the certainty that came from repeatability. One whiff of my breath after eating Doritos and he would immediately fly away, shaking his head and squawking with intense disgust. Morning breath or coffee breath produced identical results. Ralston, it seemed, could smell quite well and had rather strong preferences and discerning tastes. He very much liked the smell of peanut butter, apples, and other fruits, nibbling at my lips when these smells tinged my breath.

Try as we might, we were never able to teach Ralston to speak, though the different meanings of his amazing array of vocal sounds was usually quite simple to interpret. The closest he came to speech was his wolf whistle, which he would unleash enthusiastically whenever I whistled at Cynthia. Ralston and I could carry on quite an extended conversation consisting entirely of my initial and his echoed wolf whistles. After two or three salvos, I would give the first rising tone of the whistle and Ralston would complete the final descending tones. Ralston also seemed to know the appropriate times to use the wolf whistle. Some mornings when she uncovered his cage, Cynthia would be greeted by his enthusiastic whistle, apparently in sincere appreciation of her beauty. It was a harbinger for her of a good day.

During my sophomore year I joined the volunteer staff of the Wildlife Rehabilitation Clinic at the veterinary college. I admire and respect those veterinarians who have a passion for wildlife and work to treat and release injured wild animals. But for me, the real joy in veterinary medicine is in becoming a part of the wonderful and mysterious kinship between a beloved pet and its enamored owner. This simply doesn't occur with wild animals who, despite your best efforts to make them better, try to inflict injury upon you and attempt at every encounter to escape. However, since sophomore year in veterinary school is still largely devoid of actual hands-on work with animals, working in the wildlife clinic provided an opportunity to actually treat sick and injured animals.

One of the fun aspects of this work was raising orphaned animals that, like most of my classmates, I had attempted with limited success as a child. I don't know how many blue jays and mockingbirds, who had the double misfortune of falling out of their nests and then being found by me, had suffered under my most earnest attentions. As a staff member at the wildlife clinic, though, I had learned the right way to foster orphans. This is how a baby squirrel, eyes not yet opened, came into our lives. Cynthia and I called him Squirt. Since he had to be fed every couple of hours, he could not be adequately cared for in the confines of the wildlife clinic. Instead, I took him home so I could get up every two hours through the night and feed him through a syringe a gruel of powdered goat's milk fortified with a variety of additives. He was incredibly cute as he grabbed the hub of that syringe with both front feet and sucked at the nourishment in the wee hours, eyes still sealed shut. At least, I remember his being cute, though, in the middle of the night, my eyes too were often shut as I fed him. During the day, Squirt accompanied me to class in a small cardboard box so I could feed him between classes.

This went on for a month or so as Squirt grew, his eyes opening and his tail growing full and bushy. He followed us everywhere in the apartment, scampering from couch to chair to bed, tail flagging and uttering a throaty chuckle. Soon it was no longer necessary for us to get up in the night to feed him. He would do very well with some sunflower seeds and a prepared mixture of nutrients left outside the shoe box that he claimed as a den. These were placed inside a large cardboard box with high sides that he could not initially scale. But by the end of that first month he was venturing out of the box on his own, exploring the farthest reaches of the apartment. He loved to climb the drapes and sit on top of the curtain rod, his tail curled up over his back.

Ralston was completely unsure what to think of the intruder. He would sit on my shoulder as I fed the baby and watch with unconcealed dismay, wondering, I'm sure, why any other animal was necessary when we already had the best. He was also incredulous when Squirt would climb the curtains. Ralston, from the top of the curtain rod, would watch as Squirt scampered up the curtain like a tree trunk. But Squirt was not satisfied simply to have reached the top. He then wanted to introduce himself to Ralston, who wanted nothing more than to be left alone. As Squirt hopped toward him on the rod, Ralston would scurry toward the other end, screaming at the pursuer in full voice. This only increased Squirt's curiosity, who thought he might have finally found a playmate. Ralston would come to the end of the curtain rod and stop, head bobbing, and the intensity and volume of his screaming would reach a crescendo. Squirt was not the slightest bit put off by this display and would slowly advance, tail jerking. With nowhere else to go, Ralston would lean away as far as he could. Not until he was knocked off the end of the curtain rod would he finally give wing and fly to the rod on the other window. It was a sad day for Ralston when Squirt realized that the game could continue by jumping to the floor and climbing the other curtain.

One morning, though, Ralston's limit of patience with the impudent intruder was reached. When we woke up and went to feed Squirt, we discovered that he was not in his cardboard box. This initiated a thorough search of the apartment, which, due to its size, took very little time. No Squirt. He was not in any of his favorite places; not on the curtain rod; not on the entertainment center; not nestled down in the dirty clothes hamper; not squirreled away in the underpinnings of the couch; not on the top of the kitchen cabinets. We simply couldn't find him. The mystery was solved, however, when we uncovered Ralston's cage. There was Squirt in the bottom of the cage, tail fluffed and flagging a morning greeting as he munched hungrily on Ralston's birdseed. Ralston was huddled up on his highest perch leaning away from the squirrel with a look of disdain that was completely wasted on the young trespasser.

When this happened, we knew it was fast approaching time to release the squirrel that we had become quite fond of. So I built a wooden box that could later be nailed to a tree and began to place Squirt's food in it. Removing the familiar shoe box encouraged Squirt to sleep in the new wooden one still within the comfort and safety of his familiar cardboard box. After a few days, he acclimated to it nicely.

We also had to get him acclimated to the outdoors, a place that was completely foreign to him. On Memorial Day, we took him along on a picnic to Como Park, which was located between our apartment and the Saint Paul campus of the University of Minnesota. The park was absolutely packed with people that day celebrating the return of warm weather to Minnesota, where the winters are long and brutal. Where there was not a softball game or people throwing Frisbees, the grass was carpeted with blankets. We found a parking place and added our own blanket to the quilt-work pattern of revelers already on the grass. We had stopped at Taco Bell before coming, so we spread our burritos and nachos on the blanket.

Squirt was with us, but his eyes were huge and bulging and he trembled with fright. He refused to explore the blanket, choosing instead to stay on my shoulder, feet spread wide for support and tail still and flat. The expanse of the outdoor space, the green grass, the waving branches of the trees, the clouds, the grackles and blue jays flying overhead, the sounds of the breeze in the leaves—all the things that make up the natural environment for a normal squirrel paralyzed him with fear. I gently placed him on the grass. He jumped high like a surprised cat when the blades touched him and ran back to me, climbing onto my lap. After several attempts at introducing him to the grass with similar results, I finally tossed him from the blanket. He spun several times in the air, then landed softly some five feet from the edge of the blanket facing away from us, where he froze in place in abject terror. We found this hysterical and burst into laughter, the sounds of which oriented Squirt to us. He turned and looked in our direction. Recognizing something with which he was familiar, he took off skittering in our direction. Neither the nachos nor the burritos provided any barrier to his progress. He blew through them without breaking stride, sending chips in all directions and soiling his feet with Taco Bell Mild Sauce. Making a beeline for me, he ran up my torso as if I were a tree trunk, not stopping until he had reached the top of my head where he huddled, shivering with fright, chest heaving with effort and panic.

With time, we were able to acclimate Squirt more and more to the outdoors. Finally, we nailed his wooden box to a tree trunk in the yard of my parents' house in Hutchinson and left a supply of seeds and nuts in a feeder not far away. For the first couple of days, they saw him coming and going into his house and munching at the feeder. But after a week or so, the box remained empty and undisturbed. Three weeks later, when Cynthia and I next visited, we found three squirrels feeding at the feeder we had placed for Squirt. When we approached, two of them scampered away, tails flickering and throats buzzing in warning. The third, though, remained behind, eyeing us with interest. When we squatted down, he approached to within two or three feet of us, hesitated a few seconds, then turned and hopped unhurriedly away to join his new friends. From that time on, we could never distinguish Squirt from any of the other squirrels in my parents' yard either by sight or behavior. He had become thoroughly repatriated into his natural environment. We had been successful to the point that we were no longer needed and only distantly remembered, if at all. It made us happy in a rather rueful and nostalgic way.

Ralston, on the other hand, wasted not the least bit of sadness or emotional energy on the disappearance of his nemesis. He was very glad to have our attentions to himself and went about the task of making himself the center of attention again.

Ralston lived another year or two, succumbing prematurely to some budgie malady. I've since learned that we did everything wrong for him. A strictly seed diet is enjoyed by the bird, but does not provide a quality, balanced diet that maximizes their health. Neither did we provide any iodine, an important nutrient for parakeets that prevents the development of goiter in this species. Perhaps he died as a result of our ignorance of proper parakeet care. Whatever the cause, his passing was a sad one for us. We buried him under the spreading branches of a huge oak tree in a small neighborhood park close to our apartment. We often think of him when we see the deep blue hues of a perfectly clear, cloudless sky—the color of Ralston's belly.

Tess

Senior year in veterinary school is qualitatively different from the first three years. Actually, because of the incredibly long hours required of a senior student, it is quantitatively different as well. But the single most significant difference is the fact that you finally get to deal with actual live animals, treating real physical abnormalities. To be honest, senior students are generally far removed from truly treating the patients. But at least you are closer to the action than at any other time in your life so far.

I have often told senior students and new graduates that you learn more about a disease by seeing your first patient with that disease than from countless hours of lectures, studying notes, or reading textbooks. And this process begins your senior year in school. Tess is an example of this fact.

Tess was the first Russian wolfhound I had ever seen in person. I had learned as a boy that the largest breed of dog was the Russian wolfhound and Tess was evidence of that. Though she weighed in at about one hundred and fifty pounds, she was at that weight quite lean. Tess was young, with dark wiry hair liberally admixed with gray strands, a roan effect that gave the impression that she was much older than her two years. She was also endowed with an incredibly sweet and trusting disposition.

She was referred to the Veterinary Teaching Hospital at the University of Minnesota College of Veterinary Medicine by her primary care veterinarian for a sudden onset of rear limb paralysis. It is always tragic when a pet suddenly is unable to walk. But added to the emotional turmoil of such a disease was the logistical ramifications of dealing with a paraplegic dog that outweighed her petite, one hundred and fifteen pound owner, Celia Carlisle, who dearly loved Tess and was willing to spare no expense to see her on her feet again.

I happened to be on my neurology rotation when Tess was referred to the hospital, so I was assigned to be the senior student on her case. This sounds more important than it really was. In a teaching hospital, there are strata of medical personnel layered between the patient and the senior clinician. The owners are referred into the hospital to benefit from the expertise of the attending clinicians, specialists who have spent decades honing their knowledge and skills in their particular area of expertise. But first, they have to brave the well-intentioned onslaughts of the senior students on the rotation, followed by the interns, and finally the residents before they ever meet the specialist. There are also the veterinary technicians who provide nursing care and the kennel attendants, both of which technically fall below the students on the organizational chart. However, since they have usually been long-term employees, some of them working in the hospital for decades, and the students are in the rotation for only a couple of weeks, we poor students really ranked lower than them in the pecking order.

My role, therefore, in Tess's medical care consisted primarily in heavy lifting, bedpan duty, and completing the numerous forms, generally in triplicate, which were necessary to process laboratory submissions, schedule anesthesia and surgery, or arrange medical therapies and pharmaceuticals that had been ordered by those higher up the medical food chain. I also had the opportunity to listen in on discussions between Ms. Carlisle and the various clinicians, residents, and interns. On the off chance that I might be called on in medical rounds to answer some question of arcane medical trivia relevant to Tess's case, I was expected to be completely familiar with all the pertinent textbooks and current medical literature that might tangentially be related to Tess's disease and its diagnosis and treatment.

Tess had presented with what the clinicians wanted me to describe as an acute onset of pelvic limb paresis. This simply meant that she had suddenly developed partial paralysis of her back legs. (I have come to realize the importance of precise language in correctly describing to our colleagues the clinical signs that we doctors see, but honestly, doesn't it seem sometimes that doctors just like to make up big words that make us look smart?) The list of possible causes of this symptom is relatively long. Perhaps the most common is the development of slipped disks that place pressure on the spinal cord. But other causes include blood clots, tumors, scar tissue, abnormalities of blood flow to the spinal cord, a few infectious diseases, tick paralysis, and a poorly understood condition called fibrocartilagenous infarct. Another possibility to rule out included idiopathic disease. This category is typically included in any list of differential diagnoses and is applied to any undiagnosed condition where all available diagnostic tests have been exhausted and none of us idiots can figure out what the heck is going on. This circumstance must at all costs be obfuscated by the injection into the discourse of another large word that means something only to us.

Suffice it to say that Tess's clinical signs warranted a diagnostic protocol that included an exhaustive physical examination, a neurologic evaluation, blood work, X-rays, anesthesia, nerve conduction studies and a myelogram, during which X-ray dye is injected into the space around the spinal cord to highlight areas of compression or other abnormalities of the spinal cord. Tess underwent all of those tests, and for each one, she was accompanied to them by me, the senior student, hoisting her up onto a wheeled cart that made the transport to the different laboratories much easier. Today, we have the benefit of additional modalities like computer tomography and magnetic resonance imaging, but at that time, those options were not available to us.

I quickly developed an affinity for my favorite patient and hoped against all odds that her disease would be one with a happy outcome. After years of practice, one rule of thumb has often proven itself to be consistently true. That is, the nicer the client, the better behaved the patient, the worse the disease. This seemed especially true in the teaching hospital where the caseload was skewed heavily toward diseases with horrible endings. I hoped this was not in Tess's future.

The process of the diagnostic protocol that Tess underwent required perhaps four or five days. During that time, Tess was the ideal patient. Daily blood drawing, squeezing of her flaccid bladder to empty it, and moving her to clean up her messes or to position her for testing involved a great deal of physical manipulations that I'm sure were not comfortable for her. But Tess displayed not the slightest tendency to be anything but ladylike, despite the fact that with one snap of her massive jaws she could have made these tedious jobs much more exciting.

Taking her outside was a real chore. Two people were necessary to heave her onto a cart. I would then wheel her down a long, tiled hallway to a door beyond which was a small island of grass. The cart, though, could not negotiate the three or four stairs on the porch, so I would have to slide her unceremoniously off the cart onto the cement. I would then place a long towel under her stomach and support the weight of her back end while she walked down the steps and onto the grass with her front legs. This task required a good bit of teamwork between her and me to accomplish, a fact that she quickly learned. The two of us made this sojourn three or four times a day. She loved to be outside in the sun, nose interrogating the breeze, even though her malady made it impossible for her to evacuate either her bowels or her bladder unassisted. After a few minutes in the sun, the process would be reversed, except that I would usually have no assistance lifting her back onto the cart.

Tess's trust and connection to me grew each day as I worked with her. After only a day or two, she began to look for me specifically among the sea of unfamiliar faces, her stress settling noticeably when she found me. During each of her myriad diagnostic tests, Tess demonstrated an uncanny faith in us and patience in enduring them. Since each one was, for her, new and frightening, and I was the one common thread through them all, I would not have been surprised if she had started to eye me suspiciously each time I came around. Such was not the case, however. Instead, each day her trusting yellow eyes developed a deeper level of faith in me. For me, this was heady flattery, and I increased my attentions to her in direct proportion to the confidence she placed in me.

Tess seemed to sense that I was a novice at patient care and decided to mentor me in my education. I'm sure it didn't require any medical expertise, even for a dog, to recognize my ineptitude at the tasks I was learning. But Tess patiently endured all my unsuccessful attempts at drawing her blood, emptying her bladder, and heaving the dead weight of her back end onto the cart, fixing me with a look of grateful forbearance rather than the disdain these efforts probably warranted. She realized, it seemed, that I was an earnest, if inexperienced student and diligently tried to broaden my knowledge and experience. She graciously accepted the role of teacher with patience and magnanimity. I could tell she was grateful to me for her care, but I was just as appreciative to her for her benevolence.

While she lounged on the grass each day, I rehearsed the skills of the neurologic examination. To evaluate the presence of sensation in her useless legs, I would pinch her toes, increasing the pressure slowly until I was grunting with effort. She revealed not the slightest awareness that bone-crunching forces were being applied to her toes. To determine the level on her back at which the sensation returned, I pinched the skin over her spine, starting at the base of her tail and progressing toward her head until she rippled her skin and snapped her head back to me, her face confused at the discomfort this caused her. With a little rubber hammer, I pounded away at her knee, her shin, and her hip to observe and measure her reflexes. It seemed unfair that her leg would jerk sharply with the reflexive response to the pleximeter even though she was unable to initiate even the slightest movement by force of her prodigious will. I tested her ability to discern the position of her feet by turning her toes over, leaving her standing on her knuckles. Unlike a normal dog, which would immediately right its feet, Tess would leave her toes knuckled over, unaware of their awkward position. Combining the information gained from these tests, a skilled neurologist can surmise the extent and location of the problem causing the paralysis. I was not a skilled neurologist, but again Tess was teaching me.

As the results of each of the different diagnostic tests came back, I held my breath, fearing bad news. Blood work failed to identify any causes for her paralysis. X-rays were normal. Tess's myelogram likewise was maddeningly normal as well. Nothing, in fact, other than the obvious neurological deficits could be found. Only one clue seemed to give us any direction at all, and it was more an absence of a clinical finding rather than a finding itself. Despite all the cranking, the manipulation, the torque, or the pressure we applied to Tess's back and legs, we could elicit no pain, an incongruous fact in light of the devastating effects of the problem on Tess's ability to move or feel her back legs. The only other thing we could identify was a subtle difference in degree of involvement between the two hind limbs. The right leg demonstrated ever the slightest bit more strength to it and responded more quickly to the pinching of the toes than the left. These findings were most consistent with fibrocartilagenous infarct, which generally was painless, acute in onset, often showed asymmetry in its effects on the patient, and produced few, if any, other diagnostic findings.

While it was true that the disease had severe consequences, it came with a good prognosis. Most dogs who develop fibrocartilagenous infarct recover with time without the necessity of surgery. So after all her diagnostic tests, we transferred her case to the two best doctors in the world, Mother Nature and Father Time. Chances were very good that with a little bit of their attention, Tess would be as good as new.

Patient care does not end with the coming of a weekend. So throughout the weekend, I continued to give attention to Tess. Cynthia was recruited to assist me in getting Tess outside on Saturday. As we let her relax in the grass, I demonstrated to Cynthia my progress in learning the neurologic examination. I pinched the toes, I pounded out the reflexes, I checked the level of superficial skin sensation, and tested Tess's ability to sense the position of her feet. As I did, I provided a running commentary on what I was doing and why. Cynthia listened attentively. Summarizing my findings, the thought occurred to me that they were a little different from the previous day. There was a subtle improvement in the sensation of pain in the toes, a strengthened reflex, a bit of correction of the knuckling. Nothing dramatic, to be sure. I wasn't even convinced of it myself, but a glimmer of hope began to burn in my mind.

When I reached for the door to go back into the hospital, I realized with irritation that the door had locked itself behind us. I would have to go around the building, through the large animal hospital whose garage doors were open, up the stairs through the small animal hospital, and down the long hall again in order to open the door. It would be a detour of almost ten minutes. Though it was only an inconvenience, I was frustrated as I told Cynthia what I would need to do.

"No problem," she said. "I'll stay here with Tess while you're gone."

When I finally opened the door, Cynthia seemed like she had seen a ghost.

"What's wrong?" I asked.

"You should have seen Tess. As soon as you went around the corner, she started getting antsy. She whined and her ears went up and she looked first at the corner where you disappeared, then at the door. She was so worried that she'd been left with someone she didn't know, I thought she was going to throw herself off the cart. As soon as you showed up at the door, though, she calmed down again."

"What's wrong with that? She likes me."

"Nothing's wrong with that. But, Bruce, when you came to the door, I think I saw her tail wag just a bit." I doubted that. Tess's paralysis was profound and reflex movements are often confused by laypeople as purposeful.

But when I turned to Tess and cooed her name, I was rewarded with just the tiniest little movement at the base of her tail and a big Russian wolfhound smile. I reached out and ruffled her giant head and neck, leaving the wiry hair in an unkempt cowlick. Her amber eyes were warm and grateful, as if she knew things were beginning to look up.

By the next Monday, I was confident enough about the improvement, that I pointed it out to the intern, who alerted the resident, who presented it to the neurologist, who confirmed it himself. Tess was getting better. She was released the next day. I still cannot imagine how Ms. Carlisle managed to care for Tess until she could finally walk on her own. I can only assume that her improvement continued until she was normal again. But I don't know for sure. I never saw Tess again. Her case was one that confirmed in my mind that I did not want to become a specialist, who sees their patients for only a few days during a time of intense illness, and then never sees them again either because they died or recovered fully and didn't need the intervention of a specialist again. I wanted to be able to follow the progress of my patients throughout the entirety of their lives; to insinuate myself into the texture of their existence; to know and see what effects my work brings about not only for my patients, but for the loving and concerned families that surround them.

I remember Tess still with gratitude for how she mentored me. Many other patients have benefited from the things Tess taught me in those few days. I can still bring to mind her noble and trusting face, still sense the confidence she placed in me. And my work is directed each day by the desire to see that same trust manifested by my patients. Thank you, Tess.

The End and the Beginning

It was with a great deal of pride and appreciation that I guided my family through the halls of the College of Veterinary Medicine at the University of Minnesota. This would be the last of many such tours I had led through the veterinary hospital during my four years as a student. This was the first time, though, that I had shown the hospital as an alumnus. The previous day had been commencement for myself and the other eighty graduates who were my classmates and had become my friends.

I remembered with nostalgia the first time I had been led through the echoing halls of the university by a third-year student during freshman orientation. What had at that time seemed so intimidating and daunting now was as familiar as an old pair of shoes. For four years I had pounded my own echoes into these hallways, laboratories, and classrooms. They had been challenging years to be sure.

But the very difficulty of the effort added worth to the memories. Hard-won victories are invariably the sweetest. And yet, the sweetness is rarely savored until the victory is clenched. So, with the feel of the diploma still tingling in my hand, and the flush of accomplishment still pink on my cheeks, the walk through the school that day translated all the challenges of the last four years into the vocabulary of nostalgia.

Outside in the parking lot of the hospital was a medium-sized U-Haul truck taking up three spaces. It was loaded with the ragtag cast-off furniture that my wife and I had salvaged from both sets of parents. After this last memory-laden trip through the hospital, Cynthia and I were headed for upstate New York to begin my internship.

Dr. Bruce Coston! The title kept running through my consciousness like a song. I had been motivated by just this dream since third grade and now the initials were mine! DVM. Doctor of Veterinary Medicine.

The tour that day was perhaps the most comprehensive one I had ever given. Every nook and cranny was explored again. My folks probably had no interest in seeing the anatomy lab with its strong odor of formaldehyde and the anatomic specimens in the coolers. They had little interest in the histology lab with its neat rows of microscopes. They probably cared not the least to be paraded through the animal wards filled with patients. But the patients (some of whom I had treated just last week), the strong formaldehyde vapors, and the racks of prepared tissue slides held a powerful fascination for me. The untold hours devoted to peering into the binocular hematoxylin-and eosin-stained world of histology, the gram-stained sanctums of microbiology, and the malodorous precincts of parasitology had finally compensated me with the title Dr. Bruce Coston. I liked it!

So many memories flooded me as I marched the halls: the time spent in dissection; the hair-pulling study time in the library; the gross of gross anatomy; the minutiae of pharmacology with its drugs, side effects, dosages, and interactions; the busywork piled on me by lowly interns who were simply passing on the work assigned to them by the residents, who were in turn dumped on by the internists and surgeons; the lunchtime seminars in the autopsy amphitheater. The years in these halls had been good ones whose memories I would cherish fondly.

The favorite parts of every tour were the patient wards. Upstairs, in the small animal hospital we passed kennel after kennel of dogs and cats. A few of the dogs huddled in the back of the cages in fright, afraid that we had come to insert more needles or thrust more pills down their throats. Most, though, pressed up against the cage fronts with wide-mouthed, happy grins and wagging tails. Some had shaved patches of skin with an even row of neat stitches situated in the bald spot's center. Others sported bulky, brightly colored bandages on limping legs. Some were too ill to stand, displaying no particular interest in the people nosily trooping through.

The cats responded to our intrusion as would be expected of cats. Most lifted sleepy heads and, with looks of utter boredom or undisguised disdain, peered at us with half-closed eyes, yawning and disinterested. A few arched their backs and hissed, a defensive move designed to fend off veterinary students.

As we descended the stairs to the large animal hospital, the warm wafts of hay-scented cow and horse odors greeted us. They were sweet and familiar and welcoming. Just at the bottom of the stairs were two stalls whose current occupants were of the llama persuasion. Their long necks, erect and alert, supported heads with incredibly bright, dark eyes that followed our progress down the stairs. One curious creature caught my eye. As she chewed her cud absently, I could follow the swallowed food as it coursed its way down the left side of her long neck. Then, after a short rest, a new bolus of roughage could be seen being launched like a rocket back up the neck from the llama's rumen, and the interminable chewing would resume. The other llama had an impressive set of external hardware providing fixation for a fractured leg.

We made the rounds of the large animal wards, passing horses with carefully wrapped legs and tails, foals with rounded foreheads and spindly legs nosing mares too sick to give milk. One large gelding's belly was tightly wrapped with a bandage to protect last night's incision, inflicted in the dead of night for the emergency treatment of colic.

In one stall an enormous ox, one of a working oxen team,

stood serenely with shoulders that towered to the level of my eyes, his heavily muscled back as broad and flat as a picnic table. A petite young woman, dwarfed by the ox's bulk, was poking and prodding blindly with a large bore needle in the general region of the jugular vein, desperately trying to draw a blood sample for testing. Her attempts exposed her status as a newly promoted senior student. This bloodletting was done without benefit of restraint in any form, the huge beast tugging placidly at its rack of hay all the while, occasionally turning its head slowly and nudging her gently as a puppy nudges its master. I had done the same many times, except usually on considerably less agreeable subjects. I resisted the impulse to give suggestions. Some things you just have to learn by yourself.

Eventually we had rounded every corner of the sprawling complex and made our way back to the lobby of the hospital. As I was about to head out the door for the last time, a white-coated, diminutive man with a beard and laughing eyes rounded the corner of the hall. He smiled broadly when he recognized me.

"Well, Dr. Coston. Good to see you! Are you on your way to New York?"

I could have reached out and hugged him. Dr. McKnight had been my attending internal medicine resident during my small animal medicine rotation and had been resolute in encouraging me to seek an internship program. And now he, who possessed my complete respect, was referring to me as Dr. Coston.

"Yes, I just wanted to go through one more time. So much of my time was spent here over the last four years it seems a little strange to be leaving for good now."

"I'm glad you're doing an internship, Bruce. You've got a bright future ahead of you. In the next few weeks, you're going to feel pretty overwhelmed. I know I did. Just remember the things you learned here. Especially remember the process of reasoning you learned. You're done here, but don't be surprised to find that your real education begins next week."

Dr. McKnight extended a brisk hand to me that I grasped firmly, hoping that the strength of my grip would somehow communicate the depth of my gratitude; a gratitude not solely to him, but to all the professors, the surgeons, the internists, the ophthalmologists, even the patients who had each been so instructive in my training.

"I've got to run now, though. I've got to help a new senior draw some blood. She's scared to death." He laughed and winked in knowing conspiracy. "Good luck to you, Bruce. You'll do fine." He turned and as abruptly as he had rounded the corner he disappeared around it again.

As I navigated the U-Haul away from the hospital, I was practically overcome with appreciation for those four years of grueling work and study. I drove away with a title I had coveted for years. But deep within me I also harbored a nagging question: Had these four years, as difficult and arduous as they had been, really prepared me for practice? Or would my internship simply expose my ignorance?

With the Twin Cities quickly receding behind me in the west, I processed and expanded these concerns, mixing them liberally with my most optimistic projections of practice until I was practically in a tizzy of anxiety and anticipation. My scholastic career had reached its conclusion. Ahead of me to the east, somewhere at the end of this road, stretched a new vista of opportunity, a new beginning. Out with the old, in with the new. I pressed my foot hard on the accelerator.

Daphne

When we arrived in Rochester, New York, a few days later, we rented an apartment close to the veterinary hospital in which I would work. One thing I insisted on when we signed the lease was the option of getting a pet. Though we had to pay a one hundred dollar pet deposit, a veritable fortune for a newly graduated student who would be working at practically subsistence wages, my wife and I wanted desperately to welcome a pet into our lives.

The apartment management would not allow dogs in their buildings at all—no exceptions. I had never had a cat before. My father had been intensely allergic to cats and had never allowed even an outdoor cat on the property. In fact, it was only because of my aunt's activities as a dog breeder, trainer, and show judge that I had a dog at all. Under such circumstances I can be forgiven for my view of dogs and cats as pets.

As I understood it, dogs were the pets that God had intended mankind to have. They were noble and loyal; their sole purpose in life was to please their owners. When you heard stories of amazing animal bravery, courage and sacrifice in service to people, they invariably featured a dog. Who ever heard of a cat rescuing a child from a swollen river by swimming out into the raging torrent, grabbing the child's clothes, and dragging him to the shore? Clearly, it was the canine that deserved special consideration when it came to pets.

Cats? They were okay if you didn't deserve the adoration of a dog, or were too lazy and uncommitted to provide a pet the care they really required. If those described you, a cat was a perfect pet for you. And cats would reciprocate with the same level of diffidence. They didn't really care for you. To a cat, you were simply a fixture in the house, like the couch or the refrigerator. The difference being that, unlike the couch, your lap was heated and therefore more comfortable for them to curl up on. Humans, cats would think, were simply utilitarian drones whose usefulness was maximized by affording them every now and then the slightest attention, a rub on the leg or an occasional lap nap accompanied by an well-timed purr. Unlike them, people are able to access the refrigerator, which makes them an unfortunate necessity. Uncaring, independent, callous, indifferent, inattentive, and detached were all adjectives that, in my understanding of the feline frame of mind, fit them perfectly.

It wasn't that I was necessarily prejudiced against cats. I had an open mind. I didn't mind, for instance, if other, less informed people preferred cats to dogs. After all, now that I was a licensed veterinarian, it was in my own best interest to encourage such unsophisticated preferences. But my mind was unclouded by lapses in logic or reason.

The rigid rules of the apartment complex, therefore, presented a real dilemma for me. I would have to compromise my own firm principles and get a cat. My wife, Cynthia, who had had cats as a little girl, did not understand my misgivings. And I had not been married long enough yet at that time to realize that logic is a disappointingly poor persuasive tool.

"Okay, Cynthia. Fine. We'll get a kitten. But there are a few things that I'm going to insist on." I knew some things about cats that I was sure few without my training could appreciate. In order to save untold anxiety and frustration, I needed to fully inform my wife. "We have to get a female cat. Males have a tendency to develop life-threatening urinary tract obstructions. I deal with that enough in other peoples' cats; I don't want to have to treat my own cat for it." Though I had been in practice less than a week, she somehow managed to hide any amusement at my exaggeration and seemed to be appreciating my invaluable advice.

"I don't mind having a female cat. That's no problem," she assented. "We wouldn't have to worry so much about spraying that way either, would we?"

"That's a common misconception among laypeople." I nodded knowingly. "But neutering prevents that almost all the time anyway." Wouldn't it be nice, I thought, if everyone had the opportunity to receive such sound professional pet selection advice before they chose a pet! "Another thing," I continued, "I've always thought that calico cats are really pretty. Especially the starkly contrasting ones. That's what I want, a calico. But if we can't find a calico, the only color I really don't want is black. I've never liked black cats—and on Halloween black cats are targeted, you know."

Within a couple of weeks of this discussion, I let slip in the office that we were looking for a kitten. One of my colleagues, Dr. Denny, had a queen that had disappeared two weeks after having a litter of four kittens and his family was having to hand raise the whole litter. Would I be interested? I arranged for Cynthia and me to see the litter that very evening.

As we drove to see the kittens I reiterated my nonnegotiable criteria for any kitten we would get. "Female! Preferably calico, but any color as long as she's not black! Okay?"

"That's fine with me," Cynthia responded. "I just can't wait to have a kitty."

"I know. Just don't be so eager that you're willing to settle for just anything," I warned.

When we arrived, the family was in the yard. They greeted us and took us into their garage where muffled meowing could be heard emanating from a large cardboard box. This was opened and four tiny kittens were placed on the floor. Three of them huddled together in a tight little bemused bundle of fur and squeaked insecurely. The fourth, the smallest of them all, struck out determinedly in a beeline for the yard, head held high, eyes squinting in the unaccustomed brightness, tail held as erect as a flagpole. It tried to run, but was too young to have developed any level of coordination. The result was a gait that resembled inebriation. This, coupled with its incongruous attitude, combined to produce a comical persona. I was immediately drawn to this kitten.

The effect on Cynthia was the same, so we followed it out into the sunshine, laughing at its halting headway. In the sunlight, its coat took on a very unusual hue. The undercoat was a dark brown, but the kitten fluff that puffed out from everywhere had an auburn cast. The effect was quite striking. I had never seen a cat of this color before.

"It's beautiful!" Cynthia gasped. I could tell that she was already enamored with the cat. "And it's not black. What do you call a cat of that color?"

"I don't know. I've never seen one like that before. It's so unusual, it's kind of neat." This kitten, with its can-do attitude and sense of purpose, appealed to me. "But don't get too excited, we don't even know if it's a male or female."

I snatched the kitten up and turned it around, lifting its tail. At two weeks of age, the sex of tiny kittens can be a little difficult to determine. And with my vast three weeks of clinical experience I was, let's say, not the most skilled person at kitten sexing. "Good, it's a female." I looked again, my confidence wavering. "No . . . yeah . . . yeah, it is a female! Right?"

I turned the hindquarters toward my colleague. Dr. Denny was a veterinarian with years of experience who had completed an internship and a residency in internal medicine and was qualified to sit for specialty boards that fall. I knew I could count on his expertise. "Come on, Bruce. You know that! What are you going to do when a client comes in to the office and asks you what sex their kitten is? You're a licensed veterinarian, for heaven's sake."

I was a little embarrassed. Dr. Denny was the one in charge

of my intern class of four recent graduates. In the three short weeks we had been in Rochester, he had rapidly become a mentor to me, someone whose respect I wanted to earn. I certainly didn't want to lose face in something as simple as sexing kittens. I looked again, carefully this time. "Okay, it is a female. I'm sure of it."

Dr. Denny took another look at the evidence. "Okay then."

"That settles it. We'll take this one!" I declared as if the statement carried the weight of national security. "Do you agree, Cynth?" But with one quick glance I knew that no response was necessary. She had the kitten snuggled up against her cheek and was already walking toward the car.

In the course of the drive home, we adopted and promptly dismissed several names for the new kitten. I suggested Marie, a name that Cynthia eliminated without so much as a comment. Cynthia wanted to carry on a line of kitty names begun in her childhood, but I would not abide Princess Prissy Puss the Fourth. A number of other names were brought up and discarded. Finally, after much debate, we settled on the perfect name; one classy enough to work for her when she was mature, yet with a silly edge that would suit her as a tiny kitten. Her name would be Daphne.

A Shot in the Dark

I unlocked the door to the office and let the Stanley family into the lobby. The family was a wreck. Mr. Stanley was a short man dressed in work pants and a threadbare white T-shirt that was stretched tightly over his ample stomach. His face masked a complicated combination of concern, frustration, and other deeper scars at which I cared not to guess. He carried in his arms a young male Brittany spaniel whose face, totally unmasked, was full of fear. Two boys, a young girl, and a large woman in a cotton print dress followed him into the office. The girl, Shelly, was about six years old and kept up a flow of nonstop blathering. She introduced herself to me, then in turn introduced the dog, her brothers, and each of her parents before launching into a detailed description of the injuries her dog had sustained. Most of it I missed, but I did manage to catch the fact that her brothers had shot the dog.

The boys, for their part, were quite meek and quiet, standing carefully out of the way with heads down, only speaking to each other in hushed tones and furtively passing a BB gun back and forth between them like a hot potato.

Mrs. Stanley took up the rear of the procession. She spent half her time competing with her daughter for who could tell the story in the most detail. The other half was spent trying either to comfort her sons for their offense or define their punishment, I couldn't tell which. After doing nothing more than ushering the family into the hospital, I could already feel my head beginning to spin. Emergencies are often that way.

The entire family followed me into an examination room to sort out the story. Apparently, as boys will, Andrew and Kevin had been outside that evening having fun with their BB gun. Though they had been instructed not to shoot it at night, the excitement had gotten the best of them and they found themselves in the backyard shooting at shadows. As they targeted imagined villains in the darkness, they heard a yelp from the direction of their last target. Their dog, coincidentally named Phantom, came scurrying toward them from the shadows, tail tucked between his legs—clearly scared. Kevin and Andrew followed him into the house and furtively examined Phantom. They found a small wound on his side that oozed a little blood. They told their parents about the incident with fear and trembling and then they had called me.

Phantom was a nice dog. Though frightened, he greeted me with dignity and trust. I patted his head and was immediately rewarded with a kiss. He stood on the stainless-steel table, his tail tucked and his legs trembling with fear, his toenails tapping a staccato beat on the tabletop. I carefully examined him, trying to block out the ongoing chatter between mother and daughter. Other than the small puncture wound on his side and a mild harshness when I listened to his lungs, Phantom seemed fine. The wound, which was small, still intermittently dripped a small amount of blood.

"I think everything is going to be all right, guys." I watched Kevin and Andrew visibly relax. "You realize it could have been much worse, though. Phantom is a lucky dog. It could have been in his eye and he would be blind." I caught myself, sensing that neither Kevin nor Andrew suffered from a lack of lecturing. "Well, never mind. Phantom will survive this. It isn't unusual to find pellets in dogs when we X-ray them for some other reason.

Most of the time, the pellets lodge in the tissue just under the skin. The body just walls them off and they cause no problem. I think we should get some X-rays though, just to be sure there aren't any internal injuries."

I lifted Phantom and carried him to the X-ray room, confident that X-rays would confirm my diagnosis. I took two X-rays, one with Phantom lying on his back and another while lying on his side. This allowed me to visualize the chest in three dimensions. On the side view I could clearly see the BB sitting above the heart shadow, just where I expected it. That was where the entry wound was. As I put the other X-ray on the view box I caught my breath. I fully expected to find the BB located just under the skin where the entry wound was. But there it was right in the middle of the picture just in front of the heart. That meant that the BB was in the chest cavity itself. What to do?

I took the X-rays and went back into the examination room. I put Phantom back up on the table and carefully examined him again. With the stethoscope I listened to his heart and lungs long and hard. Just a mild harshness was noticeable with each breath. No discomfort or difficulty breathing was apparent. Phantom seemed none the worse for wear. He was alert and bright, his gums were pink, and he was active. My vet school professor's mantra came to mind and I made my judgment. "Always treat the patient—not the X-rays" were his words.

"It does look like the BB is in the chest cavity. It appears to have just missed the heart and the aorta. Phantom is a lot luckier than I originally thought. Fortunately, Phantom seems to be doing all right. There is no evidence of any immediate danger. I'm going to put Phantom on some antibiotics to prevent any infection. And I don't expect any further problems."

"But what about that bullet, Doctor?" Shelly clearly didn't buy my diagnosis. As I looked around the room I could tell that the rest of the Stanleys shared her skepticism.

I knelt down to the little girl's level and tried to calm her fears. "I don't think that's going to be a problem. The body will form a wall of scar tissue around it and it will just sit there all his life. Phantom won't know the difference. Anyway, it would be too hard on Phantom to do surgery and get it out. BBs that small can be extremely difficult to locate during surgery. We could cause more trouble than we'd solve. I'm sure that he'd just as soon we leave it there."

No sooner had the words passed my lips than Phantom lowered his head and coughed three times. On the third cough, a sharp clink was heard as something metallic fell onto the stainless-steel tabletop. A BB rolled noisily across the stainless steel and came to a stop just in front of me. In my kneeling position, the BB stopped not six inches from my nose. The room fell silent. For just a moment the entire Stanley family was focused on the BB. Then in unison they shifted their gaze to me. My explanation was immediate and definitive.

"Uh . . . well . . . that's a new one on me."

Kevin and Andrew gulped and then started giggling nervously. Pretty soon we were all laughing. The tension in the room evaporated and the family began to draw together again. Their confidence in me regenerated. Even Phantom sensed the change. He jumped down off the table and ran from one of us to the other, barking excitedly.

"Take this boy home. Give him his antibiotics and call me if there are any problems."

As I locked the door to the office after I had escorted the Stanleys out, I shook my head and laughed as I thought of that BB rolling across the table. What a story! Who would believe such a thing? I wouldn't have if I hadn't been there myself. Mr. Stanley honked the horn as a final thank-you as the car pulled away from the clinic.

My First Time

The night was suddenly filled with a high-pitched, intermittent whistle. I jolted awake and sat upright in the bed, my mind fumbling to make sense of the noise. The alarm clock? No, it was set for 6:30 A.M. and it was now only one thirty in the morning. The phone? Wrong sound. The fire alarm? No, not loud enough. Then it dawned on me—my beeper.

By now I am quite accustomed to being awakened by my beeper in the middle of the night. But in the summer of 1987 I had just started my internship in Rochester. This was, in fact, one of my first rotations through the emergency service at the hospital. As the emergency clinician on duty, my shift started at six thirty in the evening and ended at nine thirty the next morning. Most nights it was busy until midnight or so, then calmed down enough for me to catch a few winks. But that night it was not to be.

I dialed with trepidation the number that the answering service gave me. I had only been in practice for a month or two and had not yet developed the confidence that comes with experience. Mrs. Ansen was worried about her cocker spaniel, Ashley, who had been due to have a litter of pups the day before. I could tell that the bonds of love between Mrs. Ansen and her pet were strong and advised that we examine Ashley as soon as possible.

Mrs. Ansen, her sister, and Ashley arrived at the hospital about two fifteen in the morning. Ashley was a timid, sweet little dog who proved to be completely baffled by impending motherhood. She had big brown eyes and eyelashes that would be the envy of all the ladies in the bridge club. Through those lashes she eyed me coyly, carefully positioning herself behind Mrs. Ansen. Ashley was clearly in the later stages of pregnancy. Her stomach nearly brushed the ground as she walked, and her mammary glands were swollen with milk. She had that uncomfortable look unique to soon-to-be mothers that says, my bladder is always full and my lungs are not.

Mrs. Ansen described how Ashley had begun to have contractions the previous afternoon. She had had strong contractions for several hours, then they had simply stopped. I took Ashley's temperature and found it to be low—a sure sign that birth was impending.

Donning a sterile glove, I performed a digital examination of Ashley's birth canal. As I slipped my finger in, I almost immediately bumped up against a little puppy nose. Gently I probed into the puppy's mouth and was rewarded with a soft little nip.

As exciting as it was, it was also a little frightening since it was the first time I had faced a difficult birth. I had placed Mrs. Ansen and Ashley in exam room number one. In exam room number two I had several veterinary textbooks laid out on the tabletop, opened to the section on difficult whelping. Each time I had a question, I would nonchalantly leave the room and hurry next door to pore over the textbooks. Then I would stride back into the room with renewed confidence, carrying an instrument or two to justify my leaving, and proceed with my examination and treatment. They must have suspected that I suffered from uncontrollable diarrhea or some other malady that forced me to run without warning for relief.

Following the protocol in the book, I administered calcium injections and oxytocin to Ashley two or three times over the next several hours. During the wee hours of the morning, three healthy pups were born to Ashley and her owner. As each new life emerged squirming, slippery, and vocal into the world, I took it and shook the placental fluids from its airways. Then I rubbed it vigorously with a clean, warmed towel until it sang the endearing song of the newborn puppy. I carefully tied off the umbilical cord, severed it, and dipped the remaining one inch of umbilical stump into iodine disinfectant, before placing the newborn with its inquisitive mom.

It was exciting to see Ashley worry over each new little puppy. She industriously surveyed her new charge from nose to tail as if counting the toes and looking for any other abnormalities. Then she licked the remaining placental fluids from the coat and nudged the pup toward its first meal. It was an incredibly exciting night made all the more so by the fact that I had never experienced whelping before in any fashion, much less as the primary caregiver.

The scene was taken in by an exultant mother and a doting and adoring owner. But their pride paled in comparison to mine. It was an especially poignant moment for me. After the last pup was delivered, I stood drying my hands on a towel and considered the scenario. Suddenly the all-night study sessions, the countless hours in the dissection lab, every difficult test I ever took, even the abuse at the hands of interns as a lowly senior student all made sense. I no longer resented all the school bills or the low starting pay. All were a small price to pay for this: the soft, closed-eyed squeaking from three perfect pups and the proud, thankful mother's eyes as she nursed them for the first time. This would never get old for me. My whole life, since age seven or eight, had been directed by my goal to one day be overseeing this very scene.

When I recollect that night, which I often do, it is with a mixture of incredible pride and shameful hypocrisy. Ashley's was the first case of difficult whelping that I had successfully managed. It had been a victory! Though Mrs. Ansen must have wondered why I made so many trips out of the room during my evaluation, my professional pride would not allow me to divulge the fact that Ashley was a first for me. I maintained the illusion (or at least thought I did) that her case was just another in a long series of successful birthings.

As the sun came up, I felt it was safe to discharge Ashley and her litter to the care of her owner. As Mrs. Ansen and her sister filed through the front door, she turned to me with tears in her eyes and a catch in her voice and said with deep gratitude, “Oh, Doctor, this is so beautiful. It must have been quite a thrill for you the first time you saw this!”

It was, Mrs. Ansen. Indeed it was!

Daphne, the Transvestite

Daphne quickly became an obsession for Cynthia and me. The minuscule stature with that gargantuan manner was maintained as she grew larger. At first, we confined her to a small cardboard box at night, but within just a few days, she would settle for nothing less than sleeping on our bed where she would wrap herself around Cynthia's head on the pillow, sometimes disappearing completely into her hair. I must admit to some concern about this arrangement as Cynthia, then as now, slept at the depth of surgical anesthesia. I could envision the little mite being trapped and seriously injured while she slept. But I could talk neither Cynthia nor Daphne out of this sleeping arrangement and eventually learned to quell my fears.

Within a week or two of her arrival, Daphne mastered the skill of climbing onto the bed. This was quite a feat as our bed was an unusually tall waterbed that towered over her like a mountain. Crouching beside it, with all the strength in her, she would leap as high onto the side of the bed as she could. Then, with claws extended and groping, she would scale the face of the mattress cliff, literally grunting with the effort. The sound evoked Velcro being separated with the background accompaniment of nails on a chalkboard. It had the jolting effect each time of bolting me upright from a sound sleep. The first time she was successful at this climb, she reached the summit proudly, her face completely obscured by a huge cat toy she had carried in her mouth during the ascent.

From the very first, Daphne was dependent upon us, in a uniquely feline sort of way. Wherever we were in the apartment Daphne had to be there too. Sometimes she wanted to lounge decadently in our laps. But often it was enough just to be close and observe our activities from the height of an armrest on the couch in her singular sphinxlike pose. Watching her you had little doubt but that she was completely disgusted with the absurd little humans under her control, so disdainful was her expression. But the next moment she would be at your side ingratiatingly soliciting a massage or enticing you into her favorite game of fetch.

She loved to watch Cynthia get ready for work, sitting quietly on the side of the makeup table equally as engrossed as Cynthia in the chore of applying foundation and blush. As if she wanted to try some herself, she would gently paw at Cynthia's hand persuasively and quietly chirp her little purr. Sometimes, when Cynthia had her face close to her lighted mirror, Daphne's little face would appear magnified in the mirror as she looked over Cynthia's shoulder. This activity quickly developed in Daphne a firm affinity for Cynthia's makeup brushes. They became her favorite toys. We would find them all over the house. She would seldom patrol the apartment without one of them clutched in her little mouth like the kill from a hunt.

If she was asleep on the bed you could awaken her simply by tapping a makeup brush with your finger. Even while sleeping, she could immediately identify the sound and awaken with a start. When her eyes caught sight of it, she would freeze in stalk posture, flooded with the adrenaline of the chase. Her head would sink down in the universal feline prowl position. Her hindquarters would draw up under her, trembling with all the potential energy of a taut spring, and her eyes would dilate widely with intensity. She would remain in that position unendingly, waiting for you to fling the brush across the room. Then she would hurl herself from her post, careening with abandon after the fleeing prey. With all the fury of a lioness she would pounce upon the brush, gripping its neck in angry teeth, and shaking it violently until all the life was drained from it. Then she would lift it solemnly and carry it back to you across the bedroom savannah while emitting her characteristic hunting moan, finally dropping it at your feet as if she were presenting you with a feast after the long, hungry dry season. If you picked it up, she was immediately prepared for the hunt again. This game became her purpose in life. She was addicted; she was committed; she was persistent; she was ruthless.

Over time we developed variations of this game. When she was on the floor, for instance, you could throw the brush high over her head and she would fling herself in unimaginably athletic contortions trying to catch it. Sometimes she would complete gymnastic maneuvers with unbelievably high degrees of difficulty: round offs, back handsprings, backflips, or half gainers with a full twist. Endlessly she would rehearse these tricks. I generally tired before she did.

One day, about three weeks after her arrival in our home, I noticed something that took me off guard. She had adopted the pose that cats usually do while grooming their backsides: sitting on her haunches, one back leg raised high like a student requesting bathroom privileges. Down there, under the tail in the region she was grooming, I noticed an odd swelling. Alarmed, I grabbed her and threw her unceremoniously onto her back. Not only was there a small linear growth, but it was accompanied by two round appendages. I gasped and sank to the ground as the diagnosis dawned on my consciousness.

Daphne was a male! I don't recall whether I was more appalled by the fact that I now had a tomcat or that I had been so absolutely erroneous about her . . . his gender. Probably it was a combination of both, though the thought of divulging my error to my colleagues galled me more than I cared to admit.

With a great deal of hemming and hawing, I confessed the

truth to Cynthia who handled the information with much less tact and sensitivity than I thought was indicated. Her unbridled levity left me with little hope of maintaining any shred of professional dignity when this news leaked at the hospital.

The fact that Daphne was a male disturbed Cynthia not in the least. Frankly, even for me, this fact did nothing to curb my hopeless infatuation with the kitten. In fact, knowing that Daphne was a male clarified some of the incongruities of behavior that I had observed. It made more sense, I reasoned, for a male cat to be so engrossed in hunting and fetching than for a female, though it flew in the face of all the amassed knowledge of feline behavior in the pride.

The two most pressing problems this development presented for us were the need for a new name and the changing of gender pronouns when we talked about her . . . him. Much discussion ensued about the appropriate moniker for him. Spitting out names indiscriminately like a word association exercise proved fruitless for both Cynthia and myself. I was amazed that a person of her intelligence and experience would come up with names so imbecilic. She, on the other hand, felt much the same about the ones I nominated. And now, after having him with us for three weeks, we had a clear picture of his personality to guide us, which you would think would make the job easier, but instead only clouded the issue.

What we needed was a methodology for coming up with possible names, a theme to follow or a pattern to start the process. While silently driving in the car one day, both of us fed up with the epithet drivel being propounded by the other, the voice of the news reporter on the radio caught my ear. At that time, the headlines were replete with details of the Senate hearings on the Iran-contra scandal and its central figure, Oliver North. Having little political interest, these stories had been only peripheral to my consciousness.

What I did know of Oliver North, however, seemed appropriate for our nameless cat. He was a man of conviction and loyalty, one who followed that conviction with action—however misdirected. He was always dressed to the nines in his military uniform and carried himself perhaps a little more proudly than his rank called for. He was incredibly earnest and more sincere about some things than was to his advantage. At the same time he exhibited a studied disinterest in things he considered below himself. All these things described our little kitten quite well.

"Hey, Cynthia!" I broke the chilled silence suddenly. "What about Oliver North? That guy is a dead ringer for Daphne." I listed the resemblances to her mounting amusement and enthusiasm.

"That's perfect!" she replied, and the name was settled from that point on. Oliver North seemed to approve of his new name, responding to it almost immediately. As any good name does, it also lent itself easily to a number of variations, and Oliver proved himself amenable to all its permutations. He came when we called him whether we called him Oliver, Ollie, Ollie-Wall, Olive, or any number of other nicknames based loosely on the original.

Ollie had had a pretty rough start in life as orphans often do. As a consequence, his coat health left much to be desired when he first joined us. Despite its interesting color, it had the rough and unkempt quality of a parasitized kitten. I had taken him in to the hospital and started his vaccines at the appropriate times, of course, but returning his coat to normal health was a task of several weeks. Until then, we accepted his scruffy appearance knowing that with time, his unusual coat would begin to gleam with the glow of health.

Unfortunately, Ollie developed a profound case of diarrhea shortly after joining us that seriously compromised him. Such small kittens have few reserves to call on when they are ill. This was doubly true since everything he ate ran through him like an Olympic sprinter. Losing large quantities of water quickly dehydrated him to the point where fluid supplementation became necessary. This was done by injecting a saline solution under his skin three or four times daily. I also treated him with an oral liquid antibiotic to kill the offending intestinal parasites.

Ollie was anything but a willing participant in his therapy.

Though the oral medications had a pleasant butterscotch flavor (at least it's pleasant to us), he was incredibly offended by these unwelcome invasions of his personal space. This indignation was compounded by my poking him indiscriminately with what he considered to be extremely oversized needles and pumping unbelievable quantities of fluids under his skin. This procedure left him with large, camel-like humps on his back that he despised. After each treatment he would glare at me, swat me with his front claws, and emit a malignant hiss and growl. The fact that this bravado was comical to us, coming as it was from such a tiny imp, simply added insult to his injury and he would slink away under the couch, casting diabolical glowers over his shoulder as he went.

For two weeks we followed this protocol until finally his diarrhea resolved. With time he began to regain a normal healthy sheen to his coat. This, of course, we were pleased to see. But as this process continued there was something strange that I could not quite put my finger on. More and more there were subtle changes to his coat. As the gleam returned, the auburn cast became less noticeable and his brown color darkened. These changes were insidious and with our seeing him every day, they were so incremental that I didn't realize just what was happening. Until one day, that is, when I came home and the realization struck me full in the face.

Ollie's coloration had completely changed. The white on his paws, tummy, and chest contrasted starkly with the rest of his body, which was now undeniably and unapologetically black! How had this happened? By that time, however, his power over me was undisputed. I was completely under his spell. He was a part of the family and I could muster no resentment against the conspiracy.

For the first time, I completely understood my cat-owning clients. No longer were they a mystery to me. I discarded as fallacious my previous delusions about cats as pets. Gone was the idea that only dogs were worthy of our affections. No longer did I subscribe to the notion that cats are less dependent than dogs, or that they are less bonded to their owners. Abandoned was the perception that cats are indifferent and diffident to human existence, or that they interact with humans solely for their utilitarian purposes. Cats could indeed hold the same place in the human heart as do dogs. Ollie, my black male cat had seen to that.

A Cheep Shot

Strange things happen under a full moon, so the old wives' tale goes. I hesitate to take a position on this, though in my experience I have discovered a corollary of this theory that rings true enough to warrant further investigation. While strange things may not reveal themselves under a full moon, strange people certainly do. I admit that this may not hold up under scrutiny, since strange people tend to remain strange whether the moon is full or not. Of that fact I have become convinced, having had it proven to me over and over again. I suspect this is no deep revelation to you. Most often this truth is reiterated to me in the darkness of night after the office has closed.

I'm not sure why. But it seems that as the business of the day recedes with the daylight, and the radios, TVs, and children's voices give way to the chirping of the crickets, people have a little time to sit back and contemplate the deeper, weightier issues that lurk just behind the press of the day.

These are not issues to be wrestled with at desks, or at coffee breaks, nor while negotiating the traffic jam on the way to work or vacuuming the house. These themes seem to require the silence of night, solitude, twinkling stars, perhaps a stiff drink or two, and, of course, a full moon to work through. For most of us, these issues center around the great questions: Who am I? Why am I here? Where am I going? But for the full moon people, the questions, though just as unanswerable, are not as profound.

When these questions entangle themselves into the sulci of strange brains, the full moon people look for answers from known experts: people who have dedicated literally years of their lives to intense study, people who are trained to discuss complicated things in language that can be easily understood. But most important, people who don't mind dispensing their limitless knowledge at all hours of the night for absolutely no remuneration. That's when these strange people decide to call their veterinarian.

My beeper has gone off deep into the night many times to get answers to such pressing queries as: Do you think I can reserve a boarding space for my dog for six weeks from now while I'm on vacation (9:25 P.M.)? I think my dogs are stuck together, what should I do (10:15 P.M.)? Why did you test for female leukemia in my cat? He's a boy! (11:30 P.M.) How many eggs does a platypus lay (12:30 A.M.)? Or my personal favorite: What do you call a baby swan (no joke, 3:00 A.M.)? I'm sure you can spot the trend here. The later the call, the more important and pressing the question.

One such call stands out in my mind. Having just graduated from veterinary school, I had not yet become completely comfortable with my education, so each time I took a call, I experienced a certain degree of anxiety. Would I know the right answer? Would I be able to communicate it effectively? Would I be credible? Would my insecurity be too obvious? This call was no exception. The caller was a young, apparently sophisticated woman who clearly was shaken.

"Thank you for taking my call, Dr. Coston. This may sound rather crazy, but I need some direction."

"What seems to be the problem?"

"Well, tonight I got home from work late and decided to boil an egg for supper." There was an apologetic, self-conscious pause.

I waited patiently for what seemed like a long time. The silence persisted.

"And you need some direction on how to boil your egg?" I asked sarcastically, checking my watch. It was ten thirty in the evening.

"Of course not. No, but when I put the egg in the water, I heard some cheeping coming from the egg." I pulled back the shades and glanced to the east. The moon was low on the horizon and full. "I wasn't sure about it," she continued, "so I woke up my husband and he heard it too. Is that possible?"

My heart immediately went out to this poor saintly man. "Well, no, I don't think so. Sometimes there is a small pocket of air trapped under the shell on one end of the egg. It's possible that as the egg warms in the water, some of that air is escaping and making a noise. There should be nothing to worry about."

"No, that's not it, I'm sure. It sounded just like a little chick!"

"Are these eggs that you collected yourself from your own chickens?" This seemed to me to be a silly question since the practice where I worked was located in the heart of a city of several hundred thousand people. But I consoled myself in the knowledge that silly questions were apparently the order of the evening.

"No. I got them at the grocery store last week."

"Well, I can assure you that those eggs are not fertile. Eggs produced for retail sale are laid by hens that have never seen hide nor feather of a rooster."

"If they've never been with a rooster, how can they lay eggs?"

I thought about pointing out that she produced eggs regularly whether or not she was with a rooster, but realized in the nick of time that this would serve only to further confuse the already confused. Instead, I again tried the reasoning approach. "That's just how the physiology of the chicken works. They lay eggs daily. But the eggs only form chicks if they are fertilized by a rooster. Commercial laying hens are never exposed to roosters."

"Oh, I didn't know that."

"In addition to that," I continued, "all eggs are screened by trained specialists who shine a light through them looking for any sign of problems or fertility. It's called candling. A fertile egg would never make it through the candling process."

With no apparent consideration of this information, she immediately struck out in another direction. "Maybe someone messed up and confused a male for a female and the rooster grew up with the hens."

However, in a split second of clear thinking, she discounted this theory without my help. "I guess that couldn't happen, could it? The rooster would think the hens were his sisters and wouldn't mate with them, would he?"

Before I could entirely process this line of reasoning, she took off on yet another tangent.

"I should have known not to get them. The eggs were already so large I should have realized how close they were to hatching."

Keeping the phone to my ear so I wouldn't miss anything, I laid my forehead in my palm and shook my head. That I was making little progress was slowly coming clear to me.

"No, ma'am. That's not how it works. The eggs stay the same size from the time they are laid until they hatch. Only the embryo grows. But again, I'm quite sure there is no embryo in your egg. Even if there was, it wouldn't still be alive. The gestation length of the chicken is something like three weeks. From the time eggs are laid in the chicken house until they reach the store shelves is much less time than that!"

"You don't think my chick is alive? How could it be cheeping if it's not alive?"

"I don't think I'm making myself clear. Your egg does not contain a live chick!" What was initially amusement was quickly turning into frustration. "Look, even if the unthinkable happened and the hen had somehow reproduced the virgin birth, even if magically the incubation period was shortened in your egg to two weeks or less, a chick could not survive the refrigeration eggs are exposed to. Successful incubation occurs only in a very narrow temperature range. If it gets too hot or too cold, the embryos do not survive. Now, were the eggs you bought in the refrigerator section of the store?"

"Yes."

"Did you take them home and immediately put them in your refrigerator?"

"Yes."

I had found the secret: leading questions. I was making real progress here and was darned proud of it. "Good. Now, have the eggs ever been out of the refrigerator since you got them home?" The pause that followed was longer than it should have been. I began to fear that she had not followed my lead after all.

"There! There it is again! Ernest, did you hear that?" In the background I heard Ernest, who was apparently laughing too uproariously to have heard it. "Be quiet, Ernest, and listen."

I was glad Ernest was enjoying this, but my patience was wearing thin. "Ma'am?" No answer. "Ma'am . . . hello?"

"*There*!" The shriek virtually pierced my eardrum. "Oh, Doctor, I can't stand it. Do you think he's suffering?" I, of course, couldn't speak for the chick, but I certainly was. "Do you think the other eggs in the carton are ready to hatch too?"

It was no use. Clearly this was a woman who would be satisfied only with direct visual evidence. "Ma'am, why don't you just crack open the egg. Then you'll see that there is really no chick inside." Why this brilliant advice had eluded me so far was a mystery to me, but certainly this would bring this phone call to an end.

"But the egg timer hasn't gone off yet." She said it as if I had overlooked the most obvious of culinary rituals—which of course I had.

"You're right, but if it's really a chick, which it most certainly is not, and it's cheeping as you say, which is absolutely impossible, you wouldn't want to keep cooking it, would you?"

"Yeah, I see what you mean."

"So go ahead and crack it open. You'll see everything will be all right."

"What do I do if the chick is still alive?"

By this time my head was spinning, I was tired and beginning to question my own logic. I was also more than just a little bit frustrated with this lady. So I did have some excuse for confusing my adverbs, you must admit. But, honestly, my tongue just played a trick on me. It was just a slip, truly. With forced patience I finally said, "Okay. If the chick is still alive, then you'll have to put it out of its misery mercilessly."

I had meant to say *mercifully!* Really I did. Immediately I realized my slip and, bursting into laughter, I put the receiver down before she could say anything more. Perhaps it was Freudian, perhaps not. Either way, I admit it was a cheep shot.

By the way, should you need to know what a baby swan is called, the correct answer at 3:00 P.M. is a cygnet. At 3:00 A.M., however, the correct answer is an egg.

Too Little Sugar

While my internship afforded me a great deal of experience in a short time, there were definitely trade-offs. The most significant of which was the time embezzled from my wife and me. We had only been married a couple of years when we moved to upstate New York for my internship. We were still essentially newlyweds.

Our time together was especially meager during the two weeks out of every eight when I was scheduled for emergency coverage. Throughout my emergency rotation, I was kept very busy with emergencies until about midnight or so. After that, I could concentrate on caring for critical patients in the hospital, writing records, and answering the occasional telephone call. Many nights I was able to get a few hours of sleep in the doctor's quarters. After my shift I would drag myself home and flop uselessly into my bed to sleep the day away. Since my wife worked regular human hours, we were able to spend very little time together during that rotation.

Unable to stand those weeks of separation, Cynthia and I developed a strategy that allowed us to spend some extra time together. She would come to the hospital about nine o'clock in the evening and attend me on my rounds until midnight or so before heading back home to go to bed. Anita, our evening receptionist, and Kristen, the technician, granted us this luxury with only the slightest teasing and a few knowing winks and nods between them. But Cynthia and I didn't care.

Knowing how much my wife likes her sleep, I recognized how much she was sacrificing for this stolen time. My memory shades those nights in very special hues as I think back on them. As I gained invaluable experience and confidence in veterinary medicine, I fell more deeply in love with both my wife and my career.

In order to preserve my professional image with the clients that came in on those nights, we concocted a charade that Cynthia was a technician who was assisting me with my duties. To lend credibility to this charade, before each patient I would give Cynthia a quick course in the technique we would be doing so she could appear proficient. I also insisted that she address me as Dr. Coston in front of the clients. This she did despite the fact that it was completely foreign to her. This system served us very well throughout my internship.

On one such night, I received a call from a client about eight thirty in the evening. "Good evening, Doctor. This is Caroline Schleck. I'm very concerned about my cat, Louie. He's a ten-year-old Siamese and he's had diabetes for about a year now. This evening he got his insulin injection as usual about five o'clock. But then he got sick and vomited all his supper. Now he's really wobbly on his feet. Do you think this can wait until morning?"

"No, ma'am. It sounds like his blood sugar levels are low. That can be life-threatening. You should bring him in immediately!"

"Really? It's that serious? Couldn't we just give him another dose of insulin?"

"Whatever you do, don't do that! That could kill him. I really think it's a matter of life and death. Get him here right away!"

"Okay, if you really think so. It might take us about an hour or longer to get ready and come in, though."

"The sooner you get here the better, Mrs. Schleck. I'll look for you soon."

I was worried. I didn't get the idea that Mrs. Schleck understood the seriousness of the situation. In diabetic patients, the insulin shots that control the disease are not without risk. Low blood sugar, known as hypoglycemic insulin shock, occurs if there is an overdose of the insulin or if a patient gets sick after its dose of insulin. Since glucose is the brain's sole energy source, lack of glucose in the bloodstream can result in a wobbly gait and weakness that, if untreated, can progress to seizures, coma, brain damage, and eventually death.

I went to the treatment room and gathered the things I thought I would need. I set up for an intravenous catheter, a blood glucose test, and got out a solution of concentrated glucose for injection, just in case.

About this time, Cynthia arrived at the hospital for the evening. I explained the situation and described the procedures we would need to do as soon as the Schlecks arrived with Louie. She was concerned too, not really knowing what to expect or how exactly she could help. The buzzer at the front door alerted us to the Schlecks arrival.

"Remember, call me Dr. Coston," I reminded Cynthia just before I opened the door for the couple and their pet.

The Schlecks came into the examination room and placed a plastic carrier on the table with Louie inside. Unlike me, they displayed not the slightest concern.

"I'm sure we're overreacting, Dr. Coston." Mrs. Schleck was a very sophisticated, middle-aged woman who carried herself with an air of calm self-assurance. Mr. Schleck, a dignified tax attorney, smiled warmly and shook my hand.

"Shortly after I talked with you, Louie went to sleep. He's been sleeping soundly since then. Rest should really be good for him, I would think."

I opened the door of the carrier and looked in at my patient. The blood drained from my face. Louie wasn't asleep. He was comatose! With no pretense of calmness, I jerked Louie out of the box and laid him on the table. There was no response to any stimulus. His breathing was shallow and slow. His heart rate was only about eighty beats per minute rather than the normal one hundred and forty to one hundred and sixty. His gums were quite pale. He barely blinked his lids when I touched a finger to the surface of his eye. I had never seen a patient so close to death before.

With Cynthia holding up Louie's head, I plunged a needle into his neck to collect some blood. The blood glucose level was only forty. The lowest end of normal is sixty-five. Louie needed glucose; and he needed it fast! I glanced over at the Schlecks. It was clear that they were starting to understand the predicament Louie was in.

"Louie is in hypoglycemic shock. His blood sugar levels are dangerously low. Unless he gets his glucose levels stabilized immediately, we could lose him. I hope there has been no permanent brain damage yet."

Mrs. Schleck blanched and put her head on her husband's shoulder. His concern was also apparent as he tried to comfort his wife. "Should we just put him to sleep, Dr. Coston? We hate to see him suffer." At her husband's words, I saw Mrs. Schleck's shoulders shake with subdued sobs.

"Hold the vein off like this, Cynthia. We need to place a butterfly catheter so we can administer glucose." I continued my frantic work of placing the catheter, while directing an answer to the Schlecks over my shoulder.

"No euthanasia yet! Let's see how he responds to treatment first. Unless you refuse treatment, I'm going ahead with it." The Schlecks' response to this was an audible sigh of relief and silence allowing me to concentrate on my work.

I quickly injected a large volume of the concentrated glucose solution into the vein through the catheter I had placed. Holding my breath, I waited for Louie's response. I anticipated a rapid improvement to this treatment. Failure to respond rapidly would probably mean irreversible brain damage. In no time at all, I had emptied the syringe full of glucose. I waited a few seconds, my breath catching in my throat. No response.

"Cynthia, I'm going to have to go get some more of the glucose solution. Watch the patient for a second."

I turned on my heel and left the room, but not before Cynthia, my erstwhile technician, gave me a look that said emphatically and unmistakably: "I don't know what to do. Don't leave me alone with this cat." But time was of the essence, so I continued into the treatment room leaving the door open behind me.

As I was returning to the room, I heard a shrill call, dripping with urgency, barked from the examination room. "Brucey, hon, he's starting to move, what do I do?" In the heat of the crisis, Cynthia's concern had overcome her attention to professional image and she had fallen back on her pet name for me.

The knowing glances the Schlecks exchanged as I entered the room were transparent. It was clear what they were thinking: "So Dr. Coston has a little something on the side with his assistant, doesn't he?" Their grins spread as I approached Louie, unmistakably communicating their unspoken thoughts, "We know your secret."

My attention, though, was on my patient. Louie was magically reviving. Little by little his mental status was improving. Within a minute he was lifting his head and looking around the room. A minute after that he sat up and meowed weakly to his owners. "Oh, what happened? What was in that drink?" he seemed to say. Within five minutes, he was standing steadily and rubbing against my hand. When I placed a bowl of food in front of him, he ate hungrily.

I hospitalized Louie overnight for observation and sent the Schlecks home to get a little sleep before their day began. Through the night, Louie's recovery was miraculous and complete. His blood glucose quickly stabilized in the normal range and stayed there throughout the night. The next morning when I discharged him to the very grateful Schlecks, he was the picture of normalcy. Yet as pleased as I was to be sending home a healthy patient, it was somewhat sheepishly that I faced Louie's owners.

"I'm sorry I didn't introduce you to my wife last night," I said by way of explanation. "Things were happening so fast that I just didn't think about it."

But the Schlecks were clearly not buying. Through their gratitude I could still see thinly veiled amusement. They knew, despite what to them was a feeble excuse, that I had a thing going on with one of the hospital assistants. With a wink they let me know that their silence on the matter was their form of gratitude.

Chinchilla Surprise

Anita, the night receptionist at the twenty-four-hour animal hospital where I was doing my internship, handed me the record with a look of veiled amusement. Anita was in her forties, a rather quiet and retiring woman who found the stress of the emergency shift difficult. During emergencies, her face always took on, if possible, even more strain than usual. I could assess the seriousness of an emergency by how high her voice ascended the chromatic scale. Seeing humor on her face was a good thing, but it made me wonder just what I was in for.

"This ought to be a fun one for you," she said. "How many times have you treated a chinchilla?"

"Treated one! I've never even seen one before."

My job provides a degree of variety that few other jobs do. One minute I am a dentist and the next an ophthalmologist. One patient needs orthopedic care and the next one needs a proctologist. In one examination room I may encounter a one hundred and seventy-five pound mastiff and in the next room I'm met with a parakeet. If it's true that variety is the spice of life, then my life is a spicy one indeed. I've come to expect the unexpected, and frankly, I would have it no other way.

Kristen, the night veterinary technician, took the record from me and glanced through it quickly. Kristen was a recent immigrant from Germany and spoke with a heavy accent. I had come to depend on her a great deal. Not only did she know all the practice politics and policies and where all the supplies were, but she also had a wealth of clinical experience far exceeding my own that had proven invaluable to me as I learned the ropes. In the few months since my internship had begun, she had bailed me out more than once. Kristen didn't try to hide her amusement about the current case.

"Eez just a hurd leg, Dohctoor. I hev seen meny shinsheela. Theenk of eet as a geenee peeg."

"That doesn't help at all, Kristen. I haven't treated very many of those either."

"Eet vill be okay. Just let me hold eet for you. You vill see."

I followed her into the examination room trying to emanate an attitude of nonchalant confidence. Perched atop the shoulder of a stunningly beautiful young woman was my patient, Sandy. Sandy was a ten-month-old male chinchilla who was obviously quite devoted to his owner. I was stressed by my lack of experience with chinchillas to begin with. The fact that Sandy's owner was gorgeous flustered me all the more.

"Tell me what happened, Mrs. Hollis."

"Oh, it's not Mrs. Hollis. Call me Linda. I'm not married."

Of course not, I thought, my face flushing red and my mind whizzing like it was in a wind tunnel. "Okay, Linda. You say that Sandy is favoring his leg? Since when?"

"Well, just this evening he was up on my shoulder. He likes it up there. He'll stay there all evening as I watch TV. Anyway, the phone rang and when I reached down to pick it up, he fell off. He hit the ground really hard. He started dragging that leg immediately afterward and he's been doing it ever since."

"Put him down here on the table, why don't you. Let's see what we've got."

Sandy seemed resigned to his injury. Exotic pets are experts at hiding their injuries. In the wild, lame chinchillas quickly fall victim to predators, so faking health is a lifesaving necessity.

When Linda put him down, he stood still as if it hurt too much to move, his right front leg hanging uselessly at his side. Finally he began to explore the exam table on the other three legs, not even trying to move the injured leg. Either a broken bone or an injury of the peripheral nerves, I thought to myself. I could feel Kristen's eyes on me questioningly. Our eyes met and I could tell she was thinking the same thing. This was a bad injury.

Sandy made his way to the edge of the table and I instinctively reached out to prevent a fall. I was amazed at how incredibly soft his fur was—like running your fingers through whipped cream. I picked him up. He weighed less than two pounds and from the look of it, most of the weight was hair and ears. His big, round, paper-thin, almost translucent ears were held erect, framing his intensely dark, bright eyes. His little, pointed nose squirmed continuously and he wiggled his long whiskers in accompaniment. *Perky* was the adjective that came immediately to mind.

I made a point to examine Sandy just as I would any of my other patients. Though I may not have seen a chinchilla before, the principles of physical examination and diagnostic protocol certainly were applicable here. I went over him from head to toe with special care—both because I wanted to be thorough and because I was curious. The two large incisor teeth were common to all his rodent cousins. His heart and lungs sounded normal through the stethoscope, despite the fact that the heartbeat was about twice as fast as most hearts I routinely listened to, at two hundred and fifty or three hundred beats per minute. The skin was very thin, but had no bruises or bumps that might be associated with internal injuries. Though Sandy didn't appreciate it, I could feel his bladder, kidneys, intestines, and spleen when I gently palpated his abdomen.

Lastly, I evaluated the injured leg, amazed at how small the bone structures were. There was no swelling at the toes and no injuries to the pads. I half expected to feel the ends of broken bones scraping against each other, but was pleasantly surprised when I didn't. Surprisingly, Sandy didn't exhibit any significant pain when I probed up and down the leg. This puzzled me.

After feeling his leg from toes to shoulder, I was no closer to a diagnosis. Fortunately, the other leg provided a comparison with a normal leg, so I carefully examined it as well. I could detect no differences. To a little prick with a needle, Sandy responded with a quiet squeal and a wiggle of the foot. I straightened up and turned to look at Sandy's owner.

"I need to get the X-ray machine ready, Linda. I think we should take an X-ray of that leg. We'll be right back in to get Sandy for his pictures." Then turning to Kristen, I added, "Can you come help me get things set up for radiographs?"

When we got out of the room, Kristen grinned wryly. "You hev no ideeah vut is goink on, do you?" she said between giggles. She was enjoying my puzzlement way too much, I thought.

"Why? Do you?"

"Vhy, no. But you are ze dohctoor, no?"

"Thanks, Kristen." She laughed again as she prepared the X-ray machine for the procedure. "I don't get it. I sure don't feel any fractures. I felt the whole leg and there don't seem to be any painful areas. And the nerves are functioning normally. He has pain perception and voluntary movement. And there is no asymmetry between the two legs. What do you think?"

Kristen smiled and there was a twinkle in her eye, but she remained silent. I could see I was getting no help from her on this one.

"Okay, smart aleck," I said. "Let's go get some X-rays."

"Before we take these films, Linda, I want to check one more thing," I said as we strode back into the examination room. "Kristen, hold onto Sandy while I try to manipulate the leg again."

She looked at me with a question mark in her eyes and I managed a furtive shrug of my shoulders. Once again I bent over the little animal and grasped the hurt leg. As I felt around the elbow I felt the little body tremble just a bit. I carefully compared the way the two elbows felt and sensed a subtle difference in the two. Holding above the elbow on the injured side, I grasped the toes and rotated the foot back and forth to check for range of motion. Sandy squealed. I knew I was on the right track, but still wasn't sure of the problem. Again I rotated the foot, this time a little more aggressively.

There was a loud crack from the leg and Sandy's whole body jolted. Both Kristen and I snapped our heads up and our eyes met. There was alarm on her face and I felt my heart rate speed up. I've done it now, I thought. I broke the leg! I felt that bone break right in my hands. How was I going to explain this to his owner? I glanced over at Linda and could tell that she sensed something was wrong. I hoped the concern hadn't registered too noticeably on my face.

"Let go of him for just a minute and let's give Sandy a rest, Kristen."

Slowly Kristen released her hold on the chinchilla. With lightning speed and without a trace of a limp, Sandy ran across the tabletop, jumped into Linda's hands, clambered up her sweater, and perched himself again on her shoulder.

I thought Kristen was going to speak, but she remained silent, her mouth hanging open in surprise. I resisted my immediate urge to do the same, electing instead to act as if that was exactly what I had expected. In reality though, I was utterly dumbfounded.

"That should do it, Linda," I said finally. "Sandy dislocated his elbow in the fall from your shoulder. But I was able to pop it back into place just then. I would keep him in his cage for a few days so he has some time to heal, but I don't expect any more problems."

I could tell that Ms. Hollis was surprised, pleased, and impressed. "Thank you, Doctor. It's really nice to know that there is a vet around who has some experience with chinchillas. Most have never even seen one before."

Transition

Faster than I could believe, my internship drew to a close. I looked back on the time of intense work, unbelievable demands, staggering schedule, and time away from home with a surprising amount of satisfaction and pride. I had, in one year's time, logged the equivalent of perhaps two or three years of experience in most other practices. There had, of course, been times of frustration borne of sheer exhaustion. But the time had been worth it. I emerged a much more confident veterinarian, with the benefit of close supervision and mentoring that, I hoped, would make me more marketable as I pursued my career.

I toyed with the idea of staying on in Rochester and joining the staff of the hospital at which I had interned. But along with the many advantages of a large practice organization comes the inevitable politics and bureaucracy inherent to larger groups of people. Besides, though I had never lived in a small town (with the exception of Okeechobee, Florida, when I was a child in the late sixties), I nonetheless fancied myself a small town person. Besides, there is just way too much snow in Rochester!

One of my reasons for leaving Minnesota was because I didn't want to live in a place where if my car died in the winter, I might too. Rochester, though not quite as cold as Minnesota, had just as much snow, thanks to the effects of Lake Ontario. I wanted to work my way south.

An inventory of my personal list of addresses included Colorado, Tennessee, Florida, Michigan, Minnesota, and, most recently, New York, as resident states. My wife added even more states to the list: Georgia, Montana, Washington, Idaho, and Oregon. As we had both grown up PKs (preacher's kids), we each had an impressive number of moves during our growing up years. This gave us an amazing array of potential places to which we could move that had personal history and the pull of familiarity and friendships. It may seem strange then that when I began to search for permanent employment, my fingers always went to the listings in the journal for practices in Virginia, one of the few states in which neither my wife nor I had ever lived.

For four straight years during high school and college, I had spent my summers at a beautiful, rustic summer camp in the Blue Ridge Mountains of western Virginia, nestled in and hugging the walls of a small valley just three or four miles off the Blue Ridge Parkway where the width of the mountain range was at its greatest. Those years remain in my mind as golden times, shaded as they are with memories of the mountains, of carefree weeks with good friends, of summer flings, and cool evenings ringing with cicadas and lighted by the indistinguishable blending at the horizon of twinkling stars and blinking lightning bugs.

I fell in love with Virginia during those summers. More specifically, I fell in love with the Blue Ridge Mountains and the Shenandoah Valley and had nurtured since then a dream of returning to them. So with the arrival of each new issue of the *Journal of the American Veterinary Medical Association*, I flipped immediately to the job postings within the state of Virginia.

I made appointments during one week in the late winter of my internship with several veterinary practices in Virginia. Unfortunately, none of the openings were in the mountains or in the Shenandoah Valley. All of the appointments I made were in Burke, Dale City, Fredericksburg, Vienna, or other regions of the huge sprawl of Washington, D.C.'s northern Virginia suburbs. Though I received offers of employment in many of the practices in which I interviewed, I could muster little enthusiasm for any of them and continued to search.

Before heading back north to New York, I scanned the journals once again for any new listings. One ad for an opening in Charlottesville caught my eye. Eagerly I called the number listed to set up an interview only to be told that the position had recently been filled. As an afterthought, before she hung up, the veterinarian offhandedly mentioned that a colleague of hers might be looking for an associate in Waynesboro, just over the mountain. Though I had not seen any ads for this position posted in the journals, I called the number she gave me.

Dr. David Peartree was a solo practitioner who was adding an associate to lighten his load. Yes, the position was still open and he would be pleased to interview me. I arranged a time to meet him the following day.

Cynthia and I drove into town early in the morning and found the practice. It was located in the back of a Kroger grocery store with an entrance off the side of the building. Having arrived very early for the interview, we scouted the town. Waynesboro boasted a population of about twelve to fifteen thousand people and was laid out around the bends of the South Fork of the Shenandoah River. Just west of town was the northern portal of the Blue Ridge Parkway, just a few miles north of the camp where I had first become infatuated with Virginia.

Waynesboro was supported economically by a huge DuPont plant that produced Lycra, spandex, and a large middle class. The original streets of the town were wide and graceful and adorned by huge oak trees overarching the avenue. All along the street were equally large, gracious churches that are requisite to southern towns. From this center, the town had grown mainly to the west, bordered as it was on the east by the shoulders of the Blue Ridge. I thought it was perfect.

We pulled up to the practice after our self-guided tour and strode wide-eyed and exuberant into the lobby. Dr. Peartree greeted us pleasantly, introduced us to his staff, and gave us a quick tour of the practice. The emphasis here was on quick, for there wasn't much to the facility. It consisted of two examination rooms, a small waiting room, a cramped treatment room, a surgery suite, a darkroom, and a dog ward with just a few runs. Though small, it was clean, well organized, and filled, I noted, with an impressive number of patients under treatment for problems that required a skilled hand. Some of the cases had been referred to Dr. Peartree from his colleagues. It was not the facility that impressed me, though. It was the interaction between Dr. Peartree and his staff—an easy, gentle repartee that evidenced mutual respect and appreciation, generously mingled with wit and humor. The atmosphere was open and inviting and I was welcomed into it immediately. I felt right at home.

As Dr. Peartree and I discussed the job, Cynthia again went for a drive around the town. We spoke of practice and philosophy, my past and his, our expectations for working together, and other such things as are always covered in an employment interview. At the end of our discourse, I glanced down at my watch and was surprised to see we had consumed two hours in congenial conversation.

I was excited about the possibilities this job provided. The details of starting salary, benefits, and scheduling seemed superfluous to the decision I had already come to. It didn't occur to me that Dr. Peartree might not have come to the same conclusion. So I wasn't surprised when, at the end of the interview, he invited me to join his practice. I played coy, asking for some time to discuss it with Cynthia and go over the proposal he had offered.

I returned to the car with a bounce in my step after the interview. Cynthia knew immediately that I had gotten the job. I babbled incessantly in my excitement, going over all the details of the interview for her as we drove away. I was pumped.

We decided to spend the night in a hotel in town overnight so we could look for a place to live the next day. I pulled into the hotel parking lot and stopped the car. As I was about to open the door, I heard a strange sound from the passenger's seat. I looked across the car and was shocked to find that Cynthia was crying softly.

"What's the matter?" I was completely baffled. After all, if I could have chosen a place to live simply by placing my finger on a map, I could not have found somewhere that seemed more perfect to me than Waynesboro. The fact that I felt at home in the practice was simply gravy on top of that.

Cynthia put her head in her hands, "I'm not sure I can live in such a small town."

I was stunned and leaned back in the driver's seat in disbelief. Such a small town? Twelve to fifteen thousand people was ideal. Not so small as to be provincial, but not so large that you lose the homey community feel. It was exactly what I had been looking for! I thought back to the towns in which we had already interviewed and tried to picture myself in them, fighting the traffic, the pace, the impersonal, anonymous feel. I wasn't sure I could live in cities that large.

"You really feel that fifteen thousand people is too small a city?"

"You know how much I like the symphony, the theater, the choice of restaurants, the shopping in a big town. You know, stuff like that."

"I'm sure I saw a theater on Main Street as we were driving."

"No. I mean live theater."

"But, Cynth," I reminded her, "we're only about two hours or less from D.C. here. We can get to all of those things anytime we want to. And wouldn't you rather raise children in a town like this than in D.C.?"

"I know you're right," she responded. "I'll be okay. I just need a little time to get used to the idea of being here."

"Remember, this is still fairly close to both our parents." Cynthia's parents lived in a D.C. suburb and my folks lived an hour and a half away in Richmond.

Cynthia wiped her eyes and squared her shoulders. "You're right. We're about the same distance from both of them and that's better than we've ever had it before. I'm sure I'll get to like it here. Just give me some time."

Cynthia did indeed learn to love Waynesboro as much as I did. We still do, in fact. We spent almost four years there before the path of our lives led us away from it. Waynesboro treated us well. It was there that we bought our first house, welcomed two baby boys into that home, had several wonderful years in a thriving practice, and settled comfortably into the rhythms and flows of life there. In Waynesboro we found a place in the life of a wonderful, gracious church family that provided us a foundation of friendship and support upon which we still often lean. Life was wonderful in Waynesboro! We look back on it with the very fondest of memories.

In retrospect, I must smile at the conversation Cynthia and I had in the car that day. We came very close to declining the position in Waynesboro because the town was too small. Little did we know that Waynesboro would be just a stopover transition for what was to follow. In the not-too-distant future, Waynesboro would seem huge.

Out to Lunch

It was soon after our move to Waynesboro that my parents first visited us in our new apartment. We have always enjoyed spending time with our folks and do so still whenever possible. But this visit meant a lot more to me. It was, for me, symbolic.

With my internship behind me and my new career now in full swing, this visit would be something of a statement to Mom and, especially, Dad about my ability to succeed in an adult world completely on my own. You would think that at twenty-eight years of age, after four years of marriage, I would have already made that step. But, in fact, I hadn't. I must admit to being, in some things, a bit slow.

There comes a time in life when the relationship between a father and son must change from parent to friend. For many, this necessary transition involves a certain amount of trauma. My father and I were fortunate to have skirted such consternation, but in so doing, had also avoided a specific break point. It appeared, now that my lifelong dream had become a reality and was succeeding, that this move might well provide that threshold beyond which I could enjoy my father's company as a man—pleased for his approval, but not beholden to it or imprisoned by it. Most transitions for me have been so seamless as to go unnoticed. But this one was a cognizant epiphany. This visit, then, loomed large for me as a paramount symbolic event in my relationship with my father.

It would be a time, I vowed, to demonstrate to Dad my newly acquired independence. I would assume the dominant role in planning the weekend. I would be the one, for a change, to discreetly signal for the check when we went out to eat. Surely Dad would sense the shift in my thinking.

It was with these thoughts that I watched the headlights of Mom and Dad's car pan across the front of the apartment as they turned into the driveway. With head high and proud I strode resolutely out to greet them.

My dad unfolded himself slowly from the driver's seat. He stretched his arms high and contorted his face in an unhurried yawn before turning to greet me. Mom and Dad had moved to Syracuse, New York, shortly after our move to Waynesboro. Dad despised the nine-hour drive from upstate New York to Waynesboro, especially when it meant driving deep into the night.

"Glad you're here, Dad," I said evenly. We embraced for a moment and I thought my father sensed a new awareness of me in that one simple act. He broke our embrace and held me for a moment at arm's length, a bemused, questioning look in his eyes. He knows, I thought. He understands.

"Son," he said.

"Yes, Dad." I had not expected this interchange to occur quite so early in the weekend. I fairly trembled with expectation. There was a pregnant pause as he collected his thoughts.

"I've had to pee like a racehorse for the last seventy-five miles. Help me get this stuff inside quickly so I can hit the john." He turned and opened the trunk unceremoniously, grabbed the handle of an overstuffed suitcase, and headed inside.

I should have known right then that my expectations for the weekend were ill-fated. But the weight of my own naïveté pressed down on my consciousness too heavily to sway my thinking. With the determination of my newfound independence, I set my jaw and grabbed a hanging bag, following my father into the house as I had done countless times before as a boy late at night at the end of many a family trip.

The next day offered another opportunity for me. After spending the morning perusing area antique shops, we decided to go out for lunch. In my family the process of deciding whether or where to go out to eat has always been a difficult one. The men in my family have a hereditary reluctance to be decisive on this issue, choosing instead to simply grunt ambiguously at any suggestion made. This, for reasons completely unapparent to us, evokes in our spouses a surprisingly visceral reaction. The interchange went something like this.

"Honey," Cynthia began, "I was thinking we'd take your folks out to eat. Any preferences?"

"Uh . . . nah. Whatever."

"Would you rather have Italian or Mexican?"

"Um . . . either one."

"We could go to the Chinese place for takeout."

"Wuh . . . if you'd like."

Her voice was beginning to rise just a little. "Come on. You have to have an opinion!"

This of course, as any man knows, is simply not the case. There are entire categories of subjects about which a man has absolutely no opinion at all. These may include, among others, what shoes his wife wears with a particular outfit, what color panty hose she chooses, which centerpiece looks best on the Thanksgiving table, whether to use the china or the everyday dishes, or which wallpaper border goes best in the living room. Please understand, ladies, when you get only a disinterested grunt from your husband in response to your questions about these topics, that it does not mean that your husband is disapproving of your choice. What it really means is that he simply has no feelings either way. This should make you feel much better.

"I do have an opinion," I said. "You just haven't told me what it is yet." This clever comment was designed to defuse a rapidly deteriorating conversation. I was sure my intentions would be obvious and appreciated. Surprisingly, though, it did not seem to have the expected effect.

"I don't think you really want to go there, bucko," Cynthia hissed. "Come on! I need some help with this! Your folks are getting hungry. What do you want to do?"

"I don't care. Whatever everyone else wants."

"I don't know what everyone else wants!"

"Well, what would you like?"

"No way! You're not going to force me into making this decision. I'm out of it from here on!"

"Okay." I figured this would be a good way for me to take an assertive stance anyway. I strolled to the room where Mom and Dad were bent over a puzzle laid out on a table.

"Dad, we're going to take you guys out to eat. Any preferences for where you'd like to go?" I asked.

"Uh . . . nah. Whatever." He didn't look up from the game. Apparently, it's a dominant hereditary trait.

"Okay," I realized this decision would take a bold stroke from a true leader, "I'm going to order pizza. We'll order by phone, then go eat at the restaurant. Then we won't have to sit around and wait. What toppings would you like on them? Would you rather have mushrooms or onions?"

"Um . . . either one."

It surprised me how annoyed I was by Cynthia's smirks. I decided to try the new pizza restaurant in town, Pizza Inn, which enjoyed a good reputation, instead of our usual choice. I dialed their number and placed an order for two large pizzas with the toppings I thought everyone would like. After a few minutes I was able to get everyone out of the house and into the car.

We were in a jovial mood as the family filed into Pizza Inn. I made my way to the counter. "I believe you have a couple of pizzas ready for Coston, don't you?" I asked the waitress.

She looked over the names on the pizza boxes behind her. Then scanned them again. "What did you say the name was again?"

"Coston," I replied, putting on a look of bored disinterest.

"I'm sorry, sir. I don't have a pizza for that name. Could there be some mistake?"

Now usually, I'm pretty low-key about these types of things. But I made a conscious decision that part of my newfound independence would include being assertive and not getting pushed around by people.

"Well, if you don't have a pizza for us, then yes, there has been a mistake!" I replied forcefully.

The poor waitress froze under my withering gaze. "I'm sorry, sir. If you'd like us to make your pizza now, I'm sure we can extend you a discount."

"What I wanted was a pizza, not a discount!" I measured my voice to a carefully prescribed volume, enough to communicate my contempt, but not enough to disturb the other diners in the restaurant.

"Since we've apparently made a mistake with your order, the only way I can help you now is to take another order and offer you a discount with our apologies." The young woman behind the counter maintained her composure admirably, smiling sweetly at me as I scowled back at her.

"Let me see what the rest of my family wants to do," I said briskly. I turned back to my family, who seemed a little embarrassed by my show of bravado. The waitress turned and headed into the back room.

"Would you all rather wait here for twenty minutes while they make another pizza, or go somewhere else?" I surveyed the faces of my parents and my wife. They were surprisingly sullen. No one responded for a moment.

"It's entirely up to you." Cynthia turned and headed toward the front of the restaurant, apparently distancing herself from the brutish jerk accosting the waitress. I could not understand her reaction. Couldn't she see how important it was for me to finally assert myself in front of my folks? Apparently, my folks missed it to. They followed Cynthia to the door.

About that time, the waitress returned to the counter. Before

I could render my decision, she addressed me, still in the kind voice of well-trained customer service. "Sir, your pizzas are ready at Pizza Hut."

I was stunned. "Excuse me?"

"The pizzas you ordered are ready at Pizza Hut." She continued to smile.

"I don't understand."

"Well, sir, I called Pizza Hut just to see if there had been a mistake in the order." Her voice was calm and even. "The pizzas you ordered are ready at Pizza Hut."

"Oh, they are?" I stammered. I turned to walk away and then turned back to her again. "Uh, I'm sorry . . . please excuse my rudeness. Apparently, it was my mistake all along."

Unfortunately, Mom, Dad, and Cynthia, though they had moved away from the counter, had not moved far enough away to miss this last interchange. When I approached them, they were hooting. I hurriedly herded them out the door, thoroughly embarrassed.

Pizza Hut was only a couple of blocks away and we arrived and parked in just a minute or less. Soon we were seated and a waitress approached our table to serve us. I explained that we had ordered our pizzas ahead and that they should be ready. When I told her our name, she nodded and smiled broadly. Apparently news of my mistake had preceded me. By the time the pizzas arrived at our table, we had all enjoyed a hearty laugh over the situation and I had apologized for my insolence. Soon we were talking and laughing and enjoying our meal.

Before long, I excused myself to go to the restroom. I made my way into a toilet stall and was absently scanning the walls for entertainment when a strange awareness slowly began to dawn. Something that I couldn't quite place was wrong. But what was it? It slowly occurred to me that in the stall, hanging on the partition was something that I wasn't accustomed to seeing. It was a box with a lid and a decal that said PLACE NAPKINS HERE. I thought it strange that someone would bring their napkin from the table to the restroom. Slowly, like fog burning away under the strengthening morning sun, the thick vapors in my mind cleared and a startling realization dawned on me there, settled comfortably in a bathroom stall with my pants down around my ankles. I was in the women's restroom!

I took a quick inventory of my position. The good thing was that I was alone in the bathroom. If I could just quickly finish the paper work and slip out, perhaps I could get away with this unnoticed. Just as I resolved to pull this off, however, I heard the door open and at least two people trundle in. Judging by the voices and the happy twittering, I could tell it was two young girls, probably nine or ten years of age. I decided to wait them out, sitting quietly in my stall.

Giggling all the while, they made their way down the row of doors looking for an open stall. One of them pulled on the door to mine. Though it was locked, I held it firmly with all my might. The little girl hesitated in front of my door for a moment.

Then I heard her say to her friend in a snickering, smothered whisper, "Look how big her feet are!"

I involuntarily pulled my feet back further from the door of the stall, glancing down too late to realized that my size ten and a half basketball shoes would not pass for those of a woman. I cringed. The two girls melted into paroxysms of hysteria, bouncing around the stalls for a minute, punching each other, and turning on the water in the sinks before finally bolting out of the bathroom door, belting out ringing guffaws as they entered the dining area.

This was my chance. Quickly I pulled up my pants, buckled my belt and sprinted for the bathroom door, fumbling ineffectually with my zipper. I was going to make it! But just as I pulled on the handle, a woman pushed on the door from the other side and, in my hurry to get out, we came almost nose to nose on the threshold. It was hard to tell who was more surprised. At first she smiled, but then her face transformed into utter confusion and she cranked her head ninety degrees to look at the sign on the bathroom door just inches from her face. It said WOMEN. She then looked back at me with a startled, almost angry look, as if I were one of those strange bathroom stalkers in public parks.

"My mistake." I hung my head in embarrassment. "You're in the right place."

I made my way back to the table and sat down, taking a big swig from my soda. Maybe I could just let this pass without acknowledging to my family what had happened. I was unusually quiet. Cynthia eyed me with some concern.

"Are you all right?" she asked. "You seem a bit flushed."

"You have no idea." I decided not to tell. "Good choice of words, by the way."

About that time, two little girls came down the aisle from the other side of the dining room. They were laughing and elbowing each other as they slowly made their way along. I noticed as they came that they kept their heads down, their eyes on the floor. This confused me some until I realized that they were scanning people's feet at the tables as they passed. I pulled mine up and crossed my legs. But it was too late. They had spied my tennis shoes.

They stopped directly in front of me, nodding and pointing at my shoes. Their eyes left my shoes and made their way slowly up my legs, surfaced above the table, and continued up until they both looked me in the eye. They had wanted to find the woman with the big feet. What they found instead was altogether too much for them. When they realized it was not a woman at all their eyes met and in unison they doubled over in laughter and raced away, squealing and howling as they ran full tilt back to their table. After a few moments, I heard a roar of mirth ascend from that side of the restaurant.

"What was that all about?" Cynthia asked. And I had to tell the whole story.

I don't remember much else about the weekend that was to be my coming out, my rite of passage. I do recall, however, that Dad paid the tab at Pizza Hut.

The Heavy Wooden Door

A scruffy young woman and her equally scruffy boyfriend pushed the door of the hospital open sharply and stormed into the waiting room. Both were generously decorated with tattoos, dark in both contrast and content, and bedecked with multiple studs and rings in their ears. They sported a number of other body piercings, some apparent and others only imagined, the thought of which made me shiver. They were dressed in tattered jeans and dirty sweatshirts. Behind them tottered a little boy of two or three with uncombed hair and unscrubbed face, whose persistent crying and whining had no apparent effect on his parents. In her arms the woman carried a bundle which looked like wadded towels. The sounds emanating from the bundle, though, were the throaty moans of a kitten in deep distress.

"Help us!" they yelled above the din of their unhappy toddler. "Our kitten's really hurt bad!"

The receptionists guided them to a room and handed them a clipboard with some papers to fill out. I grabbed my stethoscope and followed them into the exam room, not waiting for the forms to be completed. The woman laid the patient on the table still draped in the towel, no part of him showing.

I began to unwrap the bundle of kitten, pulling back the

layers of the towel to find a small, gray and white kitten weighing only about three or four pounds. Once totally unwrapped, the kitten lay splay-legged on the table on his belly, his head bobbing and weaving in uncontrolled tremors. His unseeing eyes, one pupil huge and dark and the other a pinpoint, darted back and forth in a rapid staccato cadence. His little toes curled under in an ineffectual attempt to grab on to something that might settle the shaking and twitching of his world. His nose quivered and jerked, searching the room for some familiar smell that might help him understand the situation he found himself in. Every so often the little form would be overcome completely by the quaking of his limbs and he would knot up into a tight, quivering ball of fur that would hold its shape for an interminable time before finally relaxing again.

"What happened to this little guy?" I asked as I began to go over him gently with my fingers.

"The kid here," the woman responded, tossing a look of scorn over her shoulder at her son, "slammed the door on the kitten's head. I think it was an accident," she added, but the emphasis she placed on the word *think* showed that she actually thought the opposite.

Accident or not, this kitten was in serious trouble. Head trauma can be a dangerous injury from which many patients do not recover. With the progressively worsening cerebral swelling and inflammation, I didn't expect this kitten to survive. The biggest concern in cases like these is the pressure within the braincase that develops as the brain swells. Pressures can get so high that serious damage to important structures that control heart rate, respiration, temperature, and other vital functions can occur.

"He got his head slammed in the screen door?" I repeated incredulously.

"No, sir, it weren't no screen door. It was the solid wood front door of the house where we stay. The kid just learned to open and close it and he slams it as hard as he can every time. I came around the corner just in time to see him slamming the door. The kitten was trying to sneak back inside and wham, there he was all laid out on the floor, twitching and stuff."

"This kitten is in serious trouble," I said soberly. "That's a pretty major trauma for such a little guy to take. There has been critical damage to the brain. That's what's causing the abnormal behavior and the seizures."

"Well, can you give him some medication to get him better?" the man asked, seeming sincerely worried.

"I can do my best, but there's no guarantees in patients that have been injured this badly," I responded. "And things may well get worse than they are now. These head trauma cases can change dramatically hour by hour. We'll have to hospitalize the kitten so we can monitor its progress."

"I want you to do everything you can to save him. He means the world to us." He looked at me earnestly, eyes filled with concern.

"I have to tell you that this kitten's odds are not that good."

"I still want to try."

"It could mean several days of hospitalization. It could be expensive," I warned.

"Money is no object. We just want our kitten to be okay."

I have learned over the years that there are all kinds of pet owners. In all planes of financial wherewithal, from the ultra-wealthy to the beleaguered, some people are willing to spend their hard-earned cash on their pets and others are not. I cannot assume, based on the kind of car a person parks in front of the office or the sophistication (or lack thereof) of their speech or dress, what level of care they will choose for their four-footed family members. I have been surprised by both extremes. I have been stiffed by people who drove away in Mercedes and have been faithfully paid ten dollars a week by people who could ill afford it. What has been consistently true is that whenever someone says money is no object, it is because they have no intention whatsoever of parting with any.

"I'll do what I can, but I must tell you again, that this kitten's condition will be touch and go for some time yet. Call in the morning and I'll give you an update on his condition."

I carried the trembling kitten into the treatment room, the unexpected movement throwing him into spasms that contorted his little frame into bundles of thrashing legs and claws. This one was going to be a challenge.

And yet, in his own little way, it seemed like he badly wanted to get better. Though control of his faculties was wanting, his determination was not. With everything in him he was trying to right himself onto wriggling, spindly legs that simply refused to cooperate. When I softly spoke to him, he turned his head toward me in wildly exaggerated overshoots and corrections and meowed silently with openmouthed entreaties. This kitten was a gamer.

I laid him gently on the treatment table and, with the help of my technician, inserted a catheter into a tiny vein through which I started intravenous fluids and medications to ease the swelling in his brain. At that time, the availability of CT scans and MRIs was nonexistent for veterinary patients. Now, though I have to refer my patients ninety minutes away, these diagnostics can be pursued in the right cases. But then I was forced to treat these cases rather blindly. My interventions were mainly supportive care, monitoring and relief of pain and inflammation. The rest was largely dependent on the fight of my patient and the tedious work of my two most dependable colleagues, Mother Nature and Father Time.

I was afraid to go to the clinic the next morning, unsure of what I might find. Chances were about even for finding either an improved patient or a dead one in the cage. To my delight, the kitten was still alive and had even shown slight improvement. His pupils, though still of different sizes, were approaching equality. I couldn't say for sure, but I thought he followed my fingers as I waved them in front of his face. He certainly heard me and was able to respond to my presence, judging by the way he shimmied on his stomach toward the sound of my voice. I was pleased, and knew that his owners would be too.

Throughout the day, as I continued to provide supportive care, the kitten improved. Each time I removed him from his cage, he was able to move around a little better. True, his head still wobbled and swayed like one who was losing the war on drugs, but his vision was slowly returning and his will was stronger. By late afternoon, he could stand precariously on teetering legs for just a moment before tumbling forward onto his nose.

I was eager to update the owners of the kitten, sure they would be elated to hear how he had improved. I thought it strange that they hadn't called to check on him. When I was able to find a few minutes late in the afternoon, I grabbed the kitten's record and picked up the phone. Eagerly I dialed the number they had written down on the admission forms. I had not anticipated good news, so this would be a unexpectedly pleasant call.

"The number you have dialed is not in service. Please check the number and dial again. If you think you have reached this message in error, please hang up and dial zero and an operator will assist you." Puzzled, I redialed the number only to get the same message. A little voice began to nag at the back of my mind. I pushed it back.

I dialed directory assistance and gave the name of the client. Perhaps a recent move had necessitated a change in their phone number. No such names were listed in the phone directory, however. I would have to wait for them to contact me for an update on the kitten.

Meanwhile, the patient continued to improve each day. For the first few days, whenever the kitten tried to eat, which he did often, his little head would tremor uncontrollably with the effort and he would end up slamming his little nose deep into the cat food bowl, filling his nostrils with kitten food slurry and evoking a sneezing fit. Because of this, we had to force-feed his food and water carefully through a syringe. Once he learned to accept these undignified meals, he began to blossom.

After five days he was moving around the cage under his own steam, exploring the far reaches of his stainless-steel domain.

Clearly his eyesight was improving. Every time someone walked by his cage, he reached through the bars trying to snag the passerby with his little claws so they would feed him more gruel through the syringe. His tremoring was also improving steadily. Now, though he certainly wasn't light on his feet the way most kittens are, he was walking quite well, only stumbling when he moved his head too abruptly or was startled by a noise. Then he would fly into a discombobulated flurry of disorganized feet, which would invariably leave him in a crumpled pile of kitten. Nonplused by his collapse, he would recover promptly and quickly regain his feet. Meanwhile, my wait for a call from his owners continued unrewarded.

By the end of the first week, it was clear that the kitten was going to make a complete recovery. He had begun to eat on his own. He was also able to run around the hospital in a very ungraceful, racoonlike way, without falling at all. In fact, he became a veritable ball of uncoordinated energy barreling around the office looking for trouble. He especially enjoyed running down the hallway at full tilt, tail bushed out behind him and back arched, then quickly pirouetting and, with spinning wheels, heading out in the opposite direction.

He began to gain weight and his gray and white patterned coat was filling out nicely as well. He was a truly appreciative patient, purring and caressing your hand and cheek gently with sheathed claws when you gave him the least bit of attention.

The other thing that was very apparent by the end of that first week was that his owners were not coming back for him. They had not once bothered to call. And my efforts at locating them had all ended in frustration. The information they had provided to us, it turned out, had all been fabricated. I learned, for instance, that the street they had listed as their home address on the form was not to be found on the city map. The phone number, the employment information, even the social security number they had provided, all ended up to be fraudulent. We had been duped.

I began to entertain the idea that Ollie, our cat at home,

might appreciate a companion. He was now three years old and had been an only cat all that time. Cynthia and I had just purchased our first home and were in the process of painting and repairing it prior to our moving in. The move would provide some extra room for a new pet. I thought the idea had merit.

I would have to choose just the right time to present it to Cynthia and Ollie. At that time, Cynthia was painfully pregnant and due to deliver our first baby at any moment. Our work on the house was done each night after I was off work: painting, patching, laying linoleum, and cleaning. So excited were we at our good fortune to have found the little Cape Cod, that the hours of sweat equity hardly seemed like work at all. Since the outcome of the race between parenthood and home repairs was as yet undetermined, we worked feverishly on the house at every opportunity. Between renovations, packing our things for the move, and preparing for a new baby, Cynthia was extremely busy and not a little stressed. One evening I tentatively brought up the idea.

"Hey, Cynth, you know that little kitten I told you about that got its head slammed in the door?" I had told her the story of the injury and had kept her updated on his progress each day.

"Yeah?"

"The owners have dumped him on us."

"Really?" she responded, unsuspecting. "Didn't they seem really concerned when they brought him in?"

"Yeah, they did when they brought him in," I said. "But that was the last thing we heard from them. It's been over a week now since they came in. All the information they gave us was wrong and we have no way to contact them at all. He's doing really good now too. It looks like we're going to have to find a home for him. Man, is he a cutie!"

Cynthia raised her eyebrows and gave me a look that told me she was on to me. "You're not thinking of bringing him home, are you?"

"Well, with the new house we'll have more room. And I think Ollie would really like having someone to play with. Chances are, when the baby comes Ollie will get less attention than he's used to and a playmate would be just the thing to help with that." I had rehearsed the details carefully.

"It couldn't be any worse timing, you know," Cynthia noted correctly. "We're packing, moving, fixing the house, and having a baby. Adding another thing onto that may just send me over the edge."

"You're right. I don't have anything to urge. He's just such an endearing little cat. I've grown fond of him. But I think we'll be able to find him a home without too much trouble."

Cynthia has always been the clear thinker in our home. It is she that always sets my feet back on the ground when I come up with some overly ambitious plan or set off on some compulsive scheme. This is an attribute I value in her. It has saved me countless times from unnecessary frustration. I am always well-advised to listen to her when she reins me in. But she also has a predictable soft spot in her heart for kitties. So I was not particularly surprised when, a few days later, she asked me about the kitten again.

"Do you still have that little head trauma kitten at the office?"

"Yes."

"I'd like to see him."

"Really?"

"I've been thinking a lot about him lately. You may be right about Ollie needing a friend. If you could keep him at the office until after the baby is born and we get into the house, I might be talked into him. But I want to see him first."

"Are you sure about that?" I asked. "Because once you see him, you're going to fall in love with him."

The Firstborn

Pregnancies in our family are nothing to be taken lightly. I realize, of course, they are never insignificant events in any family. But because Cynthia and I had lost two babies previously, pregnancies are for us nerve-wracking events. The first time, during my senior year in veterinary school, Cynthia had become so ill that I was within just a few hours of losing her as well as the baby to a severe, systemic infection. It had taken weeks for her to recover. Unfortunately, the doctors were unable at that time to diagnose the cause of the stillbirth.

It was not until our second pregnancy during my internship in Rochester that the problem was diagnosed; a diagnosis that came too late to save that baby either. We suffered a second devastating loss, but there was hope for future pregnancies. Cynthia would need surgery in the second or third month of her pregnancy and then would have to be bedridden throughout the rest of gestation.

So in Waynesboro, with our third attempt, Cynthia and I had mixed emotions. We were, of course, thrilled at the prospect of finally having a baby in the family. But we also felt vulnerable and frightened. Cynthia was very concerned about finding a doctor with experience in dealing with her specific problem in our little town and did not relish the prospect of having to travel to a doctor.

When I asked about an obstetrician in Waynesboro, we repeatedly received ringing endorsements for one particular doctor in town. Everyone we asked brought up the same name. Each person told different but similar stories of skill and compassion. We called his office and made an appointment.

Dr. Martin Smith is a very tall man whose monstrous hand engulfs yours completely when he shakes your hand, not necessarily a desirable trait for an obstetrician/gynecologist. Nonetheless, we found him warm and understanding when we discussed our losses and optimistic about this pregnancy. He immediately prescribed medications to control any premature contractions and put Cynthia on bed rest. He also scheduled a surgery at twelve weeks along to correct the problem that had caused the loss of the first two babies.

The surgery went well and Cynthia settled in for a long sentence of bed rest. Of the two of us, Cynthia is by far the more gregarious, and six months of bed rest was worse than house arrest for her. Having only moved to Waynesboro a few months earlier, we had few friends we could call on to provide company for her. To our surprise and relief, our new church family and those at the office came to the rescue, even preparing hot meals for us several times a week.

After what seemed an eternity to Cynthia, who counted the passing days eagerly, we finally reached the magic threshold: thirty-two weeks. After this point, Dr. Smith told us, chances for survival, even if the baby came unexpectedly, were very good. He lightened Cynthia's sentence, allowing her limited activity and some time out of the house. It was about this time that the details of our house purchase were finalized and we went to work renovating it.

Finally, after weeks of toiling on the project until midnight every night, we proudly moved in. We were giddy with the purchase of our house and how nicely all our hard work had transformed it into a home. The nursery was ready upstairs just across the hall from our room. With its slanted ceilings and teddy bear wallpaper and border, the matching crib and changing table, the rocking chair, and the hanging teddy bear light that Cynthia and I had made, it looked beautiful. Cynthia spent many hours organizing all the baby supplies in the drawers and setting out the teddy bear decorations she had collected over the almost three years since our first pregnancy. We were ready to welcome the new addition.

One night, after crawling into bed late from working on the endless projects that came with home ownership, I was awakened abruptly by an elbow in the side and a well-controlled voice in the bed beside me.

"Bruce!" she said. "Bruce, wake up."

"What's the matter, babe?"

"I think it's time."

You've heard a million stories of couples at this time racing around the house in unmitigated panic, fumbling and bumbling and forgetting the most basic of things—like the expectant mother—in their hysteria. Though I certainly felt feelings of panic, nothing could have been more controlled than the next few minutes in our lives. No voices were raised. No intonations of crisis were evident in our discussions. With the utmost of calm composure we got up, dressed, collected the bag we had packed for this time, and made our way downstairs. I even remembered to call Dr. Peartree and tell him he would have to take the beeper for the night. Then we calmly loaded things in the car, including Ollie whom we dropped off to board at the office, and headed to the hospital.

It was ironic that after all those months of bed rest and boatloads of budget-stretching pills to control premature contractions, in the end Dr. Smith had to induce labor. Even then, Cynthia was in hard labor for eight or ten hours. Those seemed the longest hours on record. Every few minutes, my poor wife would be racked with indescribable spasms of pain that would heave her into sitting bolt upright and taking in air in short bursts. Having been housebound during her pregnancy, we had not had the benefit of any birthing classes and were not prepared for what took place.

These cycles continued for hours. She was exhausted. I did my best to help her through it, but I could barely stand to see her in such pain. With each contraction, I would offer my encouragement and coach her in her breathing like a good husband should, but with tears streaming down my cheeks. I know it was worse for her, but for me it was sheer torture.

After one particularly wrenching round of contractions, Cynthia turned to face me. There were road maps of popped blood vessels etched on her red, splotchy cheeks. Her wide eyes were also red and rimmed with tears.

"How much longer?" she asked through clenched teeth.

How was I to know? I had no idea how this was supposed to go. It already seemed like it had gone on far too long. Had it been up to me, I would have hurried the process along one way or the other. I ignored the question, choosing instead to try encouragement. This seemed to work for one or two contractions. But soon she turned to me and asked again.

"How much longer?"

I turned a beseeching face to the nurse, who, despite her experience, merely shrugged. You'd have thought she could have given even the slightest bit of direction at a time like this. But her attention was directed at the myriad monitors and beeping machines that monitored my wife's and my baby's progress.

"Just hang in there, Cynth. We're gonna get through this," I said by way of diversion. Another wave of excruciating pain came. We grunted. We groaned. We breathed. I cried quietly. Then again.

"How much longer!?" This time with more urgency.

I realized this was a question to which my suffering wife needed an answer—even if it was wrong. Cynthia is unbelievably brave and can tolerate pain at levels that would make me pass out. But she needed to know that at some point there would be an end to it. I looked her lovingly in the eye between contractions and lied through my teeth.

"Fifteen more minutes," I said with forced certainty.

"Okay," she responded, settling noticeably.

To be honest, things did really seem to start moving after that. Within just a few minutes, they moved her from the birthing room into the delivery room where an anesthesiologist administered an epidural anesthetic. I remember Cynthia telling the anesthesiologist after the anesthetic took effect that she loved him, and I remember wondering to myself whether or not she still loved me. Wisely, I didn't ask.

The nurses encouraged me to be loving and supportive by holding Cynthia's hand and stroking her hair for moral support. But I knew from past experience that when in pain, Cynthia wants to be touched by no one, and at a time like that, perhaps especially not by her husband. I knew that my best moral support could be provided by leaving her alone to concentrate on her pain.

The nurses, though, thought me distant and heartless. So, throwing disgusted looks at me, they came over and held Cynthia's hand and stroked her hair. Cynthia, who is polite to a fault, allowed them to continue, not wanting to offend them or seem ungrateful. They glowered at me, exchanging irritated smirks.

My mind was in a whir for the next few minutes. I remember the anesthesiologist pushing on Cynthia's stomach. I remember the doctor using some type of salad tongs on the baby's head. I remember him offering me a pair of pruning shears to cut the umbilical cord. I remember wondering with some alarm if all babies come out looking so gray, then marveling at how quickly the tiny arms and legs grew pink after his first lusty scream. I remember my head falling onto Cynthia's neck and my shoulders shaking with quiet sobs of utter amazement at how much my heart was already filled with unadulterated adoration for this tiny baby—our baby!

It all happened so fast! Perhaps not really just fifteen minutes as I had promised. But still, one minute our family consisted of just Cynthia and me. Then a few drugs were given, some pushing occurred, there were a lot of bright lights, and *wham,* I was a parent. There were no tests to pass, no permits to apply for. Just boom! And the next minute there was this baby, this little boy that I was now responsible for. Did they not know me? Didn't someone realize I was not nearly responsible enough for this? For heaven's sake, I was only twenty-nine!

The next minute they handed that little boy to me, all wrapped up in clean towels, right there in the delivery room in front of everyone. I looked down for the first time at my son. Let's face it, newborn children are not pretty, no matter what anyone says. The child looked like some exotic larval stage of a human with imprints of salad tongs on his strangely pointed and bruised head. His cheeks and mouth convulsed independently without any apparent direction from higher centers. Suddenly a little hand would tent the towels he was wrapped in as the arm jerked uncontrollably. He stretched his little neck and with wide, round eyes he looked me over, clearly terrified by his prospects.

Like every father before me, I looked down at this little pupa of a person and realized with utter conviction that he was the most beautiful baby ever to be born because he was mine. I held him up for Cynthia to see and furtively counted his appendages. He appeared to have all the standard-issue supplies. He was perfect!

It took a while for the doctor to batten down all the hatches after the birth and for the nurses to hose down the goods. It was, perhaps, a half hour or so before they wheeled Cynthia and the baby out of the delivery room and down the hall to her room, me trailing along, grinning like a new father. Both sets of grandparents were in the hall waiting for our arrival and immediately gathered around the gurney. There were all the appropriate oohs and aahs when the baby was held up, but my father pretty well summed up how he looked that morning when he caught his first look at his grandson.

"Well, jerk me through a knothole backwards!"

We named him Jace Eliot Coston. We had known for many weeks before he was born that he was a boy, but we had kept his name a secret until the big day. It seemed to fit him.

He and his mother stayed in the hospital for only a day or two. Before I knew it I was bringing our little red Toyota Corolla to the front of the hospital to take Jace home for the first time. I was petrified. After carefully buckling him into his car seat like a skydiving instructor strapping on a parachute, and helping Cynthia gingerly into the front seat, I carefully pulled away from the hospital. The whole way home, which was only two or three miles, I barely accelerated more than fifteen miles an hour. I slowed to a veritable crawl over every bump and pothole and stopped at traffic lights before they turned yellow just in case. The ride took us probably fifteen minutes. Cynthia found this terribly amusing, but I couldn't take my eyes off the road or the traffic to defend myself against her teasing. Finally, I eased the nose of the car into the driveway and edged slowly to a stop by our front door. Jace was sound asleep in his seat. I was dripping with sweat. One baby was home!

A few days later, I brought the other baby home without nearly so much trepidation. The little gray-and-white kitten had recovered well by then and had wormed his way completely into my heart. I brought him into the living room and set him down on the floor. He padded around the house exploring every nook and cranny, trailed step for step by Ollie, who was put off at first by the kitten's lack of coordination, a residual effect of his injury. Most cats glide across the floor, sleek, smooth, and supple, as if able to ignore the laws of gravity and the effects of friction. This kitten, in contrast, moved like a raccoon, lumbering in slow, swinging strides that slung his shoulders low and caused him to shuffle. As he ambled along, his tail hung low and stiff, sticking out horizontally behind him like an opossum. Ollie treated him like he had a disability, which, of course, he did.

The kitten, for his part, was not at all put off by Ollie's close scrutiny. From the first moment, he viewed the older cat as a friend, as someone he could admire and love—much the same way he still views everyone he meets. Ollie, on the other hand, was not convinced this relationship was going to work, and was not at all sure he was interested in trying. Each time the kitten approached him, Ollie would rear back on his haunches and scream a loud wail, spitting and hissing in unmistakable feline curses, the precise translation of which I did not care to know, nor could they be recorded here. This display did not affect the kitten in the slightest. It was as if he was too dim to interpret the obvious meaning of Ollie's outbursts. Sometimes there are real advantages to ignorance.

And yet, I noticed with time that Ollie began to play little kitty games with the newcomer, chasing him around the legs of the furniture, and wrestling with him wildly on the floor. I even happened in on the pair several times to find them laid out on the couch sound asleep, tangled up in each other's appendages. Ollie continued to yell and scream when the kitten overstepped his bounds and disregarded his elder's dignity. But even though Ollie swatted and spanked the youngster, it was always with sheathed claws.

Though Ollie took some time to adjust to the kitten, Cynthia and I loved him from the first. His personality was thoroughly enchanting. His philosophy of life was that everyone was someone he could love, and he viewed all around him as potential friends. He had an amazing capacity for affection. He would stare deeply into your eyes and fix you with a look that was unmistakably and unashamedly devoted, almost amorous. When approached, he would grunt affectionately and roll over onto his side, presenting his belly for you to rub. He loved to be held in your arms, lying vulnerably on his back, head tossed back, exposing his throat in a very uncatlike pose. Such was his trust in everyone.

He loved the baby with an obsessive devotion and became a dependable babysitter. We discovered that when Jace woke up at those ungodly, infant morning hours and began to stir in the nursery, the kitten could invariably be found at the nursery door, pawing and asking to be let in. If we cracked the door just a bit, he would sneak in, trundle across the floor, jump into the crib and lie down with the baby, kneading and purring until Jace fell back to sleep. This happened every morning for months, allowing two tired parents to get an additional hour or more of sleep.

He especially loved to crawl into the baby swing with Jace where the two of them would swing and sleep for hours. When we would wind up the swing, the cat would look up at us with a look that said clearly, "Oh, isn't this just the cutest kid you've ever seen. Don't you just love him?" Of course, he got no argument from us. That cat was the cheapest babysitter we ever had. Later, when our second son came along, he was equally dedicated to his care.

The kitten, of course, needed a name. We eagerly watched the news for some prominent figure whose name we could borrow for our newest addition. For no particular reason, the one that captured our attention was Salman Rushdie. A fatwa had been placed on his head by the Islamic fundamentalist leaders in Iran for publishing his novel *The Satanic Verses*, which they considered to be blasphemous. The reward for his death forced Mr. Rushdie into hiding and guaranteed the book's success, propelling it high on the best-seller list where it resided for quite some time. We had not read the book, nor had we ever heard of Salman Rushdie. But the story intrigued us, and we liked how the abbreviated name, Rush, fit the kitten.

We gave little thought to the assumptions that the names of our cat duo induced people to make about us. When we told people that our two cats were named Ollie and Rush, they invariably presumed us to be flaming Republicans, committed to the ideals espoused by Oliver North and Rush Limbaugh.

For some, the names were considered a badge of honor that elevated us immeasurably in their esteem. For others, the names would raise their eyebrows; and the subsequent conversation would take a decidedly apolitical turn. We assured them that the names were less an endorsement of any particular political persuasion than a way to place the pet on the time continuum of history. But this explanation was seldom accepted. For them, the Salman Rushdie story was shallow guise for blatant Republican partisanship.

I won't here tip my hand at our true political leanings. But let me suggest that whether or not you believe the Salman Rushdie story says more about your allegiances than mine. Either way, Rush was named after Salman, not Limbaugh.

Rush has been a delightful addition to our home in spite of his injury. Few reminders remain of that heavy wooden door. He still has a raccoon gait. And he's still remarkably ponderous on his feet. Cynthia claims that he never plans a landing when jumping up onto a table or down from the bed. Should he fall from a chair, he's as likely to land on his noggin as he is on his feet.

It must be admitted that Rush will never be a candidate for a Nobel Prize. Brains are not exactly his strong suit, to be sure. In fact, I have often accused him of being the first living brain donor. After being at work all day, when I come through the door, he is always the first to greet me. But, though he has done so every day for the last thirteen years, there is still a certain degree of bewilderment on his face when he looks up at me. The question on his face is clear. "Have we met?" We have chosen to ascribe his intellectual impairment to his injury, though there is room for argument on this point.

But that's okay. How smart must a house cat be, after all? As long as they know where the food and water are and how to use the litter box, additional intelligence is extraneous. For his own good, Rush is an indoor cat. This avoids the increased cerebral demands of navigation and self-defense. We have come to accept the simplicity of Rush's cognitive abilities. It is one of the things that adds to his appeal.

It doesn't take a Nobel laureate, after all, to return our affection; to proffer the vulnerable belly; to thump over on his side in greeting; to lovingly convey a silent, openmouthed hello. In matters of the heart few people, human or otherwise, are as skilled as Rush. And that goes far in assuring him permanent residency in our hearts and home. Besides, Jace, our firstborn, loves him.

The Gift

Amy was a sweet, eight-year-old girl who took piano lessons from my wife. A beautiful young lady, she had brown hair and rather sad brown eyes. She was painfully shy and spent a lot of time examining the toes of her sneakers. But when drawn out, her smile was broad and her wit quick. I liked Amy right away.

I noticed as she trailed into our house for piano lessons, dragging a backpack filled with her schoolbooks and homework, that invariably after a cursory hello to us, her eyes would work their way around the house looking for our two cats, Ollie and Rush. When she spied them she would drop her backpack and engulf them in a little bear hug that never failed to start their motors humming.

Animals, I believe, instinctively recognize a soft heart and usually reward it with affection and trust. This was certainly evident in Amy's case. It reminded me of myself as a little boy. Amy enjoyed her piano lessons a great deal and did very well in them. But I suspect that the time with Ollie and Rush was the highlight of her weekly piano lessons.

I often bumped shoulders with Amy's parents. Her dad directed a choir in which I sang, so I saw him weekly. One evening, during a break in choir practice, I mentioned to him how much Amy enjoyed playing with our cats.

"That would explain why she's been so insistent about asking for a pet recently," he said. "We really should get her a kitten. She loves animals so much, but her mom and I aren't really animal lovers."

That certainly sounded familiar. As a youngster, I had been no less persistent with my folks, whose affinity for animals was negligible. It was only by sheer incessancy, and the fact that my aunt was a dog breeder, that I ever had a dog of my own. Besides him, only a parakeet and an occasional hamster were allowed in our house until high school when PC came to live with us.

I suspect, based on my own experience, that a deep love and empathy for animals is *not* a hereditary trait. I certainly didn't inherit it from my parents. I have come instead to believe that it is a random, almost reckless gift from God to a privileged few who throughout their lives honor the Gift. The Gift does not come without a price, to be sure. For it is accompanied by the burden of seeing innocent animals who suffer at the hands of pitiless people, the responsibilities of raising orphaned squirrels and blue jays, and the crushing blows of losing special pets. But in repayment, the Gift returns a wealth of rewards from the animals that enrich our lives—rewards that are unnecessary for me to list here, for those who share the Gift already know, and those who don't, wouldn't understand anyway. I could tell Amy had the Gift. Her mom and dad may not have recognized the degree to which this Gift impacted her. But I knew.

During the second week of December, a client brought in a kitten to be put to sleep. It was flea-ridden and suffered from an upper respiratory infection that left her eyes crusted and red and her nose runny. Her ears were filled with mites and her intestines with worms, but she was playful and endearing. She didn't need a painless death! She needed someone who would afford her a painless life—someone who really cared. Amy came to mind.

I called Amy's mother and, somewhat apologetically, made my pitch. Christmas was coming and I knew just what would make Amy's Christmas special. This kitten needed Amy's attentions! I offered to administer the kitten's first series of vaccinations, nurse the kitten back to health in the hospital, and board it until Christmas. There was a long pause on the phone during which I squelched the urge to say more. Silence is often a more powerful persuader than words.

"Well," her mom finally said. "I know you're right. Amy would love it, I'm sure of that. Nothing would make her happier. Sounds like a good idea, Dr. Coston."

I was thrilled for Amy—and for the kitten, who thrived during the next two weeks. The congested nose improved; the sore eyes resolved. Fleas were eliminated and the intestinal worms that had given the kitten such a potbellied look were treated. Though the kitten's appearance improved daily, there was still an intangible air of need. The kitten needed someone's love to bring out the glow of health and open the bloom of personality. I knew she and Amy would be a perfect match.

Christmas morning dawned beautifully with a light snow blanketing the Shenandoah Valley in a cheery holiday costume. As I made my way to the hospital to treat the animals under my care, my heart was warm despite the winter chill. After administering medications and checking my patients, I tied a red ribbon around the kitten's neck and bundled her into my coat pocket.

The streets were unusually quiet, empty now as families surrounded Christmas trees in each tinseled home. Snowmen guarded some of the front yards; their carrot noses applied at odd angles, their scarves knotted all askew around icy necks. Christmas morning in the valley is always magical. It is even more so with snow. I drove slowly, the window cracked a bit so the chill of the morning kissed my cheek and the crunch of the snow under the tires was clearly audible.

I pulled into the driveway of Amy's house and got out of the car. Through the wreath framing the glass window on the front door, I could see the family gathered around the Christmas tree, a fire crackling cheerfully in the fireplace. There was Amy, eyes shining and hair uncombed, still in her pajamas, sitting cross-legged on the floor surrounded by a partially unwrapped collection of Christmas gifts.

I pushed the kitten deeper into my coat pocket. Amy's dad threw open the door and, with a glint in his eyes, ushered me into the living room. We began the staged discussion about a piece of music while out of the corner of my eye I caught a hint of dismay on Amy's face. Who did I think I was invading her house? To discuss music? And on Christmas morning of all times!

About that time, the kitten popped her head out of my pocket and jumped lightly to the floor. Amy's mouth dropped open and her hands went to her cheeks in utter surprise and absolute glee. In a moment she was across the room, scooping up the kitten in her arms and dancing a little jig around the living room. Gone was the frustration. What remained I can only define as sheer Christmas magic.

I would have liked to watch that scene longer, but it was really private magic—magic best shared by those whom you're comfortable with in Christmas pajamas and uncombed hair. I remembered shining eyes in Christmas pajamas on my own hearth around my tree at home. And that Christmas magic beckoned me away. I smiled as Amy's door swung shut.

A week later a card arrived in the mailbox addressed to me in the scrawling handwriting of an eight-year-old. It was from Amy thanking me for her kitten. She had named it Cosley after my wife and me, her "favorite piano teacher and vet." Probably her parents made her write that note thinking I would be flattered by the name she had given her kitten. And I must admit to that.

But I also knew immediately that it was more than that; more than mere flattery that motivated Amy to make her kitten a namesake. It was the Gift, you see! In her own way, Amy was thanking me for recognizing it in her, acknowledging that we shared it, accepting the rights and privileges it bestows, and affirming it again.

I no longer live in Amy's town. But I'd be willing to bet that this year as Amy sits beside her Christmas tree, her friend, Cosley, who is no doubt now graced by a dignified maturity and probably some gray on the muzzle, will be beside her on the hearth. Merry Christmas, and thank you for the Gift.

Not for the Faint of Heart

During the summer months it is not uncommon for teenagers to observe our work in the hospital. I suppose we get some eight or ten such requests each year from young people who are in the "I want to be a vet when I grow up" stage. Unlike most of the teenagers who parade through the practice in the summertime, I never outgrew the "vet" phase. Most of them eventually broaden their career scope when they recognize that not all of what we do is glamorous. One has only to catch the scent of a few squeezed anal glands, or watch us collect a stool sample or two to realize that much of our daily activity has little, if any, inherent aesthetic value. Some of it, in fact, is just plain disgusting.

It is worthwhile for young people who are entertaining an interest in veterinary medicine to see exactly what the job entails. Some young people are only infatuated with the thought of being a vet and are not prepared for the nitty-gritty of animal care. One such young lady comes immediately to mind.

Melissa was nothing if not beautiful. She had long, dark hair that hung around her shoulders in silky waves. Her eyes, dark brown and dangerously soft, were framed by thick lashes that she was adept at batting. She had long, athletic legs that she highlighted nicely by wearing shorts most of the time. These features were complimented by her generously apportioned, robust figure. Melissa, a junior in college, was older than most of the observers that come into the practice. Though I was a few years her senior and married, quite happily I might add, still these attributes did not escape me.

So it was with perhaps a little too much anticipation that I welcomed her to the hospital that day to observe. I was eager to provide Melissa with a positive experience with veterinary medicine. The role of teacher is one that I enjoy anyway, but with Melissa I was no doubt more enthusiastic than usual.

She had accompanied me into the examination rooms all morning during my appointments and had seen a variety of interesting, if mundane, cases. Several surgeries were scheduled for the early afternoon. Now this, I thought, was where I could really make veterinary medicine shine. Surgery is one of the more interesting things that we do. There has always been something intriguing to me about invading the inside of a patient, finding a specific and discreet abnormality, and deftly removing it with the scalpel, leaving behind only a neat row of perfectly spaced sutures. Surely my prodigious surgical skills would impress Melissa.

Our first surgery was a cat castration. We'd work her in easy, I thought. As I prepared the surgical materials I'd need, I gave her a rundown of the whole procedure so she'd know just what to expect. She hung eagerly on my every word, her level of interest bolstering my bravado and clouding my better judgment. I knew from experience that observers, regardless of their level of interest or enthusiasm, do not always make for good assistants.

"Would you like to assist me with this procedure?"

I remembered the strange mixture of excitement and fear that I had felt the first time I had observed surgery—the carefully controlled skill of the surgeon's hand on the scalpel; the obvious familiarity with anatomy; the nonchalant click of the hemostats on a bleeding artery. It had been so exciting and enticing to me as a junior in high school. I had been in awe of the veterinarian's knowledge and it had cemented my long-held dream of one day wearing the surgeon's gloves myself. By the look in her eyes and the quickness of her response, I suspected Melissa felt the same way.

"Sure, I'd love to help. What do I do?"

"It's pretty easy, really. After I anesthetize the cat, you hold the cat on his back just so, with his head to you and his feet and tail to me."

Cat castrations are indeed uncomplicated procedures. They are performed with an assistant holding the anesthetized animal in a prescribed position while the surgeon makes a few quick incisions and ligatures. The whole thing is over in ten minutes.

I planned to perform the surgery on my treatment table. This table was positioned in the treatment room so that it formed a peninsula with access to both sides of the table. I positioned my surgical instruments on the adjacent countertop, and positioned Melissa on the opposite side of the table from me. Four feet behind her, across a small aisleway, stood a stainless-steel bank of kennels that housed numerous other of the day's patients. The bottom cage of this bank was raised off the floor about eight or ten inches on a set of wheels that allowed us to move the bank of cages around for ease of cleaning.

While I completed the final preparations for surgery, Melissa turned her attention to the animals in those cages. A kitten reached through the bars of the cage front and swatted at her hair. A puppy beat out a staccato rhythm with his tail on the sides of his cage in an ingratiating effort to win a few pats and a soft word or two. From the back of another cage ominous growls and the foul odor of infected ears badly in need of flushing emanated from a cocker spaniel who was overly fearful at the prospects of being in the hospital.

"Okay, I think we're ready," I said, eager to demonstrate my surgical prowess. "All you have to do is hold the vein off like this and I'll give the anesthetics."

I showed her just the right way to restrain the cat and hold off the vein at the same time. I then slipped the needle into the vein and administered the injection. The cat's head sunk down in slumber as I expected. Once the patient was asleep, it was a simple matter to clip and prep the surgical site. I then unwrapped my instruments and began the ten-minute procedure.

Though my mind was completely occupied with the work, I managed to keep up a steady, blow-by-blow description of each phase of the surgery and its purpose.

This role of teaching and mentoring young minds was rewarding, I thought, as the surgery progressed. It was nice to have a positive impact on a young person's career path. I could tell by the questions she asked that Melissa was soaking up the information like a sponge. Unfortunately, I was too engrossed in the surgery to notice that, as time wore on, the questions came less frequently and with less enthusiasm. It was not until the patient began to move a little that realization dawned. Imperceptibly the cat began to slide toward Melissa's side of the table. Without looking up, I tried to correct the breakdown in patient restraint.

"Melissa, the cat is sliding just a bit your way. . . ." No response. "Melissa!"

I looked up just in time to see Melissa's glassy eyes turn up to the ceiling, her legs give way, and her body begin to sag down and back. I lunged in her direction, but was too late to catch her. She tipped backward like a felled tree. There was a loud, resonant thud, like the crescendo of a kettledrum, as the back of her head connected with the stainless-steel cage behind her. Unfortunately, her grip on reality faded more quickly than her grip on the surgical patient and he flew off the table on top of her, trailing a not-quite-yet-excised testicle behind him.

I raced around the treatment table to see if I could help one or the other of the now comatose duo on the floor. Fortunately for the cat, he had landed on her ample chest, suffering neither injury nor significant contamination of the surgical site. I lifted him quickly back onto the table. Still anesthetized, he was none the worse for wear and continued to sleep peacefully. I turned my attention to Melissa.

She was stirring ever so slightly. I knelt down beside her and fanned her pale, pasty face. Despite her makeup, it had turned a unique and interesting grayish hue. Her eyes wandered independently around the room, seeking unsuccessfully for something to focus on. Neither could decide or agree with its cohort on a suitable object and so continued its search alone. Softly and incoherently, Melissa was muttering something under her breath. So was I! I hoped my muttering was also indecipherable.

I gently patted her cheeks. "Melissa!" And a little louder. "Melissa. It's okay. You'll be fine."

I don't think she was convinced. I don't think she was even processing input. Finally I noticed that her eyes seemed to be once again traveling in tandem and the muttering began to take on genuine, though unrepeatable, meaning. I began to breathe a little easier.

As she began to gather her wits about her, she reflexively stretched her arms over her head and straightened her legs. This was just the wrong thing to do! Since her feet were pressed up against the base of the treatment table, the thrust of her legs propelled her head and torso toward the bank of cages. I gasped as I watched her arms and head slide under the cages. Had she not been so amply endowed, she would have disappeared under them up to the waist. Instead, she came to rest with only her bosom stopping progress. Instinctively I reached to grab her and pull her out, but there were only two available appendages, and those were neither appropriate nor functional for that purpose. I stopped myself just in time.

I stammered out a weak plea for help from the hospital staff and between three of us we were able to extricate her from her predicament. Heroic measures were not required, though there was some doubt when, as we pulled on her legs, one nostril caught the underside of the cages, distorting her face into Halloweenlike contortions. But with one of us turning her head to the side while the other two each tugged on a leg, she came out rather well.

Melissa was mortified when she revived enough to realize

what had happened. After I had finished my surgery, I called her father who promised to come and drive her home. She was in no state to do so herself. While we waited for him to arrive I was able to stem the blood loss from the minor gash on her scalp.

I tried to comfort her with assurances that these things happened all the time and she had nothing to be worried or embarrassed about. But gone was the eagerness and interest she had so recently exhibited. She hardly spoke at all; only once, in fact, to request a little privacy and promise she'd be back the following week to observe some more.

But Melissa didn't show up the next week. Or the next. In fact, I don't think I've ever seen Melissa again. I do think about her every now and then when I think about that sickening thud or see the resultant dent in the treatment room cages. And I hope, for her sake, that she is somewhere enjoying her career as an account executive or hairstylist or lawyer or bank teller or sales representative. I'm sure she's productive and successful in whatever capacity she now works. But I'd be willing to bet a dime to a dollar that she's not a vet!

And Along Came Another

Eight or nine months after Jace was born, I was busy unpacking the groceries one evening when I was surprised to find in the bags among the toothpaste and deodorant, an early pregnancy test. At first I was confused and wondered why in the world Cynthia might be buying an early pregnancy test for one of her friends. Then the implications hit me and I sank into a chair. I looked up to find Cynthia smiling at me conspiratorially.

The next morning, we were thrilled to find that the home pregnancy test was positive. Before we knew it, we were once again seated in front of Dr. Martin Smith's desk discussing a plan for a second successful pregnancy. Dr. Smith's tack was not to mess with success, planning surgery again at about twelve weeks along, just as we had done for Jace. Surgery was to be followed again by rest for the remainder of her pregnancy. What was hard for Cynthia the first time around was doubly so the second. During Jace's pregnancy, having just moved to town, she had known practically no one. This time, however, having lived in Waynesboro for more than a year, she had developed a close circle of friends with whom she very much enjoyed spending time. She had also become very active in the life of the church and leading many of the children's ministries. Bed rest made these activities impossible.

A difficult pregnancy became all the more challenging with Jace, who at the time was an active, demanding tot less than a year old. Dr. Smith gave strict instructions for Cynthia not to lift any weight more than ten pounds and not to walk up or down the stairs. These seemed like impossible restrictions with Jace needing so much of her attention.

Fortunately, Jace was exceptionally compliant. He quickly mastered the skill of climbing up the stairs himself with Cynthia scooting up behind him one step at a time. Getting down the stairs was accomplished by Jace's climbing onto Cynthia's lap and together they would slide down on her fanny from step to step. He also learned how to climb in and out of his crib and into the bathtub without Cynthia's help. These skills became a game that Jace grew to love and that allowed Cynthia to negotiate the house without breaking her ground rules.

Once again, individuals in our church coordinated their efforts to provide us a home-cooked dinner one or two evenings a week. The rest of the meals were thrown together by yours truly in a culinary style that can best be described as bachelor survivalist—a style heavy on peanut butter, cold cut sandwiches, cold cereal, and takeout.

It was exciting to watch once again the progress of Cynthia's pregnancy. Though her pregnancies have always been difficult, she nonetheless loves carrying babies. Her small, five-foot-two-inch frame does not hide pregnancy well, and it was not long at all before her poor stomach looked like it would burst. One day her father walked into the house and was surprised at how much larger she had become since he had last seen her.

"Oh, Cynthia," he said empathetically. "It looks like you've swallowed a watermelon."

Feeling like the watermelon analogy was inadequate to fully capture her level of discomfort, she responded, "Oh, that's not the half of it. It feels more like a watermelon and two cantaloupes."

Jace found the whole process nothing short of astounding. For hours on end he would place a small hand on his mother's stomach and squeal in glee whenever he felt his little sibling move against it. Then he would bend over the growing tummy and sing little nursery songs to the baby.

Because of her condition, even though she was on high doses of medication to prevent it, Cynthia had to be admitted to the hospital to halt premature labor on multiple occasions. When we finally reached the point in gestation at which the baby's safety was assured even if he came early, we were greatly relieved.

One day I was seeing patients in the hospital when I looked up and was surprised to find Cynthia, with Jace in tow, standing at the front desk. She was calm and quiet, waiting for me to finish my conversation with the owner of my last patient. After bidding my client good-bye, I turned to her with a confused face.

"I think it's time!"

My mind deserted me. I flew into action, racing around the hospital leaving hasty, unintelligible instructions with the staff for the patients in the hospital and throwing records randomly in all directions. Finally, the staff chased me out the door. I whisked Cynthia and Jace into the car and headed for the hospital, stopping quickly to drop Jace off at the home of one of our friends.

In the maternity ward, they hooked monitors up to Cynthia, placed a catheter in her arm, and waited. And waited. And waited some more. It hardly seems fair, after months of bed rest to prevent premature labor, to have to induce it with drugs when it's time. But once again, that's exactly what they had to do.

In case you don't know, dads are so much extraneous baggage during a time like this. I tried to be supportive and helpful. Really, I did. But I could sense when I caught Cynthia's eye between groans and contractions, that she blamed me for this. This, of course, was reassuring for me, but did nothing to help her through.

I had seen television programs where fathers coach their struggling wives with the breathing exercises they had learned and practiced in childbirth classes. But we had never attended any, partly because of Cynthia's restrictions, but I suspected mostly because Cynthia didn't trust me to contain my inappropriate remarks or maintain adequate respect during the classes. No doubt, she was right, but this left me woefully unprepared to be any help at all during her time of need.

I remember thinking that it would help Cynthia if I reminded her that the result of all this pain would be worth it in the end. I reached for my wallet to show her a picture of little Jace. Surely that would make it all worthwhile in her mind. But she saw what I was doing and cut me off in the middle.

"Put it away!" she said flatly.

"But I just thought you might be encouraged to see the finished product."

"Put it away!"

I put it away and busied myself again with my totally ineffectual efforts at assistance, panting at all the wrong times, and generally getting in the way. Somehow, despite my bumbling contributions, Cynthia produced another beautiful baby boy later in the day.

Okay, maybe beautiful isn't the perfect adjective. Frankly, he looked like a little gangster. He had heavy, pouting cheeks that drooped precipitously at the corners and eyebrows that furrowed spontaneously over eyes that he couldn't quite seem to open. Unlike Jace, who had peered around the room with bright, round eyes almost immediately, this boy was content to keep his eyes shaded from us, as if disappointed with the parents he had drawn. And yet, he was perfect to me all the same. He had a full complement of fingers and toes and was healthy in every way. I could not have been more proud.

While the nurses were cleaning him up in the nursery, I scooped up big brother Jace, who had just begun to talk. His grandmother had picked him up from our friend's house and brought him with her to the hospital. Rocking him gently in my arms, I introduced him to his little brother through the glass window. Jace was enthralled and watched intently as the baby got his first bath, a process that did not please the baby at all. We had settled on a name weeks before, having known the sex from sonogram images, but had chosen not to make it public until he was born. I pointed at the little naked form on the table.

"That's your brother, Jace. His name is Tucker Wade Coston."

"Kucker?" Jace repeated, not quite able to wrap his tongue around it.

"Yes. Tucker Wade Coston."

"Hey, Jace's name is Coston, too."

"That's right. Everyone in the family's last name is Coston. Tucker is in our family now. He's your little brother."

"Kucker Coston," he repeated quietly to himself.

In just a couple of days, Tucker came home with us. Being the second baby, the trip home didn't take quite as long. I was not nearly so apprehensive as I had been with Jace. Life quickly settled into the busy, but comfortable rhythms of night feedings, diaper changes for two, mealtimes, and laundry.

Jace accepted Tucker into the family with amazing willingness, even though this new intruder demanded a lot of his mom and dad's time. It took a while for him to get Tucker's name down pat. One day, the four of us were relaxing in the family room. Cynthia was resting on the couch as I changed a lightbulb and Jace busied himself with toys on the floor. He stopped and looked up at us with a puzzled expression.

"Baby's name is Kucker?"

"That's right, Jace," I replied. "Tucker Wade Coston."

He thought about this for a moment. Then he turned to us again for clarification.

"Kucker Wave"—and he motioned with his hand as if waving good-bye—"Coston?"

Cynthia and I roared with laughter, tickled at the connection he had made in his mind. What did he know of Wade? He didn't realize it was in honor of my brother, Daniel Wade, who had passed away long before he was born. He only knew the word *wave*. And he was totally confused as to why his lame parents would name his brother Wave. Our laughter did not please him in the least. He brought us up short with a stern look and an indignant finger in our faces.

"No! No!" he said. "No funny! You not laugh at Jace!"

They say that having two babies does not exactly double your work, and I think that is true. I think it quadrupled it—especially when the boys were only seventeen months apart. Life was good, but we were two tired parents. We found that we could get more rest if we let Tucker sleep in our room in a bassinet or in the baby swing. This prevented him from waking Jace when he got hungry in the night and avoided the frustration of being serenaded by two crying babies.

I'm not sure how other tired parents divvy up the parental duties, but Cynthia and I took turns getting up and attending to the babies every night. Somehow, despite sleep deprivation, we managed to keep a fairly accurate accounting of whose turn it was to crawl out of the warm bed to calm one or the other of the kids.

One night, I remember hearing one of the babies crying. In my sleepiness, I realized with relief that it was my turn to ignore the cries. I waited impatiently for Cynthia to respond. Cynthia, I may have mentioned, sleeps like a rusty old truck in a junkyard. She seemed to be snoozing blissfully. I turned over to look at her and, about that time, received a thump in the ribs from her elbow.

"Bruce," she said in a thick, sleep-drenched voice, "can you get Jace? I'm feeding the baby." She never opened her eyes.

I thought this an exceedingly unfair request and rolled out of bed in disgruntlement. As I passed the baby swing, I glanced down to see Tucker sleeping peacefully as it rocked back and forth. Rush was sprawled across his lap, purring loudly.

"You're not feeding the baby, Cynth!"

I tossed the comment out mainly to make me feel better, realizing that in her slumber, she would undoubtedly miss it. But she smiled up at me sweetly and glanced down with closed, sleepy eyes into the crook of her arm, as if to prove to me the veracity of her statement. I followed her gaze. There nestled down deeply into Cynthia's embrace was Ollie, sleeping as soundly as I wished I was, and creating a burden roughly equivalent to Tucker's weight in her arms. I was too tired to be amused, and trudged into the nursery where Jace was rolling around sadly in his crib.

I changed him and rocked him to sleep again before making my way back to our bedroom. As I rounded to my side of the bed and plopped wearily under the covers, I swear Cynthia was trying to burp that cat. But even then, it wasn't funny until the next morning.

Nine Minus One

As I walked into the house one evening after being at the office all day, Ollie greeted me at the door as he usually did. Something about his gait, though, caught my eye. Each time he placed his front right foot on the ground, there was a noticeable head bob. Ollie was limping. I questioned Cynthia about the problem, but she had not noticed anything out of the ordinary.

Over the next few days I watched Ollie's lameness carefully. While it didn't seem to get any worse; it certainly didn't improve. I examined his leg from toe to shoulder. The only thing I found was a small pinpoint of thickened tissue on the pad of one of his toes. When I put any pressure on it, Ollie would pull his foot away, yowl in pain, and bite gently at my hand. Then he would fix me with an icy stare as if to say, "What in the world are you doing, you big oaf? If you think, just because you're bigger than me, you can poke and prod and cause pain, then you've got another thing coming." And with that he would stalk off, casting angry glances over his shoulder to see if I was following.

I wanted to avoid, if possible, bringing Ollie into the hospital for treatment. Admittedly, Ollie is not an easy patient. In our hospital we have devised a rating system for ranking the patients' personalities. It's a simple one to five ranking based on the patient's temperament in the hospital. Patients that love to see you, that adore your attention even if it involves taking a rectal temperature, that don't even stir when poked with a needle for vaccinations, that lick your hand or rub against your leg in gratitude for even the most uncomfortable of procedures, these patients are assigned a one on the scale. On the other end of the temperament scale are the patients we rank as fives. These animals are direct descendants of the Devil himself. They are often equipped with extra claws and teeth that, since their last visit to the office, they have systematically honed to razor sharpness for the sole purpose of mercilessly shredding and eviscerating veterinarians and veterinary technicians. These are the patients that begin growling and hissing as soon as their owners turn into the parking lot. By the time they enter the clinic, they are cocked and ready, itching for a fight. On this scale, my staff had designated Ollie a six.

Now at home, Ollie is a lover. Intensely devoted to us and strongly bonded, he is calm and collected. Though a little arrogant, as cats tend to be, he is nonetheless affectionate and responsive, attentive to our moods and feelings and solicitous of our attentions. In the office, however, his personality changes completely. He despises being handled and examined. He loathes restraint in any form. And he directs this angst against the providers of his medical care—even if that provider is me. Instead of the adoring looks he showers on me at home, in the office his eyes are daggers, his attitude criminal, and his behavior nothing short of psychotic.

I monitored Ollie's limping for several weeks hoping for improvement so we could avoid a hospital showdown. It didn't improve; it worsened. The spot on the pad enlarged slowly. Soon he was having difficulty coming down the stairs or jumping down off the bed. Instead of enjoying his usual wrestling games with Rush, he became more and more surly with him, swatting him fiercely at the gentlest invitation to play. It was quite unlike him and I knew that the time had come to do something.

My plan was a conservative one. I would take him to the office, get some quick blood work, anesthetize him, remove the growth on the pad, have it biopsied and, since he would already be asleep, clean his teeth. Though it was a reasonable and prudent plan, I decided it was best not to discuss it with Ollie. Instead, one morning without warning, I scooped him up in my arms and took him to my car.

This, of course, was a dead giveaway. Ollie never rode in the car unless he was coming to the hospital for either medical care or weekend boarding. He knew immediately something was up and swore at me unapologetically on the ride in. But the serious growling didn't begin until we entered the waiting room.

"Oh, no! You're not bringing that dangerous vermin in here, are you?" The staff did not particularly enjoy being the object of such intense hatred. Ollie's growling continued as well!

As I do with all my surgical patients, I carefully examined Ollie prior to the procedure. It is an impressive thing to hear feline growling amplified tenfold through a stethoscope. Over those malevolent hisses I could plainly hear something else in the heart. Instead of the steady lub-dup of a normal heart, I heard shhh-dup. Ollie had a heart murmur!

I was not terribly concerned. Many animals develop a mild heart murmur with age that generally poses few risks. I was sure such was the case with Ollie. I would take some chest X-rays, do an electrocardiogram, and monitor it over time. The rest of the exam, other than the foot, was unremarkable. With difficulty and a great deal of swearing and cursing (in both English and felinese) Brenda, my technician, and I were able to draw some blood for a preoperative profile and administer preanesthetic antibiotics and sedatives.

Once the sedatives took effect, Ollie was much easier to handle. He was not exactly a happy drunk, to be sure. He maintained a steady, low deep growl all the while, but his reflexes had slowed enough that we were able to administer the intravenous drugs that slid him into a deep sleep and allowed us to place a breathing tube into his trachea. The technicians busied themselves attaching the leads that would allow us to monitor his

EKG during the procedure. Brenda and I chatted nonchalantly as she completed the task.

I glanced down at Ollie and stroked his sides. He looked so innocent and safe like this, I thought. And yet, as these thoughts swirled around in my mind something struck me as odd. Something was wrong! My heart jumped into my throat. Ollie's chest wall wasn't moving. He wasn't breathing. I looked at his mouth. His tongue was blue. I was dumbfounded. With the advent of newer drugs and protocols, the availability of sophisticated instruments like our electrocardiographic monitor and pulse oximeter, and the addition of licensed and specially trained technicians, anesthetic complications have become a rarity. But here in front of me lay my own cat in crisis!

I was paralyzed with fear and concern. My years of experience and training seemed to evaporate in the face of this emergency. Helplessly I watched the blue hue of Ollie's tongue darken. My mind seized up and I could summon only the vaguest of ideas of what to do.

After what seemed an eternity, my autopilot finally kicked in. I began external chest compressions, gave oxygen through the tube in Ollie's windpipe, and started some drugs to stimulate his system. Within just a minute or two, Ollie began to breathe on his own, his color improved to normal, and his heart rate and rhythm normalized. My color, heart rate, and rhythm, on the other hand, did not recover quite so quickly.

I slumped into a nearby chair and waited for the carbonation to clear from my veins. It had been a close call. I watched the normal pattern that the electrocardiographic monitor traced with relief. The pulse oximeter showed normal oxygen levels in the bloodstream now. Ollie's tongue was once again a healthy pink.

"Dr. Coston." Brenda interrupted my mental meandering. "What do you want me to do now? Should we just wake him up?"

"No," I said after a long pause. "The hurdle has already been cleared now. He's stable and he wasn't down long enough to have posed any risk. We may as well just go ahead and finish what we started."

I set to work on the foot while Brenda began cleaning his teeth. Carefully I incised around the growth with a scalpel blade. The growth penetrated a few millimeters into the pad itself, but I was able to dissect around its perimeter and lift it from the surrounding tissues. The pad was easily closed with a couple of fine sutures. Brenda finished cleaning the teeth within a few minutes of my placing the last suture. The whole procedure had taken less than twenty minutes.

I hovered over Ollie during his recovery like a hen over her eggs. This proved totally unnecessary, however, since Ollie woke up uneventfully. When he was able to lift his head and look up at me with unmistakable recognition, I knew we had consumed one of his nine lives.

Woodstock

Traveling south on Interstate 81 from Washington, D.C., one Saturday afternoon, a green highway sign suddenly captured my attention and I snapped my head to the right to see if I had read it right.

WOODSTOCK 1 MI.

My wife and I were just a few short minutes shy of our destination where we were scheduled to perform music in an afternoon program in just a couple of hours. Cynthia was eager to arrive so that she could tune Harpo, the only thing that really sparks my jealousy. Her harp is taller and better looking than me, and has been with her much longer than I have. Harpists have a saying that they spend half their life tuning their harps and the other half playing their harps out of tune. She has found that by arriving at a venue an hour or two early, Harpo is allowed time to acclimate to the room and thus will hold a tuning longer.

WOODSTOCK 1 MI.

The sign had brought back a long-forgotten conversation between myself and Dr. Peartree. He had mentioned offhandedly that he thought Woodstock might be an underserved community in which a veterinary practice might thrive. The conversation had taken place months before and I had not given it a moment's further consideration until that green sign jogged my memory. I turned off onto the exit ramp.

"What are you doing?" Cynthia asked incredulously.

"I just thought I would drive through Woodstock," I said nonchalantly, as if this had been the plan all along. "David once mentioned that he thought Woodstock might be a good place to start a practice."

"We can't do that now! We've got to be at the church in half an hour or Harpo won't hold a tune worth two cents."

I knew she was right, but the impulse was too strong, I turned left and headed toward town.

"Woodstock is pretty small. This shouldn't take long. Besides, we probably won't like it anyway, and then we won't have to make a special trip back later to find that out. Give me just five minutes."

For the previous six or eight months it had become increasingly clear that the practice I had been in for more than three years was not going to meet our long-term goals. Cynthia and I, after much discussion, had decided to start a practice of our own. I had spent several months scouting out locations and office space in the state capital, making significant progress with each visit. But upon returning from Richmond to our little town in the valley, I invariably felt depressed. I was just not a big city person. The thought of working in the hubbub and pace of such a large city put a little tremble of trepidation in me that I was having a harder and harder time ignoring. I was just beginning to recognize the cause of my discomfiture when I passed the sign.

WOODSTOCK 1 MI.

Turning left off the highway headed us almost due east, directly toward the Massanutten range of mountains that bounds the eastern flank of the town, giving it its unique flavor and sending the North Fork into the indecisive squirms that form the Seven Bends of the Shenandoah River for which the area is known. They are not large mountains, to be sure, rising only about nineteen hundred feet at the pass by the fire tower, but with their shoulders reaching out toward the highway, they give interest and texture to the valley floor, and depth and warmth to the eastern skyline overarching the town. I loved them immediately.

Passing the colony of fast-food restaurants that feed the travelers on the highway, the road dipped down a slight incline before intersecting with Main Street, just a mile or so from the interchange. A sign pointed left to the historic downtown district but it was fairly easy to see from the intersection that only a few buildings dotted the outskirts of town to the right. We turned left.

Within just a few blocks, the character of the community began to emerge. It was a chamber of commerce kind of day in town. The street was lined with Bradford Pear trees whose leaves that time of year were a beautiful port wine color and shimmered in the light breeze. On the right, the County Memorial Hospital occupied a slight rise with a large, green skirt of beautiful lawn flowing down to the street. Next, on the left, we passed the stately and elegant buttresses of a military academy with an obviously long and storied history. Just beyond it the street was bounded on each side by beautifully restored, older homes with wide, wrapping porches; the kind found so often in southern communities where history is treasured and preserved and the whims of commerce over time have been kind, but not excessive.

A quaint restaurant on the right, with a heavy wooden sign of some age bearing the name the Spring House, was the perfect transition to downtown Woodstock. The historic downtown district comprised only about four or five blocks of small businesses centered around a towering, white courthouse with a green slate roof and turrets reminiscent of antique prints depicting small towns throughout the country. The downtown corridor itself was indeed a throwback to antique American towns, its two-story, brick storefronts hosting family enterprises of every sort needed by a small town—furniture stores, law offices, a local newspaper, and real estate offices with pictures of homes and plats of salable land taped to the front windows.

One façade was constructed to resemble a Swiss chalet and housed an optometrist's office. Sandwiched in the eight or ten feet between two buildings was the local dry cleaner's shop with a neon sign announcing the special of the week, which probably hadn't changed in many a month. There was a family restaurant with tables up against the windows, a florist's shop, and a printer, with the odd dentist, physician, and chiropractor scattered among the rest. It was the kind of downtown you rather expected to see in black-and-white, like old episodes of *Mayberry R.F.D.*

The sidewalks trickled with pedestrians: a group of cadets in uniform from the military academy; a woman arm in arm with her elderly mother heading into the furniture store; a young man with a camera and a clipboard dashing into the newspaper office, probably behind deadline; and a boy on a bike with a baseball bat over his shoulders, holding onto the handlebars carelessly with one hand. Not that many, really, but enough to keep the doors of commerce swinging; and not so many that hands weren't raised in greeting or smiles exchanged with faces you recognized even if the names you did not. You could feel the familiarity just driving through, the intimacy and calm of a small community. It felt like home, though not mine; as if I had been brought home from college for a visit by one of the local favorites and I was being welcomed by association.

At the north end of town we passed two small car dealerships and a dated, but well-cared for shopping center with a full parking lot whose anchor store was a Ben Franklin boasting a lunch counter. We turned around in the parking lot of a large, red-brick school building and, with few comments, drove back through town again. Looking down the side streets, we could see homes on either side of Main Street stretching east and west up the hills on either side.

It was a bustling, healthy, and thoroughly comfortable little town. It was large enough, as the county seat and home of the community hospital and courthouse, to attract the bulk of the business from the county, both professional and commercial. It was small enough that all the benefits of a small town could still be enjoyed: tight community experience, the civic pride, the unhurried greetings at the grocery store from those you know.

We turned back toward the highway and passed again the phalanx of national chain restaurants: McDonald's, Wendy's, Pizza Hut, Hardee's, and Kentucky Fried Chicken—all the fatty food groups. Then we turned once again onto the entrance ramp to the southbound lane of Interstate 81. The entire detour had taken less than ten minutes.

I loved Woodstock immediately. Since this had been an unplanned tour and had put us a little behind for the day, I knew Cynthia was a little put out with me. I tried, probably unsuccessfully, to keep my enthusiasm in check. We drove south on the highway quietly until I could take it no longer.

"That was a neat little town, wasn't it?"

"I wish we hadn't taken the time to drive through now." Cynthia was not letting me off the hook easily. "Now we're going to get there much later than I had wanted to."

"I think we'll still get there in time. We're only about twenty minutes away now. What did you think of Woodstock? I really liked it a lot."

"It had some good points, I have to admit. We'll have to come back some time when we can spend some more time exploring."

I settled back into the seat as I drove along, pleased that I had taken the detour and pleasantly surprised that Cynthia had liked the town. In my mind, I instantly shifted my new venture from Richmond to Woodstock, and immediately I felt better about the future. I had never relished living in such a large city. Woodstock felt just right.

Within a few days we were driving through the town again. This time we were not pressed for time and we could really explore. We started by driving slowly through the downtown area again.

Then we followed the main drag out of town both northward and southward to get a feel for the outskirts. There weren't any.

We stopped at a local convenience store and looked in the phone book for the location of the veterinary practice in town, then found our way to it. It was a large, substantial brick building with white columns out front and a sweeping curved driveway. I was impressed—and a little discouraged. Would such a small town have room for two practices? Especially when the first one was apparently doing very well?

We drove through many different neighborhoods, each with its own character and flair. On the hill to the west above Main Street we found the city park with a pool, basketball and tennis courts, a huge wooden play station that we knew the kids would love, a baseball diamond, soccer field, and picnic shelters. The kids would be in heaven there.

We parked along Main Street and went into an office marked VOTER REGISTRATION to see what information we could glean. They gave us population numbers for the entire county and each little burg within it. These would allow us to determine the number of full-time small animal veterinarians the area could potentially support. We then found the chamber of commerce office and were greeted warmly by the woman behind the desk who filled our arms with as much information as we could carry about the town and its surrounding attractions.

At each place we stopped, we coyly asked each resident about the local veterinarian. Did they have animals? Did they see the local vet? Did they like him? The answers we got were across the board from ringing endorsements to guarded responses, just as one would expect.

At the town offices we asked to see the zoning statutes and a town zoning map so we could scout out possible sites for a practice. With these in hand, we drove through these areas looking for a storefront or building for sale or lease that might suit nicely. Finding none, we stopped in at a realtor's office and asked if there were any available buildings with the correct zoning.

Only one building in the whole town that was zoned correctly was on the market. It was a 1919 vintage two-story frame house on the north end of town. It had a paved parking area for four or five cars and was empty, but it was very small. Being the only available spot in town, we nonetheless made an offer on it.

Cynthia and I had been enormously blessed by the friendship and confidence of two retired couples in our church in Waynesboro. They had taken very grandparently shines to Cynthia and me. Dr. Peter Good, a retired, gray-haired physician who had delivered hundreds of the children in Waynesboro, took me under his wing and tutored me on matters of finance, business, and personal philosophy. I could not have had a better mentor in these things. His kindness and wisdom had made him a well-respected figure in town and a revered individual in our church, overseeing its finances and contributing to them as one of its founding members.

Mike and Alice Johnson, who my kids knew as Farmer Mike and Grandma Alice, were kindhearted and supportive in every way. They loved to have us come to their home for dinner after church. Grandma Alice was famous for her skill in the kitchen and had a magical freezer from which amazing meals of enormous proportion seemed to emerge as if spontaneously generated. We seldom passed up their invitation. The boys loved to visit them too because after the meal Farmer Mike would start up the tractor and take them for a ride around the farm in the bucket of his front-end loader.

For some strange reason, these otherwise astute and prudent people believed in me and were convinced that my efforts would be eventually successful. Amazingly, they offered to finance me in my venture even though my plans meant our moving an hour and a half from their town. Being the equivalent of a junk bond at that time with no capital to add to their generous sponsorship, I could never have opened the doors without their financial support. They could not possibly comprehend how much their kindness and backing meant to me then—and now.

When I told them about the building I had located in Woodstock, they were less than enthusiastic about spending top dollar on such an old house, which would then need extensive remodeling. They encouraged me instead to look for a lot on which to build an office. However, anticipating being unemployed within just a few weeks, I didn't feel that the extra time it would take to build a building was a luxury I could afford. We waited for a response to our offer.

Several days later the realtor called us. The sellers had not accepted our offer, she told us. They had decided to sell the building to a local resident for several thousand dollars less than we had offered. We were stunned and discouraged and considered aborting our plans altogether. Dr. Good and Farmer Mike and Grandma Alice, however, were not deterred. With their encouragement, we made a greatly reduced offer on a piece of property on the south end of town and were astonished to learn that our offer had been accepted.

Over the next several months, as work on the new office progressed apace, I engaged in part-time relief work at practices in the Washington, D.C., area. While this kept the bills paid, it served mainly to reinforce our decision to settle in a small town. Each time I left D.C. and headed into the valley, I breathed easier and my steps were lighter. As I watched the building take shape, I became increasingly excited. My goal since the age of ten or eleven had always been to be a veterinarian with a practice of my own in a small town. I was now just a few short weeks from realizing that dream.

Organizing the details of a new practice was an overwhelming proposition. From stocking the shelves with all the supplies and materials, to ordering surgical equipment and selecting the appropriate vaccines from the numerous products on the market, to hiring and training new staff members, everything kept me incredibly busy over the next few weeks.

I placed an ad in the local paper for two employees, and to my astonishment, I received one hundred and eighty applications. Sifting through them and selecting candidates to interview simply from those applications was a daunting task. After interviewing about twenty applicants, I selected two whom I thought would be great. One of them resigned after working for only a few months. The other works for me still, as office manager, after more than eleven years.

Finally, in March of 1992, we opened the doors of Seven Bends Veterinary Hospital for business, naming the practice after the seven bends of the Shenandoah River. In the beginning, things were sparse. But my spirits and my expectations were high and I went to the office each morning in satisfied disbelief that I was working for myself in my own office.

Walkabout

Florida in January! We were living the high life. After two years of hard work, we had finally rewarded ourselves with a trip to Florida. It was the first real vacation we had taken since opening the practice and we had looked forward to it for months. Temperatures were icy in the valley when we left, which made us yearn even more for more temperate climes. Snow had fallen, blanketing the valley, so we felt particularly decadent as the plane took off.

Our plans were scheduled around a huge veterinary conference where I could focus on continuing education seminars for a few days. In the evenings, I would join my family for relaxation and a meal on the town. We had also planned a few extra days before and after the conference to take in some of the sights that make central Florida a vacation hot spot.

There were just a couple of issues that gave us pause in leaving home for ten days. The first was hiring a relief veterinarian to cover the office in my absence. Starting a practice from scratch as we had done is somewhat similar to raising a child. You get extremely attached and worry about it when you are not there to take care of it. So finding someone to cover the office for ten days was akin to hiring an au pair to care for my kids. It made me nervous. My staff was also concerned.

After checking references and talking philosophy with a number of candidates, I had made arrangements for a woman with a great professional reputation and a good bedside manner to cover for me. We had gone over all my current cases. I had left copious and detailed notes and instructions. I had prepared her in every possible way.

The other thing that worried us was our pets. We, of course, didn't like leaving Ollie and Rush for extended stays like this, but we felt confident they were in good hands in our boarding kennel at the hospital. You can't leave two unchaperoned cats in your house for almost two weeks, after all. So, though Ollie hated being there, we took him and Rush in on the way out of town and settled them into their cages.

Rush was a favorite of the office staff as his personality was so loving. Ollie, on the other hand, though a shameless lover at home, was all teeth and claws at the office. So aggressive was he while in the office, that the staff had to use a broom to shoo him out of his cage in order to clean it and replenish his food and water dishes. He was definitely not a preferred patient.

The seminars, the relaxation, the attractions, and the unaccustomed family time quickly overshadowed these fears once we reached the warmth of sunny Florida. We were having a wonderful time. On the sixth evening of our vacation, we were having supper at a wonderful Italian restaurant when I found an available pay phone and called the office.

"Hello, Susan. It's Doc C."

"Hey! How's it going? Are you having fun?"

"Yeah, we're having a blast. The weather here is great this time of year. How's it going with the relief vet?" I almost didn't want to hear the answer to this question, convinced there were going to be wrecks for me to clean up when I got home.

"She's great! The clients love her and the staff loves her! And she really knows her stuff. I think we should hire her full time."

That was a good thing. It took a lot of pressure off of me on my return. "How are the cats?"

The pause that followed was altogether too long. I thought the connection had gotten cut off.

"Susan?"

"I'm here. There's a problem with Ollie."

My mind searched the possible problems that may have arisen. I knew he had a heart murmur, but he had had it for many years and it had not bothered him before. Perhaps he had developed a urinary problem. That was a fairly common malady.

"What's wrong with him?" I asked, concerned.

"Well . . . we can't find him."

This was not what I expected. "You can't find him?"

"No. He's not anywhere in the hospital."

"That can't be. He must have gotten out and is hiding somewhere in the basement." At that time, the basement of the hospital was unfinished and filled with household items we were storing. There were countless nooks and crannies amid the things down there that a cat would love to disappear into.

"I don't think so, Doc. He came up missing two or three days ago and we've left food down there and spent hours moving things around. I don't think he's there." There was another long pause.

"I don't get it. How could he just disappear?"

"I don't know, either. The only thing we can figure is that his cage didn't get completely closed one night and he got out. Then he waited around by the door and slipped out when they opened it to take out the garbage."

I made my way back to the table, feeling confused and worried. Thinking how to break the news to the family, I sat down. Cynthia saw the look on my face right away. "Something wrong?"

"Yeah. Ollie's lost."

"What?" Her fork stopped in midair and she snapped her head around to look at me. "They lost him?"

"Yeah. Apparently he sneaked out of the cage and somehow

made his way out the door without anyone seeing him. They haven't been able to find him now for the last three days."

The remainder of the vacation sped by. We continued to have fun, but never far from our consciousness was the question of Ollie's whereabouts. I remained convinced that he was in the basement hiding from the staff and that when I returned, he would gratefully come out and make his presence known. I nurtured this idea optimistically for the rest of the trip.

Our return to the valley was greeted by some of the coldest temperatures that had been seen for many years. The drive from the airport back home was a dangerous one, our car skating precariously on a thick coat of ice that paved the interstate. Every few miles we saw a car or truck settled deeply in the ditch at the end of a long skid mark in the snow. We had to drive especially carefully to make it home safely. A trip that should have taken only an hour and a half took almost four hours. We arrived home in the wee hours of the morning, too late to go to the office.

The next morning when I arrived at the office, I found things as I had expected. My bulletin board was filled with messages from clients about their pets, notes on cases seen by the relief veterinarian, and messages from colleagues and vendors. On my desk was a stack of records almost a foot high that needed my attention and follow-up. Every staff member, it seemed, had some matter of urgency that they had to discuss with me pronto. It is always the same when I get home from vacation. I sometimes wonder why I bother to leave at all.

Despite all these pressing demands, my first order of business was to go down to the basement to look for Ollie. Surely he was down there. I couldn't imagine how he could have sneaked outside when we were always so careful not to let a patient escape. It had never happened before. Certainly my own cat wouldn't be the first.

I descended the stairs calmly and began to gently call Ollie's name and shake a tin of treats. Ollie loved cat treats and a shake of the tin seldom failed to bring him running from wherever he was in the house to enjoy his favorite tidbits. I slowly made my way around the basement in this fashion, but no black cat came out to greet me as I had hoped. I began to move the items we had stored there. Nothing. After a good half hour of searching, I realized that Ollie had indeed escaped.

The next six weeks were long ones. Every trip to the office and home again, every shopping excursion, every errand to the post office or to fill the car with gas, every jaunt around town was dominated by our tireless scanning of the terrain for a glimpse of that missing black cat.

Many times Cynthia and I screeched to a halt on the side of the road and vaulted out of the car to chase a stray cat that matched Ollie's description, only to find that it wasn't him. I chased more cats onto the porches of their homes than I care to admit, abandoning my pursuit only when, with huge, frightened eyes, the poor terrified creatures wailed with panic and scratched on their doors to be let in. No doubt we developed a reputation among the cat population as crazed kidnapping lunatics to be avoided at all costs.

We did everything we could think of to locate Ollie again. We wallpapered the local bulletin boards with posters offering a reward for his return. We canvassed the neighborhood for blocks around with flyers and pictures. We contacted the local humane society and gave a description of him. We notified all the area veterinary hospitals to be on the lookout for him. And we kept looking and searching and hoping.

One afternoon I got a call at the office from Cynthia. Her voice was choked with emotion, devoid of light or hope. I knew immediately she had bad news.

"I think I found Ollie," she said flatly. "It isn't good."

"Where did you find him?"

"He's been hit and he's dead." There was a long pause. "He's about a mile south of the Woodstock exit on the west shoulder of the southbound lane of the highway. I didn't have the stomach to pick him up. Do you think you can go and get him?"

"Okay." My stomach lurched. I felt defeated and my mouth

went suddenly dry. Without a word of explanation to my staff, I grabbed a cadaver bag and left the office. The drive to the site Cynthia had described was an emotional one. I tried not to dwell on the fact that I was going to collect the remains of my friend who had met a grisly end on the highway, but it was to no avail. Keeping my eyes on the emergency lane, I hardly realized that my speed had dwindled to a mere thirty-five miles an hour on the expressway as vehicles roared by, their lights flashing. Even at that slow speed, I didn't recognize the small black lump of fur on the roadside as a cat until I had passed it. I pulled far off the road and backed up.

Carrying the bright blue cadaver bag, I walked over to the dead cat. Sure enough, it certainly looked like Ollie. His black-and-white tuxedo markings were easily recognizable. The white stockings were exactly right; the white shirtfront came up on his chest to just the right level. The contrasting white whiskers were identical.

Except for the fact that this cat had been completely flattened by the massive trauma of being struck by a speeding vehicle, it looked just like Ollie would have looked lying asleep on the bed. My heart was broken as I squatted down beside the little body and stroked the cold black fur. Tears were streaming down my cheeks as the semis and cars whizzed by at seventy miles an hour, the chill wind of their slipstream hitting me fully in the face. I was cold inside and out. Oddly, it struck me at the time that I hadn't bothered to get my coat.

Just as I was scooping him up to place him in the bag, I snagged my finger on one of his front claws, surprised at how much the jab of the sharp nail hurt in the cold wind. With the force of a knockout punch, it hit me.

This was not Ollie! Ollie didn't have front claws! I drew in a breath of cold air sharply and my heart leaped. Ollie was still alive somewhere, the certainty of this realization jolted me. And yet, I could not leave this Ollie look-alike here on the side of the road. With a much lighter heart, I scooped up the fallen kitty and placed him in the bag. He would at least have a proper burial.

The ride back to the office was lighter, but no less emotional. Though I was elated not to be bringing Ollie's body back, the fact that I was no closer to a resolution was surprisingly difficult, and the waves of relief flooding over me induced a few more tears.

By the time I arrived at the office, however, my spirits had improved. I strode into the office carrying the dead cat in a bag. My employees greeted me cautiously, confused by my unexpected departure; perplexed even more by my relieved and smiling return, swinging a little kitty corpse in a bag. I raised the bag with a smile.

"He has claws. It's not Ollie."

Five or six weeks after Ollie's mysterious rapture, I walked into the examination room on a Friday afternoon to vaccinate a cat. I found my patient, Kinko, on the tabletop quietly grooming his foot. I stopped in my tracks. Kinko was a carbon copy of Ollie with his strikingly beautiful black-and-white dress clothes. Since I had attended Kinko from kittenhood, I knew it wasn't Ollie, but the figure of Kinko resplendent in his formal attire brought Ollie's absence immediately to the fore.

"Oh, Miss Cooper," I blurted. "Your kitty looks so much like my Ollie, I can't even believe it. I was so startled because Ollie's been missing for quite a while now. We've been looking for him night and day for weeks." We chatted absently during the remainder of the examination and the procedure. When they left, I thought nothing more of the encounter.

The next day, around two o'clock on Saturday afternoon, my pager went off as I was driving in the car with my family. Aggravated by the interruption on my day off, I dialed my pager voice mailbox to retrieve the message. It was from Miss Cooper. Probably a vaccine reaction, I thought, remembering the appointment the previous day. It is not unusual for cats to get a little punk for a day or so following their vaccines, though it's usually no big thing and passes without any treatment. I called Miss Cooper to check on Kinko. She answered the phone on the first ring.

"Hello, Miss Cooper. This is Doctor Coston returning your call. Is Kinko acting a bit punk after his vaccines?"

"No, he seems just fine. That's not why I'm calling," she said.

"Oh? How can I help?"

"Well, didn't you say yesterday that you had lost a cat that looks just like Kinko?"

"Yes, I did." My ears perked up.

"Well," she went on, "there's been a black cat that looks like Kinko's twin hanging out at the 7-Eleven for the past few weeks. I stopped to get gas today and remembered seeing him there. I looked around and didn't see him, but maybe you should stop by there. I wouldn't have thought a thing about it, except that he looked so much like Kinko."

"You're kidding!" I hit the brakes and swung my car into a parking lot. I had just passed the 7-Eleven. "I'll go there right now. Thank you for calling."

Afraid to get my hopes up, I told Cynthia and the boys about the call. Within just a minute or two, I was pulling up outside the convenience store. The family stayed in the car as I went in.

"I understand there is a stray black cat that's been hanging around here lately," I said to the woman behind the counter. She looked up at me with utter apathy.

"Yeah, there has been," she replied. "It's been a real nuisance too, always trying to sneak in whenever someone comes in the door. I've had to spray him with the hose to keep him away."

I could have decked her. It was late February and had been very cold with temperatures around fifteen degrees outside. I shuddered to think of Ollie, the penultimate house cat, out in those temperatures, much less after having been hosed down with cold water.

"Have you seen the cat lately?" I glared at her.

"No, but that crazy lady that rents the downstairs has been feeding the fool thing. That's why he stays around. I keep telling her not to."

I pushed the door much too hard on the way out and rounded the corner to the back of the building where a separate entrance serviced a small health food store below the 7-Eleven. The woman who operated the store was a pleasant, robust woman with graying hair and an engaging smile. I asked her about the black-and-white stray I had heard about.

"Oh, yeah, that cat was here for several weeks. He was a real lover. He wasn't the typical stray cat that comes around here so often. He was much too people-oriented. Someone lost that cat, I'm sure. You know, I think he was even declawed." My emotional roller coaster began to climb a hill of hopefulness.

"You haven't seen him lately, then?" I asked, my stomach in my throat. The coaster crested the hill and started on the downslope.

"Well, after he'd been around for a while, I tried to find him a home. Just last week, I finally found someone who would take him. I gave him away."

"Who did you give him to?" I queried. The downslope reached its nadir and the car began to swoosh upward again. This was proving to be quite an emotional ride.

"I don't know the name," the woman confessed meekly. Whoosh! Another downward rush. "But they run the discount cigarette store on Main Street. Check with them."

Shouting a thank-you over my shoulder I sprinted back to the car. As I drove the few blocks to the cigarette store, I relayed the information to my family. They huddled together and sent up a hopeful prayer.

Cigarette stores are not places I frequent. I was not used to the acrid smoke hanging heavy in the air as I entered the store. Trying to quell my rising enthusiasm, I approached the counter.

"What are your favorite smokes?" the brusque woman behind the counter asked, turning to scan her inventory.

"Oh, I'm not here for cigarettes," I responded. "I think you may have my cat."

I described how Ollie had been lost and how we had searched for him over the last several weeks. I described his markings and personality in as much detail as I could. Then I waited, holding my breath.

"That sure sounds like the cat we have at home now," she

said. "I'll call my husband and have him bring the cat in. If it's your cat, I want you to have him back. But if it is, we'll sure miss him. He's a great cat."

I went out to the car and told Cynthia and the boys the news. They were ecstatic. Soon the whole family was inside the store waiting the arrival of the cat that could be Ollie. We passed the fifteen or twenty minutes relating anecdotes of Ollie and his many charms. The woman too told endearing tales of Ollie's time in their home.

Presently, a large white pickup truck with dual tires pulled up in the parking lot, a man in his late forties behind the wheel. In his arms was a familiar black-and-white face. Cynthia, the boys and I crowded around the truck. Ollie meowed excitedly through the window when he saw us.

Before he had even stepped out of the truck, Cynthia whisked Ollie out of the gentleman's hands and buried her face in his tummy, tears of relief and joy streaming down her cheeks. The boys danced an excited jig around her legs and jabbed with little fingers at their kitty's sides. I put my forehead on his and listened to the beautiful sound of his contented purring, his front feet kneading bread in Cynthia's hair. No reunion could have been more fortuitous or more delightful. Despite our merriment, however, I couldn't help but notice a tear of a different sort sliding down the cheek of the kind woman behind the counter.

That night, Ollie assumed his accustomed place on my chest. It was his habit to spend a little quality time sphinxlike on my chest each night, purring heavily and leaning hard into my caresses. I had so missed these times in his absence, and now that he was home, I lavished attention on him for longer than usual, with Cynthia joining in. Ollie never skipped a beat once he was home, taking up his place of dominance over Rush as if he had never been gone. For his part, Rush seemed glad to have him home too.

I wrote the cigarette lady a letter of gratitude the next day. I expressed our sincerest appreciation for her kindnesses to Ollie for providing him a home when he was a runaway. As a token of our appreciation, I offered to provide, at no charge, the complete kitten health series including vaccines, stool testing, feline leukemia screening, deworming, and surgical sterilization for a new kitten. But she never took me up on my offer. I can't say that I'm really surprised. After all, what cat could replace Ollie?

The mystery of how Ollie ended up at the 7-Eleven remains unsolved to this day. Never before then, and never since, has any patient escaped from our care in the hospital or boarding kennel, though it is true that Ollie's Houdini act increased our precautions immeasurably thereafter.

Though we got three or four inches of snow the night he made his escape, Susan found no footprints outside the building the next morning. The 7-Eleven is well over a mile and a half from the hospital. Getting there required him to negotiate the crossing of at least two busy four-lane roads. How he did that without suffering the fate of his twin on the expressway I'll never know. Finally, in the span of the weeks he was missing, the valley was hit with some of the lowest temperatures in memory.

I'd give a lot to hear the tale from Ollie's perspective and to fill in the details of his time on the lam. Unfortunately, he's not talking. He does, however, seem to appreciate more than ever the warmth of the hearth with a roaring fire, the soft comfort of the pillow by Cynthia's head at night, the convenience of ready and available meals, and the absence of cold water sprayed at him from a hose in subfreezing temperatures. We're not taking them for granted either, I can assure you.

Resurrection

About ten o'clock one brisk fall morning between appointments I stepped to the front desk and glanced at the schedule. There was not a single available appointment. It was going to be a harried day, I could tell. Already that morning, I had hospitalized a vomiting patient that needed X-rays and blood work, a very disgruntled cat waited in the cage for us to collect urine for testing, and several surgeries were scheduled for later in the afternoon. As I was pondering how I could possibly attend to all the patients ahead of me, Lisa, my technician, interrupted me.

"Your next appointment is in pretty bad shape, Dr. Coston. I think you ought to come in right away."

"What's going on?" I questioned.

"The owner really doesn't know. The dog has just been losing weight and getting worse over the last couple of weeks. Right now her temperature is only about ninety-eight degrees and she can't stand up."

The dog, Sandy, was a five-year-old setter mix that belonged to Mrs. Rhodes. Since this was Mrs. Rhodes's first visit to our office, I introduced myself as I entered the room. But as I glanced at the patient, my mind was immediately processing the case, leaving little of my available attention for pleasantries.

Sandy was mortally ill. She barely lifted her head as I entered the room, and then only in response to the sound. Her uncomprehending eyes roved the room blindly. Her breath came in short gasps that were punctuated at the end by a little grunt of discomfort. Watery fecal matter, flecked with blood, escaped unchecked from her rectum. Her gums, dry and parched, were a pale, pasty white when I lifted her lip. Through the stethoscope I could hear that her heartbeats were subdued and irregular. With a gloved finger I examined her rectum. Though there were no masses or lumps found, when I removed my finger, there was noticeable blood and numerous small worms squirmed.

"Things don't look good, Mrs. Rhodes. Sandy is very ill. I'm not sure yet what is causing this problem, but just based on her clinical condition at this time, I'd say the odds are against her." I watched Mrs. Rhodes's face carefully for a hint at what she was feeling. It is always difficult to be the bearer of bad news. Doing so with compassion and sensitivity is one of the constant challenges of my occupation. Responding appropriately to the emotional state of the client is key to that skill. Mrs. Rhodes was very worried.

"I think we should hospitalize Sandy, start an IV and do some blood work, and maybe some X-rays to see if we can figure out what else is going on in addition to the intestinal worms."

"Do you think she's going to make it?" I could see a trail of tears making its way down Mrs. Rhodes's cheek. She dabbed at it apologetically with a crumpled tissue.

"I think our chances are about fifty-fifty. But they'll be even less than that if we don't get started immediately. I'm going to take Sandy into the treatment room. I'll let you know if her status changes."

Picking up my patient, I turned and headed to the treatment room. I instructed Lisa to prepare for an intravenous catheter. Quickly she slipped the catheter into the vein in the front leg and started administering fluids. She also drew blood for a complete blood count and serum chemistry profile to evaluate the function of the different internal organs and collected a stool sample to identify the parasites I had seen. Antibiotics were started, as were medications to fight shock.

Sandy, though, wasn't responding well. Her mental status deteriorated even as we worked. I hooked her up to an electrocardiogram monitor just in time to see some abnormal beats develop in the heart rate. Things were not looking good for the home team and I was getting really worried.

Just then there was a sudden catch in Sandy's respiration. Then her breathing stopped entirely. I looked at the cardiac monitor. The heart rate was dropping precipitously. I promptly, but with little optimism, started cardiopulmonary resuscitation. While Lisa gave chest compressions, I slipped a tube into Sandy's trachea through which I administered oxygen, and began artificial respiration. Through the catheter I rushed emergency drugs into Sandy's veins, hoping to stabilize her heart and start her respirations again.

The only response was a further drop in heart rate. Frantically I barked orders at my staff. At my direction Lisa sped up the oxygen delivery, hastened chest compressions, and squeezed the bag of IV fluids to speed the flow of shock-fighting fluids. I even gave epinephrine through the endotracheal tube. Despite all our efforts, we were losing the battle.

After fifteen or twenty minutes of frantic effort, it became clear that we were making no headway. The rhythm on the monitor showed only two or three ineffectual beats of the failing heart every minute. Then the green line flattened altogether. I dropped my hands and gave up. Numbly, I stopped the flow of the fluids, switched off the oxygen machine and disconnected the tubes to the endotracheal tube. We were all exhausted and demoralized!

It is always hard to lose a patient. But after a frantic, adrenaline-charged emergency situation, it is an incredible disappointment when those efforts are futile. I tried to comfort myself with the knowledge that there was really nothing more I could have done. But those thoughts rang hollow as I stood over my lifeless patient.

"Go ahead and care for the body," I said to Lisa. Though I knew it would be an unpleasant task for her, mine would be even more difficult. "I have to go and call Mrs. Rhodes. I'll see my next appointment first, though." The frenetic activity of CPR had put me behind schedule. Fifteen minutes' delay from having to make an unsavory call seemed a reprieve.

Finally, with a heavy heart I closed my office door, sat down at my desk and cradled my head in my hands. Desperately, I tried to gather my thoughts before I picked up the phone and punched in her number. I listened to Mrs. Rhodes's phone ring with an increasing sense of foreboding. When she answered, her voice was bright and chipper.

"This is Dr. Coston at the veterinary hospital. . . . I'm afraid I have some bad news. Sandy didn't make it. She went into cardiac arrest. We tried our best for about twenty minutes to save her, but we just couldn't get her heart started again."

A knock at the door interrupted my thoughts. Not a good time, I thought. I tried to ignore it, but the knocking grew louder and more persistent. It was irritating at a time like this to be so rudely interrupted. It wasn't at all like my staff to be so insensitive. They knew I had come in here to make this difficult phone call. I made a mental note to discuss it at the next staff meeting. Finally the door was pushed open and Lisa stuck her head in, waving to get my attention.

"Dr. Coston," she whispered at me loudly. I tried to wave her off, but she tapped my knee until I put my hand over the phone.

"Can't you see I'm making an awful tough phone call? Can't this wait just a minute or two?" I hissed.

"But, Dr. Coston, Sandy came back!"

Stunned, I barely managed to stammer, "Can I put you on hold for a moment, Mrs. Rhodes?" Then, dropping the receiver onto the desktop, I sprinted incredulously into the treatment room.

My patient was lying placidly on the table, the clips for the EKG still in place from our attempts at resuscitation. In disbelief

I looked up at the monitor to see a normal heart rhythm traced by a bouncy green blip on the screen. Even though the endotracheal tube had been removed from her airway, Sandy was breathing regularly and with no difficulty. The oxygen was reading at 97 percent saturation.

Not daring to hope, I quickly gave her another examination. What had been critical just a few moments before was now boringly normal. Respiratory rate, heart rate and rhythm, the color of the gums, pulses were all within normal limits. She was even beginning to show signs of regaining consciousness. I was dumbfounded! With a much lighter heart, I returned to Mrs. Rhodes who was still holding on the phone.

"I can't explain this, but Sandy has somehow regained consciousness. Everything has stabilized, and for the moment, she is doing much better."

Of course I was careful to paint a bleak picture for Sandy's future. I explained the high likelihood that she had suffered severe brain damage during the time her heart and lungs had stopped. I underscored that we were absolutely not out of the woods yet; that she might well crash again at any time. But, as if to make me look sillier still, Sandy made a miraculous and complete recovery within three days. The only abnormality I ever found was an overwhelming burden of intestinal parasites. Within ten days, Sandy was a thin but otherwise normal dog once again. And she never looked back.

But I did. And, since Sandy is still a patient of mine, I still do. Each time she comes in for her routine vaccinations and deworming, which, by the way, she never misses now, I have to shake my head and laugh at the time my patient, to spite me or despite me, resurrected herself.

Farewell to Cy

The beginning of this story started unexpectedly several years ago while we lived in the town house across the street from the office. Cynthia burst through the office door one evening carrying a screaming, slashing mite of a black kitten wrapped in a towel. Its right eyeball was protruding grotesquely through the lids, making the cat look like an extra in a horror movie. The strong odor of putrid infection emanated from the tiny bone-thin skeleton. The ears, which were plastered back in an angry snarl, were smelly and filled with dark, dry discharge.

"Where do I put it?" Cynthia was close to panic by this time.

We found an empty kennel and flung the hissing pile of fury into it. I recognized the kitten as one of the many strays that subsisted by begging scraps and foraging the garbage from the apartment complex behind our town house. For the past several days, we had seen this same small black kitten coming up onto our back porch to sneak longing peeks at Ollie and Rush, our well-fed indoor cats. My wife had noticed a stick protruding from its right eye two days previously and had tried in vain to capture the wild kitten so we could stop its suffering.

Now we had the cat in a kennel at the hospital. It wouldn't

have to suffer much longer. I looked through the bars of the kennel door and was greeted by a malevolent hiss from the tiny feral cat. I turned around to get the bottle of euthanasia solution from the shelf and was met by several pairs of sad eyes belonging to my staff and my wife.

I recognized immediately from their looks that I was outnumbered and beaten. I did try vainly to protest, but soon found myself drawing some blood from the kitten to test for the feline leukemia and feline immunodeficiency viruses. I was fairly sure the tests would be positive for one or the other (or both) of them. Then the decision would be crystal clear. To my surprise, however, both tests were negative.

"Okay, okay." I didn't really want to put the kitten to sleep anyway. "But *if* we can get this kitten back into shape, and that is a big *if*, we have to find it a home. We can't have a loose cat in the office all the time. It's just not professional."

I suspected that my hard guy charade fooled no one. By the knowing glances exchanged among my receptionists and Cynthia, I knew they recognized my show as mere bluster.

The eye was too damaged to save and required surgical removal to prevent the infection from overwhelming all her organs, possibly even extending into the central nervous system. The ear infection was severe. The presence of both bacterial infection and ear mites made it a difficult one to treat.

With her face shaved for surgery, one eye gone, a row of sutures sewing the eyelids closed, and ears greasy from her medications, she was arguably the ugliest creature God ever gave breath. We chose carefully the clients to whom we showed our new charge. We hoped—at least I did—that a few of them might show an interest in adopting the cat. But most reacted with unadulterated revulsion. I can't say that I blame them really. She was truly pathetic.

As time went by, she began to come out of her shell. At first, she just hissed less. But as the human contact required by her frequent treatments continued, she began to enjoy the attention. Soon she would come to the front of the cage and rub against our hands. Then she began to play. We grew to enjoy her more than ever we imagined. In no time at all it became clear to me that any real attempt to adopt this kitten out would probably result in staff mutiny, perhaps involving violence directed at me.

Most veterinary hospitals have adopted mascot strays, orphans, or abandoned patients that become ad hoc staff members. They sometimes pay for their keep by becoming unwilling blood donors or de facto receptionists. But usually they are shameless moochers of free food, medical care, and the attentions and adulation of a steady stream of clients.

If this cat was to become the hospital cat, she would need an appropriate name. Many were proposed and promptly abandoned. Then, in jest, someone suggested Cyclops. Though her single eye was not centered in her forehead, as a descriptive the name certainly fit. By consensus we decided to call her Cy for short.

With her surgical scar healing and her hair growing back, Cy quickly became a landmark in the office. Her favorite spot was reclining regally on the counter of the reception desk where she surveyed each patient brought to the office. Clients came to expect her greeting when they arrived for their appointments.

She showed absolutely no fear of or frustration with any of the animals that formed a steady stream of trespassers into her domain. She seemed much more interested, in fact, in the dogs that came in than the cats, whom she often snubbed. Even the largest dogs, Rottweilers and German shepherds, did not intimidate her. She would stroll right up to them and rub against their legs or flop down on her side and roll over, exposing her tummy to them with utmost trust. They would eye her suspiciously and shoot questioning glances at their owners, who were amazed at the bravery or foolishness of the cat and the meek responses of their otherwise aggressive pets.

Cy was also quite an accomplished nursemaid, taking it as her personal responsibility to closely monitor postsurgical patients of every variety. As they recovered from anesthesia, she would lie down with them or, just as often, on them and watch them carefully as they regained their faculties. Many were the times when she donated blood to transfuse sick, anemic cats, a role that she loathed.

I often teased the staff that Cy was not paying her way as the hospital cat. Few cats of her age have had to go through as many surgical procedures as she did. Including the eye removal, spay, declaw, major ear surgery, and others, she went through no less than seven surgeries. And, let's face it, she was not exactly a paying customer.

One day in March, three years after her fateful entrance, we noticed that Cy's appetite had fallen off. For Cy, whose bulk had so often brought accusations of poor family planning, this was not at all normal. On physical examination, I felt a mass in the region of her small intestines that was larger than a golf ball. It was a totally unexpected finding in a cat that was only three years of age; one that called for rapid action.

That very evening she was once again under the knife. As I parted the ample fat within her abdominal cavity, I found an ominous round lump engulfing a section of her intestine. With care, I removed a six-inch section of intestine to which the tumor was attached, sewing the cut ends together again. With her young age, I was confident that results of a biopsy would prove the growth to be a benign one. Cancer is usually a disease of elderly animals. I was shocked, therefore, when the biopsy report came back. The growth was a leiomyosarcoma, an uncommon, malignant growth of the muscle of the small intestine. Microscopically it appeared to be very aggressive. A dire prognosis was given.

Cy bounced back from surgery quickly and was eating normally and feeling well within just a couple of days. I was cautiously optimistic that the problem had been averted, hoping against hope that, despite the biopsy report, we had removed the entire tumor. Sometimes surgery can be completely curative in these cases.

Just to be sure, chemotherapy was initiated with a multiple drug protocol. Cy underwent weeks of intravenous therapeutic toxins in hopes of eradicating any remaining cancer cells. She was plied with pills of unusual size and potency that made her irritable and partially bald. Overall, though, she remained in good spirits and happy. With veterinary cancer patients, our goals of therapy don't allow much leeway for nausea or discomfort. Throughout chemotherapy, quality of life issues remain our highest priority. Things were looking up.

Then sadly in early July, despite our best efforts, Cy's appetite again dropped off. We repeated an exploratory surgery and found that the tumor had spread to the region around the previous surgical site, including some closely associated lymph nodes. With a heavy heart I removed as much visible tumor as possible. This time, though, there was little hope that surgery would cure the problem.

Soon the disease progressed to the point that further treatment was futile. Cy was suffering horribly with severe abdominal pain. Her appetite was completely gone. We had no choice. Our decision was unavoidable. I drew the thick, pink euthanasia solution slowly and injected it into her vein; a task made all the more difficult by the tears welling in my eyes. It was all I could do to continue seeing patients that day. My heart was too heavy. The staff and I kept a supply of facial tissues at the ready all day.

Later that same day a family brought in two kittens in a large, dirty cardboard box. They had been found as strays down by the river and the owners were hoping to improve the upper respiratory disease enough to find them an adoptive home. They were insistent, though, on allowing me to examine only one of the kittens. When I asked why, they reached into the box and pulled out a thin, gray kitten that weighed no more than two pounds.

"We know this one won't make it. There's no hope for it. We're just going to take it home and shoot it."

About that time it turned its head toward me and rubbed lovingly against my hand. I recoiled. The right eye was ruptured and protruded through the lids. Fleas crawled at will through the greasy, thin coat. The ears were full of mites and the nasty debris that they generate. Visions of another tiny kitten crowded my consciousness and my eyes began to cloud again.

"I'm sorry, but I won't let you shoot this kitten. I'll take care of it for you."

Immediately I saw the defenses go up in the eyes of the father.

"It won't cost you anything." I spat out the words, then turned on my heel, and carried the little kitten gingerly into the treatment room, depositing it into the waiting and empty hands of my staff, whose eyes were still red and brimming.

"Get a feline leukemia and feline immunodeficiency virus test on this kitten, will you?"

Beside the hospital, if you looked in the right spot, you would find a small, square, polished stone with the inscription: *Cy, Everyone's Friend.* Under it is buried our special cat, Cy. She has been greatly missed for her many contributions to our hospital. Clients still ask where she is sleeping and why she hasn't come out to greet them. It smarts just a bit when they do.

But now we introduce them to a gray kitten whose right eye is also missing. She is recovering from her ear mites, her fleas, and her intestinal parasites well. She has learned to play, to beg food from the patients in the kennels, to greet clients at the front desk, and to walk across the computer keyboard just like Cy. Here we go again. What else could we call her? Her name is Ditto.

Ollie and the Ball Valve

It was almost midnight as we drove into our driveway. We were all tired. Everyone in the van was asleep except for me, and I was dangerously close to slumber. We had spent the day with friends in a town two hours away and, though we had debated staying the night, had eventually opted to make the long drive home in anticipation of the comfort of our own beds. As the headlights illuminated the living-room window, I looked for the two familiar feline faces of Ollie and Rush who were invariably waiting for us. Though only Rush was sitting on the back of the couch, I was too tired to give it much thought.

As Cynthia and I carried our two sleeping boys into the house, Rush greeted us eagerly at the door. Ollie's familiar little closed-mouth mew, though, was strangely absent. After depositing the boys in their beds, Cynthia and I began to scour the house for Ollie. With each empty room our anxiety increased. It was Ollie's habit to sneak out of the house. Perhaps he had slipped out while we were loading up in the morning and had been gone all day. I was loathe even to give voice to my fears. In the basement I turned on the light of the toy room. Surely he wouldn't be here; he seldom came downstairs. But when I called his name, I heard a quiet, weak squeak from the corner. Ollie turned his face up to me and called again. I knew immediately something was seriously wrong.

He was too sick to complain much as I carefully lifted him and carried him up to the living room. He remained limp in my arms. Silent, openmouthed cries told us clearly of his misery. A quick examination revealed the problem. When I felt his stomach, he winced noticeably and I felt a rock-hard lump in his abdomen the size of a softball. His urinary tract was obstructed. Unable to empty his bladder, it had filled to capacity. When this happens, back pressure develops within just a few hours, which causes the kidneys to fail. We had been gone more than eighteen hours. This situation was now critical! I had treated this emergency in many patients. I knew all too well how quickly cats can succumb to urethral obstruction.

I scooped Ollie up and immediately headed for the hospital. Once there, I injected a small amount of anesthetic into his vein and he drifted into unconsciousness. I then quickly slipped a urinary catheter into his urethra and sutured it in place. The bladder began to drain. The urine was bloody and had a foul odor. Antibiotics and fluids were administered before Ollie began to regain his composure.

It took me much longer to regain mine. Ollie was seven years old and had come to hold a very dear place in our family's collective heart. It was Ollie who had nursed us through the second of our two unsuccessful pregnancies, created much-needed diversions for me during my grueling internship, and helped us raise our two boys. His habit of jumping up on my chest as soon as I lie down each night and tenderly placing his right paw against my cheek had become a cherished nighttime ritual. It was Ollie who had changed my mind about cats from a perception of them as elusive, independent, and uncaring to a recognition that cats can be just as responsive, demonstrative, and dependent as dogs.

He even proved to me that cats can be trained. Cynthia had wagered that she could teach him a trick. Confident that cats were so incorrigible that I would never have to pay up, I foolishly bet a set of strings for Harpo. Cynthia's beautifully ornate harp was the one extravagant possession that we owned. I say this with no vanity as it was something that Cynthia brought with her to our marriage. Harpo preceded me in her life by decades. A set of strings for Harpo was an exorbitant proposition during our first year out of school when money was scarce. Cynthia taught him how to roll over on command. This was a trick that he performed with obvious disdain, bearing it with an air of reticent embarrassment in order to get the proffered treat.

The thought of losing him—especially like this—shook me deeply. I stayed at the hospital by his cage until Ollie had recovered sufficiently that I was confident he would be all right through the night. Cynthia was sitting up waiting for me when I returned home at about two in the morning. I assured her that Ollie's condition was stable and his prognosis was good. But we both shuddered to think that had we decided to spend the night at our friends' house, Ollie most likely would have died. The thought was too horrible to contemplate. Neither of us slept well that night without our tuxedo-clad, black-and-white feline on his designated pillow by Cynthia's head.

Two days later, Ollie's condition had stabilized adequately to remove the urinary catheter. That evening there was a joyous reunion at home between Ollie and the family. All of us, including Rush, were delighted to have him home safe and healthy. For his part, Ollie acted as if nothing out of the ordinary had taken place. He seemed to disdain all the attention, heading instead toward the food bowl. That night he assumed his place on my chest and I sighed contentedly, pleased that things were back to normal. A bullet had been dodged.

But the next morning, Ollie was lying meekly in the closet crying with the same weak, openmouthed groan that I remembered from only a few days earlier. Feeling his bladder confirmed my suspicions. He was blocked again!

Back to the hospital we went. Another catheter was placed. More fluids were administered. Antibiotics were continued. For Ollie, who absolutely despised the hospital and all the people in it (including me), this was unspeakable horror. Hospitalizing Ollie was not a treat for the staff either, truth be told. The hospital Hyde side of his Jekyll and Hyde personality manifested itself again, making his treatment not only difficult for the staff and me, but downright dangerous.

After two days, I again removed his catheter, keeping my fingers crossed that he would not obstruct again. But it was not to be. Within just a few short hours, he was once again straining painfully and unsuccessfully in his litter box. I was worried. Recurrent obstructive episodes often require major surgical reconstruction of the lower urinary tract with lifelong implications. I wanted to avoid that in Ollie if at all possible.

Before relieving the obstruction this time, I took an X-ray of his bladder to see if I could discover the cause of the recurrent problem. I put the film up on the view box. The bladder looked clean. There was no evidence of any pathologic anatomy or bladder stones. The . . . wait! What was that? In the tip end of the urethra, obstructing the outflow completely, was a very small stone. About the size of the tip of a ballpoint pen, it had been acting as a ball valve for the bladder.

Just at that spot, the diameter of the male cat's urethra narrows dramatically. It was there that the small stone jammed, plugging the urethra and stopping urine flow. When I inserted the catheter, I had pushed the stone back into the bladder where it caused no problem until it passed down the urethra again and jammed to a stop in the same place each time. That stone had to come out!

Once again I administered anesthetics to Ollie, aware each time that his raging heart murmur made these procedures increasingly risky. With trembling fingers I made an incision into his abdomen. Though I had performed this procedure many times, it seemed somehow more difficult when my scalpel incised the same white tummy that I loved to rub at night.

The bladder was inflamed and angry because of the three obstructive events it had suffered in the last few days. Carefully I sliced into it with my scalpel, and then enlarged the opening I had made with surgical scissors. After I emptied the bladder of its blood-tinged urine, I introduced my gloved finger into the bladder itself. Bladder stones are typically scooped out easily with a finger or a sterilized spoon. I groped around the inside of the bladder, but I couldn't feel the offending stone.

I searched again. Nothing. I felt my forehead flush and start to moisten with nervous sweat. Where was it? I felt around again, frantically this time. Still nothing. I had my technician flush a little fluid through the urethral catheter that was in place. As she did, I felt a tiny ping and a subtle grating as the stone bumped up against the forceps that I had placed in the bladder. Carefully I grasped it and pulled it out of the bladder.

I was amazed at its size. Though it was only three or four millimeters in diameter, it was responsible for all this pain, suffering, and unmitigated worry. I hurled it into a stainless-steel container for laboratory analysis. I then flushed the bladder completely with more fluids. Having satisfied myself that there were no additional stones, I set to work suturing the bladder and the abdominal wall. After placing the last suture, I straightened my sore back and stretched slowly. Surgery had gone well and Ollie had pulled through.

His recovery was rapid and complete after the surgery. Within just a day or two he was back home again, taking up his usual place on my chest each evening and sleeping on his pillow by Cynthia's head.

I took the small stone home to show Cynthia and the boys. With the X-rays and the stone, they made a great example of the danger to cats from even minute stones.

"Cynthia," I said, "usually we send these stones to the lab for analysis so we can determine its chemical makeup. Then we can come up with the best way to prevent the stones in the future. But I was thinking of keeping this one as an illustration for clients. I could show them the X-rays and the stone and it would highlight how dangerous even small stones can be. What do you think?"

She looked at me as if I was an unwashed buffoon and

shook her head in disbelief. "You're sending that stone to the lab, bucko. I'm not too concerned about your little show-and-tell. Get a little rock off the driveway if you'd like. But you're sending that one in! This is Ollie we're talking about, remember."

I sent the stone to the lab. Analysis revealed it to be one that could be prevented by feeding a specific diet that, fortunately, Ollie enjoyed.

After surgery Ollie needed antibiotics for ten days; one pill twice a day. He hated taking the pills. Had I not been an expert at administering them, there's no way on God's green earth he would have gotten the entire course. So intensely did he loathe taking his medicine that after the second day he began to gag violently after I popped the pill into his mouth. He would retch frantically, mouth open, tongue extended, and stomach heaving. He never actually brought anything up, but the gagging occurred like clockwork each time, like he was trying to throw up his toenails. Then he would glare at me with undisguised disdain and stomp from the room.

That we found this amusing was, to Ollie, a further unforgivable indignity. This Oscar-worthy performance actually got worse each day. By day five, he would go through the same rigamarole at the mere smell of the pills. By the end of the antibiotics, he would do it, Pavlovian, if we simply shook the pill bottle within his hearing. It was pitiful. We laughed every time, much to Ollie's chagrin.

I requested the laboratory to return that small stone to me when the analysis was completed. I keep it in a little bottle on my desk. Like everyone else, I often face challenges and frustrations. Some of them are great giants that seem to overwhelm me and shake my very foundations. They make me feel like crawling into a corner and emitting weak, openmouthed squeaks. I strain and I cry in my little box. I develop rock-hard lumps in my stomach. At these times I tend to look for great big causes for such overwhelming problems. Sometimes they are big. But the small stone in this little vial on my desk reminds me that sometimes tiny things can make for major blockages.

Most of the time, though, I'm not quite that philosophical. Most nights, life is pretty doggone good as I climb into bed with a satisfied sigh. It's especially good when Ollie, dressed in his tuxedo best, jumps on my chest, lies down purring quietly all the while, and gently puts his right paw with its warm, soft pads on my cheek. That's enough for me, thank you very much. No philosophical musings could improve on that.

An Angel Among Us

Every now and then we encounter people who impact us profoundly. They are special people! Perhaps they personify a particularly noble attribute or encourage our loftiest aspirations. Maybe they challenge us to reassess our core values or stimulate our creative tendencies. Whatever their effect on us, we are left ennobled by our interactions with them. Such people are nothing less than angels. Don't misunderstand me, I'm not being mystical here. But anything less seems a bit of a disservice to the contributions they make.

Such a person is Sadie Thrice. My first introduction to Sadie was distinctly ordinary. While standing in the lobby one day, I watched a van drive into my parking lot and park, all askew, directly in front of the entrance to the office. A short woman in her early seventies emerged from the van. She was slightly stooped and dressed in baggy jeans and a faded blouse. A shock of gray hair was piled on top of her head in a disheveled bun and wrapped with a wide headband.

She ambled unhurriedly around to the passenger door and proceeded to unload a large plastic laundry basket, fitted with a homemade wooden lid, which served as a cat carrier. The current occupant was an obviously well cared for kitten. Since then

I have seen that same basket innumerable times, filled with a long line of equally well cared for animals of all persuasions.

I honestly don't recall my first impressions of Sadie. With her unique fashion statement, her widow status, and her eccentricity, I suppose I could have been a little condescending and patronizing to her. I certainly didn't recognize that I had just met an angel.

Sadie is graced with one of the most generous spirits I've ever known. The objects of this extraordinary generosity are usually the forgotten, insignificant, throwaway creatures, human and otherwise, that are all too common in our society. Her heart is too big and too soft to let a homeless kitten or stray dog ever go without a good dose of her kindness. This fact is evidenced by the twenty-six cats and five dogs with whom she shares her home. Many of these bear testimony to her compassion in the scars and maladies from which they have recovered. Counted among her crew are two diabetics, one totally blind cat, and several others with distinct and obvious handicaps.

Countless are the times when Sadie's kindness has moved me and left me humbled. The office staff and I have become so accustomed to her thoughtfulness that it often fails to surprise us anymore. Now when she exposes her heart to us yet again, we just wag our heads in amazement and dismiss it with "That's Sadie!" One particular episode will serve to demonstrate just who Sadie is.

I had just finished my examination of Lucy, a bone-thin coonhound that Mr. Leach had finally decided needed some veterinary attention. Each rib could be easily traced as it coursed its way from her razor-sharp spine down to two rows of hugely enlarged teats, evidence of her recent and ongoing maternal activities. Bulging behind the ribs was a remarkably potbellied stomach. The hips and pelvis jutted out prominently, tenting the thinned skin. Perched atop the thin neck was an equally thin head, framed by two pendulous ears. Despite being the subject of blatant human indifference, Lucy's eyes were soft and warm and searched each human face for commiseration.

Lucy was not sick, however. She had simply had the misfortune of mothering a litter of fourteen unplanned and unwanted puppies and, during the nursing process, had sacrificed her nutritional health for theirs. I had explained to Mr. Leach the importance of good nutrition in her recovery and had recommended to him vitamin supplementation and premium dog food. But though it seemed to pain him, I could tell that providing optimum nutrition for her was not going to be his highest priority.

As I escorted Lucy and her owner into the lobby after my examination, I was pleasantly surprised to find Sadie there waiting for an appointment. As was her custom, she was busy interviewing the other waiting clients about their pets' medical conditions. After each problem was thoroughly probed, she would expound on how much better they would soon feel.

"I've got a cat that had that problem one time. Darlin,' he was so sick! I know just how you feel. But don't you worry about a thing. Dr. Bruce will help him. My TomTom is doing just fine to this day, God love him." And then she would move on to the next person.

Sadie's back was turned to my patient as Lucy emerged from the examination room. I wondered just what her reaction would be. She turned, caught sight of Lucy, and immediately let out an audible gasp.

"Oh, my sweet puppy," she said in a quiet, high-pitched wail.

Then she covered her face with her hands. I could see her shoulders shake. The next thing I knew, Sadie was on her knees with Lucy's boney head cradled in her hands, kissing the gentle muzzle. Lucy's thin, knotty tail responded with a hearty wag. They stayed in that embrace for what seemed a long time. Then Sadie turned her face to me questioningly. It was streaked with tears.

Mr. Leach was clearly uncomfortable with this display. The rest of the clients were focused on the scene as well and a hush descended on the room. Even the background music seemed to become distant. The last person to hear the overwhelming silence was Sadie. When she finally did, she realized instinctively that Lucy's owner was embarrassed. She turned to him.

"I'm so glad you're getting your dog taken care of, God love her. It just breaks my heart to see them like this. And I know it must break your heart too. What's wrong with her?"

The poor man was speechless and Sadie turned to me, her face a query.

"Lucy is going to be okay, Sadie," I responded. "She just had a huge litter of pups and just gave them everything she had. All she needs is some good food, some vitamins, and a vacation from the pups."

Sadie clasped the man's hands in hers and looked deeply into his face.

"Lucy is one of God's creatures, you know. Now you just do everything Dr. Bruce says and I'm sure she'll be just fine. I know she will, in fact. My Gigi looked just like that when I got her from the county dump. But she's fat and sassy now. Lucy will be just fine." She patted his hand comfortingly.

"I'm just glad there isn't anything more serious wrong with her," he said, recovering some composure. "Fortunately, it's nothing a little more Big Red dog food can't cure."

Sadie shot a quick glance at me. I shrugged furtively. She turned her attention back to Lucy and Mr. Leach.

"Now if Dr. Bruce wants you to feed a special food to Lucy, you should do just that. God love her, she's not going to gain her weight back on that Big Red food, now is she."

Without another word, Sadie strode over to the shelves that contain the premium pet food my hospital stocks.

"Which of these foods is best for Lucy, Dr. Bruce?"

I hesitated for a moment, but was quickly and silently chastened with a look from Sadie that could not be misinterpreted.

"I have recommended that Lucy be fed the growth formula," I replied.

Sadie leaned over a twenty-five pound bag of the puppy food I had indicated. Her stooped frame had difficulty lifting the heavy bag. With effort she dragged it over to the stunned man and leaned it against his leg.

"Now you take this food and give it to Lucy. If this is what it takes to get Lucy better, then I want you to have it. And don't you worry a bit about it. I'm paying for this bag myself. It'll be my little gift to Lucy, God love her. And I won't take no for an answer." She turned to me again.

"And didn't you say, Dr. Bruce, that she needs some vitamins too?"

"That would be ideal, yes."

"Well, can you show me which of these is the right one?" she asked as she went to my display of nutritional supplements.

I lifted a small bottle of the appropriate vitamin supplement and handed it to Sadie. She took it, but shook her head vigorously and immediately placed it back in its place on the shelf, grabbing instead the larger bottle with three times the number of pills.

"She'll need more than that, I bet!" She handed the bottle to Mr. Leach like a pharmacist, complete with personalized instructions. "Give them to Lucy just like Dr. Bruce told you to. She really needs them, God love her."

"Oh, no, ma'am," Mr. Leach protested weakly. "I can't let you do that!"

"Sure you can, honey," Sadie responded. "And I will too."

"Well . . . I don't know what to say. Thank you very much. That's very kind."

And with an amazed shake of his head, one with which my office staff and I were by now well familiar, he picked up the dog food and the bottle of vitamins and took it out to his car. Lucy followed along on the end of a thick chain. Sadie watched them walk down the stairs, then turned back to me. Tears were once again making their way down her cheeks.

"Oh, Dr. Bruce, it just breaks my heart. God loves them so much . . . and so do I. Will she really be okay?"

I reached down and tried to give Sadie a big hug. But she wriggled free. Quickly she ran across the room to the food shelves. Grabbing a second twenty-five pound bag, this time lightly, she pushed the front door open and ran down the stairs, waving and yelling at the car that had just begun to pull away from the curb. I watched as she opened the passenger door and threw in the second bag of food, slamming the door behind her. Without waiting for any dialogue, she turned and made her way up the stairs and into the lobby again, breathing heavily now.

"Sadie, you're an angel," I said as I once again enveloped her in a hug.

My eyes were misted over, and I glanced around the lobby to see how others were reacting. I was not the only one affected. Mrs. Frost was daubing at her eyes with a tissue.

"And yes, Lucy will surely be okay now," I said. "You have provided her with just exactly what she needs."

"Aren't you precious." Sadie laughed a quiet, self-conscious laugh, suddenly aware that she was the center of attention. "No, I'm no angel, Dr. Bruce. I'm just a little old lady with a mushy heart. But I just can't help it. Now you just put both those bags on my bill today. Don't forget the vitamins either. And don't you give me a discount either, honey."

Sadie would be upset with me if she knew it, but I did apply a discount to those two bags of dog food and those vitamins. You see, I'd already collected my profit from that sale. I had been brushed with angel's wings, God love her.

Ollie's Final Fight

It was my favorite time of the morning. I could feel the vibrating hum of Ollie on my chest as I traced the lines of his cheek and shoulders with a sleepy finger, his head cocked attentively, arching himself extravagantly against my touch. Few things are more comforting and cozy than a contented cat purring on your chest. Ollie's ceremonial morning greeting was one that I cherished.

It had become a ritual. Each morning after the alarm clock had awakened me but before I had climbed out from the warmth of the covers, and after Cynthia had turned the water on in the bathroom so the cats could enjoy their morning drink from the running water in the sink, Ollie would make his way slowly from the bathroom to the foot of the bed where he would jump up and ascend to my face. To do this he would balance on my leg and walk up my body like a gymnast on the balance beam. Once on my chest he would stop and look deep into my face until I opened my eyes. When I did, he would chirp a quiet greeting and lie down like a sphinx on my chest, purring deeply. He seldom wavered from this routine, and it never failed to remind me how special Ollie was to me.

Only one thing interfered with Ollie's sunrise rite—and he

hated it. Rush, Ollie's longtime friend and erstwhile nemesis, had for years observed his mentor's morning custom. I'm not sure whether he was jealous of my attention, was challenging the superiority of the elder statesman, or, like many a younger sibling (I know because I am one), just wanted to bother and annoy Ollie. But he had developed the habit of positioning himself stealthily at some point in the bedroom, crouched like a leopard behind the clothes hamper or hunched on the floor behind a carelessly discarded shoe as Ollie made his way from the bathroom to the bed. His goal each morning was to attack Ollie somewhere along the course of the trail and bowl him over, arms wrapped tightly around Ollie's neck, back legs rabbit-kicking his tummy as they rolled over onto the floor in a roiling heap. If he timed it just right, he could catch Ollie in midair before he had made it up onto the bed and thus multiply the effect fourscore.

Over the years, the rules of engagement had been codified, so both of them seemed to understand them completely. Rush never attacked once Ollie was already on the bed, for instance. If he missed his opportunity during Ollie's trek from the bathroom, he would wait patiently for the moment between us to end and for Ollie to jump from the bed and make his way down the hall to the food bowl for breakfast. Once this occurred, all treaties were null and the enemy was once again a target of opportunity.

For his part, Ollie seemed to purposely ignore the arrogance of the underling. Though he had grown accustomed to the ambush, he maintained a careful air of studied indifference to the danger, never bending to the temptation of defensive maneuvers, as if ignoring the pest would someday convince Rush to seek satisfaction from a more anguished opponent. Why it never occurred to Ollie that this strategy was invariably a miserable failure I never understood, but each time the weight of the hunter pounded him to the ground again, he would screech a strident, dismal yowl dripping with juicy expletives unprintable in books of this sort. When he was finally able to extricate himself from the grip of the younger cat, he would face him down with a few well-placed right hooks to the chops. Rush would stand his ground, ready to pounce again, one front foot raised like a pointer on bird, eyes squinting at the blows pummeling his jowls. After hissing vehemently several times with open mouth and glinting canines, Ollie would slowly turn and make for the bed again. It often took two or three of these interchanges before he finally made it onto the safety of the demilitarized zone.

This morning—the Friday after Thanksgiving—promised to be a busy one for me as the day after holidays often are. The sequels of such feast days as Thanksgiving and Christmas too often involve sick dogs and cats whose owners have lavished too many gastronomic novelties on the unsuspecting tummies of their pets, leaving veterinarians to clean up the inevitable gastroenteritis and pancreatitis cases that can result from such indiscretions.

With Ollie perched atop my chest humming contentedly, I remembered the scene around our Thanksgiving table. Our family's custom is to give voice to the many things for which we are grateful before the feast commences. Among the many things I had listed was Ollie, whose noble and inspiring spirit had so enriched our lives for almost eleven years. His presence was especially appreciated that day as he had just been relocated after one of his wanderlust walkabouts that had lasted a week or longer, during which Cynthia and I had fumed and searched and brooded. His return had been such a relief, such a striking answer to prayer, that I could not but list him among our blessings that year.

I replayed in my mind the frenetic game Ollie and I had played the night before. He loved to play chase. He found the round disk of light on the floor from a flashlight beam irresistible. He loved to have me send the disk around the floor, the furniture, and the walls with him in hot pursuit. He would throw himself into amazing contortions trying to capture and stand on that little spot of light. He had been so completely absorbed in the game that we had taken the video camera out and recorded a few minutes of his antics, laughing with abandon at the silliness of the sport. These memories made the ritual that morning especially sweet and unusually prolonged.

Finally though, with the pressures of the day calling me, I gently slid him off my chest and headed down the stairs for breakfast. On the way down the stairs, Rush attacked again from behind the door jamb of the hallway bathroom, slamming Ollie down. Rather than fighting back, he just cursed loudly and hissed, running down the stairs ahead of the assailant. I laughed appreciatively as I turned back to get my slippers.

Sitting on the edge of the bed to put my slippers on, I heard an ungodly guttural croak and a distinct thud. The sound sent ice streaming into my veins and I felt my mind grow cold. I knew immediately something very wrong had taken place. I raced down the stairs, calling to Cynthia over my shoulder as I took them two steps at a time.

At the bottom of the stairs I turned right into the kitchen from where the sound had emanated. On the cold blue ceramic tile of the kitchen floor, I could make out the end of a black tail trailing straight and still behind a prone form, partially hidden from view by one of the kitchen chairs. Rounding the table and pushing the chair aside brusquely, I found Ollie lying on his right side, eyes large and unseeing, pupils dilated fully. His mouth was gaping with the awful, unfruitful gasps of agonal breathing. A little pool of urine was collecting behind him on the cold tile. The sight was horrifying!

I dropped to my knees beside him, squeezing forcefully on his still chest to stimulate the stalled heartbeat. Scooping up his tuxedo-clad form in my arms, I encircled his mouth and nose with my lips and blew air into his lungs, continuing the chest compressions with one hand. Between breaths, I pleaded in a terrified, shaky voice for Ollie to wake up, to breathe, to somehow respond to my frantic efforts at resuscitation. Being at home, I had no other tools to assist me in my struggle. No oxygen. No epinephrine. No bicarbonate. No endotracheal tube to allow forced ventilation. No intravenous catheters. None of the things that might have made a difference in the face of life and death. Only my hands and my lips and my lungs and my breaking heart.

They weren't enough. After what seemed an eternity on the cold tile, my aching hands went limp and my lungs could blow no more for the choking grief that came with the realization that my friend was gone. Gone despite all my training and expertise; despite my gritty determination and earnest effort. Though I had often resuscitated the crashed pets of my clients, my experience had failed me when my own beloved companion lay dying before me. I held him up to my face and buried my cheeks in his soft coat.

I became aware of my family around me. Cynthia's face was drawn and strained, her hands clamped tightly over her mouth, tears now making their way down her cheeks. My sons were hovering, not quite sure what to do with the sight of their stricken parents and their departed pet, the first time in their short lives they had been confronted with death. I realized that Tucker had, in an effort to do something helpful, used one of Cynthia's good kitchen towels to soak up the urine on the floor. I loved him for it. Jace stood wringing his hands and shifting his weight from one foot to the other, a frightened and confused look on his face. I locked eyes with him and nodded a somber confirmation.

"I'm so sorry, guys. Ollie's gone. I couldn't bring him back."

"But, Dad," Tucker's voice was high and pinched and choking back tears. "What happened?"

"I think it was his heart, Tee. We've known for a long time he's had a heart condition. And it's the kind of problem that can sometimes cause the heart to suddenly give out. It just quit. And I couldn't get it started again."

I pulled him close to me, his petite torso heaving with sobs bigger than his whole world. I remembered such wrenching tears on my own father's shoulders when, as a boy only a few years older than he, my very first dog had passed away, coincidentally also from heart disease. I recognized in him the bewilderment, the emotional turmoil, the mixture of astonishment and curiosity, of horror and wonder, the marvel and mystery of facing for the first time the specter of mortality. I didn't want him to know this reality of life so soon, so young. I squeezed him close, sadness for this loss of innocence joining my bereavement over Ollie's passing. Within arm's reach, I looked and saw Cynthia with Jace similarly engulfed in a comforting embrace, kissing his head and rocking slowly back and forth.

We stood over Ollie for quite some time like that before I finally placed him gently in a cardboard box, curled peacefully as if asleep, and covered him with a towel. After completing my preparations for work, I placed the box on the seat beside me and drove slowly to the office. With a heavy heart I carried it into the office and without a word, set it down on the surgery table.

The mood among the staff was decidedly different from my own, with cheerful prattle about the events of the holiday in each of their homes. Susan, my longest tenured staff member, took note of my somber bearing and the box in my arms. Thinking I had brought in a patient from the lobby, she came over and glanced nonchalantly into the box.

"Who is that?" she asked, then gasped and jumped back. "Is that Ollie?"

Unable to speak, I nodded weakly, head down. Susan moaned audibly and immediately enveloped me in a comforting hug. "Oh, Doc. I'm so sorry." I buried my face on her shoulder and for the first time I broke down.

Throughout the decade plus that Susan and I have worked together she has seen me through many a difficult or frustrating situation, always with wit and wisdom, sensitivity and compassion. But never have I appreciated her more than the Friday morning that Ollie lost his last fight. Countless times I have watched her comfort clients whose pets had passed. I had seen her fight back tears of her own over a special patient lost, the broken bonds of companionship between people and their beloved pets. I had watched her with a great deal of respect and even a little pride. But now I was the one with the broken heart and her compassion was directed at my pain, the tears that she was unable to fight off were for my own pet, my dear Ollie.

The appreciation I felt, and feel still, for Susan's understanding and compassion that day was overwhelming. It reminded me again of the significant place that pets assume in our lives, the degree of emotion invested in their short time with us, and the value there is in honoring the iron fetters of attachment between people and their pets. It has always amazed me when my clients, after having to put their dear pet to sleep because of intractable pain or some untreatable malady, bring me cookies, send flowers, or write a note of thanks, as if my role in their pet's demise was worthy of praise. Now I know from a different perspective how healing it can be for someone else to validate the depth of your loss and give you permission to grieve in deep and earthshaking ways when the fragile circle is breached.

It is a vital role I play in the cycle of pet ownership, different and more melancholy, but no less necessary and certainly more profound than the puppy shots I administer or the lifesaving surgeries I perform throughout the course of a pet's life. Having always felt the weight of the chore, it is a duty that I now take even more seriously, having lost my Ollie. Unfortunately, not every ill can be salved, not every pain relieved. I find myself all too often within the fragile circle being called upon to snip its tattered strands, to gently release the fetters of companionship. It is a grievous task, to be sure. But one that I am qualified to complete not because of my professional training or my experience. My qualifications arise only because I am willing to do it from within the circle rather than from without.

Ollie's ashes inhabit a small, rectangular tin with a black cat decorating its lid. Though it has been several years since that Thanksgiving holiday, the tin resides still in my sock drawer. I still haven't had the heart, or perhaps I have too much heart, to bury the little coffin in my yard. I plan to some day. I'll have a short ceremony—just our family—and lay Ollie's ashes to rest in my backyard overlooking the Shenandoah Valley. It will be just the right place for him.

And though we'll bury his ashes, nothing will lay to rest the memories I have of him. They're not so crushingly painful now, after the passing of a few years. Now they are sweet and melancholy and nostalgic and center around all the good times we shared. Each year when we decorate our Christmas tree, there is a touch of sadness when we find his little toy, one of Cynthia's makeup brushes that he so loved to chase and carry, still crushed and crumpled from his adolescent games of reckless abandon. It has now been converted into an ornament, hung reverently in a prominent place on our tree.

Rush is now the elder statesmen. And when the young bucks, Webster and Flinn, bowl him over with their surprise attacks, I laugh at the memory of his ambushing of Ollie. What goes around comes around as they say.

Why do we do it, you may ask? Why suffer so deeply for just a few fleeting moments in time with our pets? Of all the memories I nourish of Ollie, none are more treasured than when, in the morning as I lie in bed before throwing off the covers, I close my eyes and feel the precious weight and the reverberating buzz of that tuxedoed kitty on my sleepy chest. Every tear, every sadness, even the bitterness of parting, when viewed through the prism of that memory is a price too small.

Holly

I walked into the examination room and extended my hand to Mr. Barney Webster. He gripped it, returning a firm, honest handshake, and beamed an ebullient smile at me. I was immediately struck by the warmth and openness of Mr. Webster. He seemed, in fact, to radiate warmth, so ruddy was his face, the redness highlighting wide cheeks and extending from his eyebrows on to his balding head. He wore thin wire spectacles and had short cropped white hair that rimmed his head just above the level of his ears. At sixty-eight, his posture was still proud and he stood up to his full six-feet-two-inch height without a hint of a stoop to the shoulders. Sharp creases danced at the corners of his eyes and mouth, lines earned honestly through years of ready mirth.

Mr. Webster, dressed casually in a collared golf shirt and polyester sports shorts, brought to mind a football coach, one whose players may have complained about him, but respected him nonetheless with esteem generally reserved for men of great influence and authority. I noted incidentally a silver medical alert bracelet on his wrist and thought it incongruous. His legs were lean, muscular, and deeply tanned. He carried not an ounce of extra weight anywhere on his frame.

"I'm pleased to meet you, Mr. Webster," I said.

"Please, no one calls me Mr. Webster." His voice seemed to bounce with a chuckle that bubbled just under the surface of his smiling, crimson face. "Just call me Barney."

"That's a mighty fine-looking pup you've got there, Barney."

Clutched in the crook of Barney's left arm was a tiny, short-haired dachshund puppy about eight weeks of age. She was also slim and red, but her eyes were full of anxiety, flitting from her owner's smiling face to my white coat without moving her head. It was clear that she thought I was up to no good and needed to be watched. There was no real malice about her, just caution, so I tried my favorite trick.

"Barney," I said, "put her down on the countertop and let's see if we can win her over."

I've learned over the years to emulate dog behavior at these times. I put my face down close to the tabletop and cooed and whistled at her. She looked from me to Barney and then began to tentatively wag her tail. Soon her whole south end was writhing and she sidled up to my face and began to lick my nose. I've used this trick for years and it seldom fails to charm even assertive dogs.

One of these days, I'm sure I'm going to get my nose bloodied, but so far I've managed to be quick enough to avoid snapping teeth when my technique proves too bold. I learned this trick from watching dogs greet each other by approaching cautiously and smelling each other's breath. (Well, okay, they smell other orifices also, but I haven't gone that far yet.)

Before long, Holly was smiling, her mouth open, eyes bright, and tail flagging wildly. With new puppies, we usually get at least one visit during which we vets are greeted with eagerness and accepted as a friend. This was her first visit to the office and she had not yet learned to associate the sights and smells of my office with the inevitable pokes and sticks and indignities of a checkup. I wanted her to remember me fondly in the future. I took her and held her in my arms. She writhed in excited puppy ecstasy, slathering my face with her tongue. She seemed as exuberant and good-natured as her owner.

"What have you named her?" I asked.

"That's Miss Holly." Barney laughed at her display, obviously pleased that she liked me. "I don't think she cares much for you."

"What a wonderful little dog!" I exclaimed, totally won over by her charm. "You're going to have a great time with her."

"She's already the queen of the house," Barney confessed. "And we've only had her now for a couple of weeks."

I examined Holly carefully from head to toe, careful to screen for common congenital or developmental abnormalities. All checked out well. During the examination, I plied Mr. Webster with all the appropriate questions designed to identify any hint of problems. No, Holly hadn't had diarrhea. Yes, her appetite was normal. Well, she had vomited once, but that was after she had gotten into the trash and had eaten some leftovers. She had been normal since.

"Have you had any particular problems with Holly so far, Barney?"

"Not unless you include weeing on the floor and biting our fingers," he responded. "But that's just being a puppy, I suppose."

One of my favorite aspects of practice is seeing a puppy or kitten at the first juvenile visit and watching that baby grow through infancy, adolescence, adulthood, and on into its geriatric years. I enjoy each phase and value the opportunity to witness the development of the bond that forms between my patient and its doting owner. As protector of that bond, I often develop with the client a depth of understanding and appreciation that makes practice life come alive with significance and meaning. I could sense that working with Holly and her owner would be especially rewarding. And indeed it has been—beyond anything I could have imagined.

Holly grew from an engaging, energetic puppy into an equally engaging and thoroughly enchanting young dog. I saw her through her series of first inoculations and performed her spay. Somehow she maintained throughout an eagerness to see me and an unabashed infatuation with me, forgiving graciously the insults I piled on her in the name of her health care. Holly grew normally, though not very big.

"Some day," I would tease Barney, "when she gets to heaven, Holly will have real legs that go all the way to the ground." Barney would laugh appreciatively and tweak one of Holly's ears. And Holly would yip back at Barney and smile a toothy grin over her shoulder.

"They may not be long. But you should see her run!" Barney would respond. "She goes on walks with me in the woods every day. And she just loves to chase everything she sees. Leaves falling, ground squirrels, birds, everything. She takes out after them with her tail high and barking like a hunting dog. She just sails along the ground with those long ears flopping. It's the thing in her life that keeps her going. I love to watch it."

I learned to expect from Barney the same easy smile, quick laugh, and appreciation for my attentions that I received from Holly. It's often true that dogs assume the personalities of their owners. And it was certainly true in Holly's case. Each visit was spent in easy conversation with Barney, much of which centered on Holly and her continued development. An equal part of our time, though, was spent sharing our personal philosophies of life and swapping stories of family and business. Not surprisingly, Barney's approach to life was reflected in his eyes and laugh and the devotion to Holly that he displayed. The more I learned of Barney, the more I appreciated and respected him.

I learned, for instance that Barney operated a sign production company in a large metropolitan city and had been hugely successful. With people to run the day-to-day operations of the business, he had migrated to the valley where he spent his days recuperating, relaxing with his wife, and pursuing his hobbies of fishing on the Shenandoah River that flowed by his house and riding his Harley-Davidson motorcycles. He had six or eight hogs in his collection, each of which was completely chromed out and meticulously maintained.

Recuperation for Barney was a full-time job in itself. A few years previously he had undergone surgery to remove a cancerous growth from his pituitary gland. The prognosis at the time had been grim and his doctors had told him no patients had survived more than five years after the surgery. Barney had devoted himself to the study of pituitary function and had, with the help of several specialists and holistic doctors, put himself on a regimen of multiple hormones, vitamins, herbal therapies, and concoctions of pills and injections of all types. It was this regimen of treatments, in fact, that accounted for the extremes of facial redness he displayed most of the time. He had become an expert in all things pertaining to pituitary hormones, a point of no small significance, for he had long since passed, twice over, the time when his doctors had forecasted his demise. His treatment protocol, it seemed, was working wonderfully.

"I feel better now," he would say, "than I felt when I was twenty years younger. And the difference is, now that I've faced death, I really appreciate life."

And it was obvious that Barney did indeed appreciate life. His enthusiasm for it was infectious and I looked forward to each appointment when I noticed Holly's name on the appointment book. At each visit I noted how much deeper the bond between the two had grown. Barney looked at Holly with proud eyes and soft ones. And Holly clearly adored him in return. I'm not sure how much exercise her short legs got at home, but whenever I saw her, those legs seldom touched the ground. When they did, she would run tight, fast circles of joy around him before jumping up and planting her squat front legs on his shins to be picked up again.

This pair, I thought, would be wonderful to share the process of a lifelong relationship with. I was enjoying the beginning thoroughly. Though the future was at the time obscure, the present was enough. Little did I know.

What's in a Name?

I have a real problem with names. Don't get me wrong. I like names; really I do. I've had one all my life and have become rather attached to it. Had I been a girl, my mother had vowed to name me Geraldine Matilda. But alas, I was born with an X and a Y chromosome, proving once again that there is indeed a God and that He is fair, just, and above all merciful.

My problem with names is that I have a mental block about remembering them. It's true. You could introduce yourself to me and I promise that within just a minute or two I would be able not only to forget it, but also to embarrass myself several times by trying to assign a new one to you. In fact, I've essentially quit introducing people to each other since the time I introduced my wife (of seven years) to some colleagues and called her by the name of an old girlfriend. I can still see (through swollen and bleeding eyelids) the look of confusion on their faces at my wife's reaction.

I do fine with faces. When I recognize someone in the grocery store, chances are I will remember that they are clients, that they have two dogs and a new kitten, that one of the dogs had a laceration on the left front foot two years ago that required suturing and that their oldest son plays on the high school golf team. But there's a better chance that I'll fall into a volcano on the cereal aisle than that I'll remember their name.

Over the years I have developed a number of ploys to mask my name disability, some of which have gotten me into even deeper trouble. One of my favorites was to coyly ask how they spelled their last name. I gave that one up when one elderly woman eyed me coolly and spelled, "S-m-i-t-h!"

Lately I have simply taken to pretending that I instantly know them, hoping that as the conversation progresses the name will magically pop into my head and I will be able to seamlessly spew it out as if I had known it all along, instead of what really happens (my every neuron bursting with effort, the strain of which causes me to break into an immediate cold sweat testing the efficacy of my deodorant to its outer performance limits).

To add one more layer of complication to it, each client may have several pets, all of which have their own names. I have discovered that many clients suffer incredible affronts if I don't immediately recall Fido's name. Please be gentle with me. I'm sensitive about my handicap.

In my office, I cheat. You may have thought that the records doctors carry into the room are for maintaining meticulous notes of our patient's medical progress. No, indeed! The main purpose of the records in my office is so I can easily greet you and your pet by name.

I have found that the names people give to their pets tell me a great deal about them. I never miss the opportunity to pursue the story behind a unique name. Almost always I am rewarded with a story that endears the patient to me all the more.

For our part, our family has taken to naming our pets according to figures that are prominent in the news at the time we get the pet. This system works very well for us. It plants our new pet firmly in the sequential time line of history and gives us permanent perspective on the current events of that time. Let me be clear that the choices we make reflect only the prominence of the namesake at that time. It is not, nor should it be construed to be, an endorsement of that person's views or politics.

A few years ago I acquired a rather sad-looking cockatiel whose wing had to be amputated because of a serious injury. Poor bird! We were challenged to come up with an appropriate name for him. We finally settled on the name Bakker. It fit him perfectly! This was about the same time that Jim and Tammy Faye Bakker got their wings clipped.

Currently, Rush has been joined, in chronological order, by our cockatiel, Chessie, who was named for Ceauşescu, the Romanian dictator who, with his wife, was executed during a Christmas uprising by his own subjects; Webster, the cat, who is our token Democratic rogue named after Webster Hubbell who was sentenced to jail time for his Whitewater activities ("They can indict my dog, they can indict my cat, but I am not going to lie about the president"); Flinn, the feline, was named after Kelly Flinn, the sacked female pilot who lost her wings for lying about an extramarital affair in the armed forces. And finally, our dog, Starr, was named on the day that Kenneth Starr's report came out of the independent counsel's office. That week was a busy news cycle, so our family had to vote between Starr, Maggie (Mark McGuire had just hit his record number of home runs) or Lewey (after Monica Lewinsky). I won't tell you which one had my vote.

Many people have touching methods of naming their pets. Dogs with names like Richard or Lucas or Raymond are often living memorials to a much-loved relative. My brother-in-law and his wife named one of their cats after a favorite great-aunt, Ella, who shared with the cat an especially gentle, quiet spirit. This worked well for them, though they aborted this method with their next cat whom they call Arthur, but whose full name is Arthur Barther Boo Bear Orange Creamsickle Lion Wilkins Pattersly Arturzino Snuffleuphogas, a name that just rolls off the tongue.

Favorite pets who have passed on are often immortalized by having their replacements named Jr. (or the Third, Fourth, and so on). As a child, my wife had a series of three cats named Princess Prissy Puss the First, Second, and the second Second.

Kids often are responsible for some of the most unique names.

I have patients named Church, TooToo, Green One, and Ball, all of which were named by their youngest masters who either could not yet pronounce their intended names or had developed, at a very young age, a rather sadistic sense of humor.

Other people take a rather highbrow approach to naming their pets. The highly literate will often give names that simply underscore my ignorance.

"Oh, that name comes from Greek mythology. But of course you knew that." Or, "You remember your social sciences, don't you? Nefur-Temu was the African goddess of the hunt and the continental symbol of intertribal cooperation."

Oh, sure, I knew that too. Thanks so much for reminding me once again. I'm sure I'll be referring back to that several times within the next few days.

Musical people have a unique language to draw on for their pet names. Of course, the specific genre of music they prefer influences the names they give. These names vary from Jazz to Elvis to Allegro. One elderly lady, wearing a stole and pearls with a dainty teacup poodle named Pianissimo on the end of a bejewelled, thin leash, gave this explanation for the name.

"She was just so very, very quiet for the first week I had her. Now that she's settled into our house, I should change her name to Crescendo."

Some stories I would just as soon not know. Once a couple came in with their three-month-old puppy. They were young and unkempt. Both sported hair of approximately the same length, color, and hygiene. Both displayed equally unacceptable tattoos on their arms. But both also demonstrated an infatuation with their puppy who obviously returned their affections. When I asked where the name had come from, they exchanged embarrassed glances and told me exactly why they had named their puppy Trojan. I'll spare you the details.

One young couple who brought in their new puppy were still in deep discussion about its name. It was a chow chow with fluffed, teddy bear hair, a smiling face, and a tail that curled up over his back.

"We need your help with his name, Doctor," the woman entreated me earnestly.

"I'll help in any way I can," I replied, expecting to lend some insight into the personalities of chows or clarify some fine point of coloration or conformation. "What can I do?"

"Well, my husband wants to name him Buddy!" She glared at him as if he was the epitome of dull-witted imbeciles. "But I think that's silly. Everyone names their dog Buddy. This dog needs a name that's unique. Something more sophisticated and enlightened."

Her husband impatiently rolled his eyes. Her face was pursed with the strain of the ongoing debate between them.

"Buddy just won't do. He needs something that suits him better, don't you think?"

"Well, what do you want to name him?" I asked, not wanting to damn the one without first hearing the other.

"I think we should name him Enid." She gave a self-satisfied smirk and nodded her head curtly at her husband.

"Enid, huh?" I turned to the pup without hesitation and stroked his cheek. "Your name is Buddy. I'm writing it down in your record—in ink."

My technician burst into laughter; the husband pumped his arm triumphantly; the wife harumphed noticeably. I'm pretty sure Buddy looked relieved, though.

The transition of practicing in Virginia after being in New York introduced some interesting confusions. Once a young woman came in with a new puppy for its first vaccinations. During the course of my initial history and physical examination I asked her what she had named the young Labrador retriever.

"Bayer," she replied.

I was confused. "Bayer?"

"Yeah, Bayer." Nothing could have been more routine for her.

"That's an interesting name, Bayer." I said. "Do you work for the drug company?"

Now she seemed confused. "No. I work at the gas station. Why did you think I worked at a drug company?"

"Well, not many people would name their dogs after a brand of aspirin. I was just trying to figure out why you named him Bayer."

"He was just so cute when I first got him, I thought he looked like one." This apparently was supposed to clear up the mystery for me. It didn't.

"You thought he looked like an aspirin?"

We were clearly talking around each other. "No, a Bayer."

So confused was I that I decided to revert to my tried-and-true method for clearing up these misunderstandings.

"So I can get this right on the record, how do you spell Bayer? B-a-y-e-r?"

She laughed. "No. B-e-a-r!"

Now that I think about it, he did kind of look like one.

Infectious Holly

Oh good, I thought, as I looked over the receptionist's shoulder at the appointment book. Holly has an appointment this morning. That will start my day off well.

Some people just tend to reset your thermostat when you spend time with them! You can be in a foul humor, but they just seem to know how to defuse it, and by the time they leave, things look better. Barney Webster was one of those people. And Holly, his dachshund, was another. Not that I was in a particularly poor mood that morning, but I looked forward to seeing them nonetheless.

As I lifted Holly's record from the pocket on the wall, I glanced down at the receptionist's notation after the date. Holly was here for me to check her skin. Good, I thought. At least it's nothing serious. I pushed the door open and walked into the examination room.

"Barney," I bellowed, extending my hand. "So good to see you this morning."

Holly would have none of it. Squealing and wiggling, she broke free of Barney's grip and ran across the countertop, not stopping when it did, and jumped into my outstretched hand. Not quite prepared for this, I lurched to catch her, throwing the record unceremoniously onto the floor. I just barely snagged her before she suffered the same fate. I held her up to my face and she writhed and groaned and licked my cheek in greeting.

I indulged this behavior unapologetically. I'm convinced that everyone should be greeted like this at least once every day. And all willing dog owners are, which helps to explain the popularity of man's best friend. If all spouses learned to greet each other with this kind of enthusiasm, perhaps without the licking and the submissive weeing, no doubt this country would have far fewer divorces.

As I held her at arm's length, though, I noticed something on her tummy. With her little hind legs hanging down and reaching for the tabletop, her belly was completely exposed to me. It was splattered with ugly round, red, dime-sized, crusty spots. A few pimples could be seen among these lesions as well.

"Oh, Holly," I said, sighing. "You've got some ouchies on your tummy, don't you?"

"You see 'em, huh?" Mr. Webster grimaced as he rubbed her abdomen in these areas. "Poor puppy. They really itch her too."

As if to illustrate his words, Holly suddenly doubled over and began to bite at one of these spots with her front teeth, leaving a little wet spot on her tummy before she quit and turned again to me.

"How long has that been going on?" I asked.

"Well, I first noticed it last week down in Florida," Barney responded. "My mom still lives down there and we go down every so often to check up on her. I thought it was fleas at first, but I haven't found any on her. She keeps getting more of those spots. It looks like chicken pox."

"Yeah, it kinda does," I agreed. "Fortunately, dogs don't get chicken pox, though. This is called superficial pyoderma. It's a bacterial infection in the skin that starts out like this pimple here, and then opens and crusts over like this, and finally heals from the center out leaving a little target like this." I pointed out each phase of the problem on Holly's belly as I talked. She absently scratched her hind leg at the air as I did, relishing the attention.

"Will it go away?" Barney asked, concerned.

"Oh, yeah," I assured him. "She'll need some antibiotics. But these generally clear up nicely. The problem, though, is that it sometimes comes back. This is often a secondary problem, taking advantage of the changes in the skin from some other problem."

"Other problems? Like what?"

"Well, fleas for instance. Or allergies, or mange, or hormonal diseases, or any number of other things." I noticed Mr. Webster's face beginning to be shaded with anxiety. "But I certainly don't see any sign of any of those things right now. This could also be just a simple skin infection that will completely resolve with proper treatment."

"How will we know the difference?"

"Time will tell," I said. "We'll treat for the infection and see if it comes back. If it does, we'll look for underlying causes and try to control those. The bottom line, though, is that this condition generally has little effect on their overall health in other ways. They're otherwise perfectly happy."

I prescribed a course of antibiotics and some medicated shampoo and sent the pair on their way to the receptionists to pick up the antibiotics and to make a recheck appointment in two weeks.

When they returned for their recheck appointment, I was greeted in the same way by a squirming puppy. This time, though, her tummy was smooth and clear. The only hints of the infection were a few fading dark targets where the skin had pigmented from the spots of infection. I assured Mr. Webster that those, too, would disappear with time. I was pleased that our treatment had been successful.

Six weeks later, however, Holly was back in with a recurrence of the same superficial skin infection. I looked her over carefully again. No other abnormalities could be identified that explained her recurrence. We repeated a course of antibiotics and special shampoos. Her condition cleared up again quickly.

Over the course of the next six or eight months, poor Holly

had no less than four bouts of the identical skin infection, each of which responded beautifully to treatment. We looked for underlying causes carefully with skin scrapes, fungal cultures, diet changes, allergy testing, and blood tests. No problems were found. Finally, after ruling out the usual culprits, I concluded that she suffered from an unexplained malady in which skin infections simply repeated themselves very frequently. I scheduled an appointment to discuss the implications of this diagnosis with Mr. Webster.

"With all these recurrences, Barney, I suspect Holly has chronic recurrent idiopathic superficial pyoderma." I waited for his response with a gleam in my eye.

"You don't say." Barney smiled back at me. "Could you say that in English?"

"Sorry." I laughed. "Doctors like to make up long names for things we can't otherwise explain. It makes us feel smart. All that means is that Holly has repeated skin infections and none of us idiots can figure out why."

"Well, it's certainly not for lack of trying."

"You're right. We've done a lot of testing and ruled out a lot of problems, but never identified the specific cause. And frankly," I admitted, "we probably never will."

"So she's gonna be miserable like this off and on all her life?"

"Usually we can find ways to minimize the episodes, but she'll probably always be prone to infections in her skin."

These problems are frustrating for pets and owners. But they are also frustrating for me. I like to think every problem is curable, but that's just not the case—for my patients any more than for humans. And it's those cases that especially gall me.

"There are a couple of things we can try. Hopefully, if they work, the episodes will be less frequent and less severe. But you'll have to work at it."

"I'm up for anything that will help Holly. You just tell me what to do."

"Okay, the first thing we'll do is start a series of shots that will hopefully reduce Holly's sensitivity to the bacteria. I'll give the first one today, but I'll have to teach you how to give them at home from now on."

Mr. Webster cocked his head questioningly. "You want me to poke her with a needle?"

"I'm afraid so."

He thought for a moment then laughed his ready, ruddy laugh.

"Well, I'm sure I can do that for Holly. I've been giving myself hormone injections once a week for ten years or longer. Can't be much harder than that."

I gave Barney a primer on giving Holly her shots and sent him home with a supply of needles and syringes and a vial of vaccine against the bacteria that caused the skin infections. He was very religious about giving Holly her shots twice a week, and over the next several months the frequency of her infections decreased significantly.

Mr. Webster became an expert at giving the injections. Both he and Holly adjusted to them. She even seemed to sense that they were helping her. Barney reported that if he forgot, Holly would bug him until he gave it to her.

All in all, Holly's treatment was a success. She still had an occasional skin infection, but much less often than before. When she did, it was less severe than it had been and cleared up faster with less powerful antibiotics. I was pleased with the results. More important, Holly seemed happier too. And Mr. Webster, though he had to poke his little friend with a needle twice a week, was tickled.

The Old Bait and Switch

"I need to see you right away, Doc Coston. Raisin is bad."

It was about eight thirty in the evening and I had just gotten home after a long day. Mrs. Warren didn't sound at all like herself. Usually she was a calm, quiet, rather self-possessed woman. That night, though, I noticed the sharpness of near panic in her voice.

"What's happened, Mrs. Warren?" I was concerned. Raisin wasn't just a patient. He was a friend.

"Raisin . . . he's all tied up! I just don't know what to do."

"Tell me what happened." Mrs. Warren's description somehow failed to bring a diagnosis immediately to mind.

"Fish hooks! Can you help?"

The rising hysteria in her voice made it clear to me that I was not going to get the full story until the problem was solved.

"Of course, Mrs. Warren. Bring Raisin right over to the hospital and I'll meet you there."

It is not terribly unusual for a kitten to get tangled up with fish hooks. Their insatiable curiosity and the delicious smells of the bait and the fish make fishing tackle all but irresistible to them. As I drove to the hospital, I pictured the typical case—

usually a hook through the lip that is quickly taken care of. I'd be home in just a few minutes.

Mrs. Warren, a professional antique collector and dealer, was in her mid-forties. She was lean and sophisticated and carried herself in ways that convinced you she had been an accomplished athlete in her youth. Her hair was blond, with a hint of dark at the roots, and was pulled into a short ponytail.

Her daughter, Margo, though now a stunningly attractive collegiate, was at the time in that transition period of adolescence when a girl's legs are a little too long and a little too thin. Her movements were still gangly, but you could begin to sense the gracefulness that has since emerged. She sported braces with bright blue bands that she made no attempt at concealing when she smiled. She tucked her long, straight hair behind her ears in a nervous, repetitive gesture that revealed her anxiety.

Mrs. Warren and Margo, were waiting for me at the hospital when I arrived. Both of them were noticeably shaken. Wrapped tightly in a towel was Raisin. He too was visibly shaken. His eyes, rimmed with white and with widely dilated pupils, were just visible peeking out of the folds of his shroud. The towel heaved rapidly with each panting breath.

In the examination room, Margo placed Raisin, still swaddled in his towel, on the table. I gently unwrapped him, surprised at how quiet and still he remained. It was not till the last layer of the towel was released that I discovered why. Raisin couldn't move!

Under his chin were several rusty fishing lures tangled into an angry knot. Raisin was hooked securely through the left upper lip, the right lower lip, an ear, the right front leg, and the left rear foot. The hooks fettered him so tightly that struggling was fruitless—and Raisin knew it. He was also liberally peppered with other wounds on his feet, his ears, his cheeks, and even his tail. These bore testimony to his vigorous struggle for freedom. Despite his predicament though, he looked up at me with eyes full of trust, arched his back against my petting and purred loudly.

With a few quick snips of my wire cutters and careful manipulations of the fish hooks, I was able to free Raisin from his cuffs. In no time at all, he was wandering around, without a care, leaving little bloody footprints on the tabletop from the wounds he had sustained.

Now that he was no longer coiled into a convoluted knot, you could appreciate what a fine specimen Raisin was. He too was an adolescent—thin, muscular, and angular. He was an exceptionally supple and athletic cat. A gray tabby, he was decorated with sharply contrasting black pinstripes of surprising width. The pattern was so stark and strikingly symmetrical that the effect set Raisin apart. And he seemed to know it. He carried his head high and, except for a cocky kink at the tip, kept his tail at military attention. He sat down, wrapped his tail around his haunches statuelike, and began to lick at his front paws, cleaning the blood from the pads. He was the picture of contentment and gratitude. Mrs. Warren, just as grateful, was more vocal.

"Oh, I'm so relieved! He looks so much happier now. Oh, Doc Coston, it was awful."

"Do tell me what happened." My curiosity was piqued.

"Well, you probably know how focused I am on antiques. Collecting them is my passion. Over the last several years now I have accumulated quite a collection of antique fishing lures. Some of them are really valuable"—she paused for a moment—"like the ones you just cut into pieces."

"I'm sorry. I had no idea."

"Don't worry about that. It had to be done." Mrs. Warren pardoned me nonchalantly with a wave of her hand. "Anyway, I wanted a way to display my collection. So I bought an antique wagon wheel and attached my fishing lures to it in a kind of rustic arrangement. It looked pretty cool! I hung it on the wall over my couch in the family room."

Though I was having a hard time understanding how rusty fish hooks and an old wagon wheel somehow constituted art, the scene was starting to come clear to me. "You don't mean that he knocked that whole wagon wheel down off the wall do you?"

I asked incredulously. I couldn't imagine how a cat as small as Raisin could have managed that.

"Well, not exactly. Margo and I were in the kitchen doing the supper dishes when we heard a loud noise in the family room," Mrs. Warren continued.

"It was more like an explosion," Margo interjected. "It sounded like someone was pounding on the wall with a baseball bat. At the same time you could hear an earsplitting screech, like a little kid screaming. I thought someone was being murdered. Then everything went silent again. It scared me to death." Margo's eyes filled with tears as she relived the nightmare. She couldn't go on. Mrs. Warren took over the narrative.

"We ran into the family room not knowing what to expect. At first we couldn't find what had made all the racket. Then we saw him. It was awful, Doc Coston! Raisin was hanging from the wagon wheel all caught up in the fish hooks like he was when we brought him in. And the more he struggled, the worse he got caught. Finally, he just gave up and hung there like he was being crucified. We were able to get him down and wrap him up in the towel, but every now and then he would thrash around again. That just got him tangled worse and worse!"

My mind conjured up the scene of that poor cat hanging like an ornament from a Christmas tree. I could see Mrs. Warren and Margo bumping into each other in their haste to rescue him from his peril. Oh, to have been a fly on the wall (the other wall, of course) that night! As I pictured the debacle, I began to get tickled. Involuntarily I began to laugh quietly, my shoulders shaking.

Mrs. Warren and Margo stared at me slack-jawed, with wide and surprised eyes. Their reaction to my mirth struck me as hilarious and I laughed all the harder, now loudly and deeply from my belly. This was soon too much for them and, now that the situation was no longer so dire, Mrs. Warren and Margo began to giggle too. Directly we were all sharing a hearty laugh. Even Raisin seemed to sense the humor in the situation.

"Well, folks," I said, finally recovering some composure, "Raisin is none the worse for wear. He's going to be just fine. Maybe a little embarrassed, but fine. The bleeding has stopped completely now and the wounds are superficial. I'm not even worried about infection. Just keep an eye on the cuts and make sure they are healing well. But if I were you, I'd hang that wagon wheel where he can't jump up to it so this doesn't happen again."

"Don't worry," Mrs. Warren assured me. "It's not going to happen again. I'm not going to put those lures back up. I can't afford to have you cut any more of them into pieces. I don't think I even want to collect them anymore. I've learned my lesson and I hope Raisin has too. Hopefully he won't be so quick to make the same mistake again."

"I'd like to think so, Mrs. Warren," I said. "But that would give him credit for more sense than most of us have, wouldn't it. Seems we're all suckers at some point in our lives—some of us more than others."

And as often happens, I learned more from my patients than I cared to admit. Now when I'm presented with something that looks just too good to be true, I think of Raisin, hog-tied to himself by those valuable antique fishing lures—a victim of his own greed. And it's a little easier for me to avoid the old bait and switch.

Slipped Disk

"Dr. Coston, Barney's on the phone." My receptionist seemed unusually concerned. "I think something is seriously wrong. Can you talk with him?"

I was writing records at my desk and still had a couple of hours of work ahead of me. This sounded pressing, though. I grabbed the phone. "Barney, what's going on?"

"Hello, Dr. Coston." He did sound stressed. "I'm hoping this is nothing serious, but I have a feeling I should be worried. I'm down in Florida right now with my mother. This morning Holly couldn't get up at all. She's down in the rear legs and just a'squealing when I lift her. I'm afraid she must have pulled a muscle. Should I give her an aspirin?"

"When did you first notice problems?"

"She seemed a little drunk on the back legs a day or two ago, but I just thought it was the heat down here."

"Oh, Barney, this doesn't sound good!"

I was worried. Dachshunds have unusually long backs, much longer in relative terms than most dogs. And while this gives them their unique physique, it also places an inordinate amount of stress on their spine. They have a high rate of disk problems, some of which can be very serious. From what Barney was describing, it certainly sounded like Holly had suffered a ruptured intervertebral disk that was impinging upon her spinal cord and causing paralysis of her hind end. If so, this was bad.

"If you squeeze the toes on her back feet does she feel it?"

"No, she doesn't seem to respond at all."

"Okay, Barney, you need to get her to a vet down there right away! I mean pronto. And it needs to be somewhere that does neurosurgery." I couldn't mask the concern in my voice. "It sounds like she's ruptured a disk and is paralyzed in the rear. Her best shot at recovery is immediate surgery! Don't waste any time."

"So you don't think I ought to get her up to you?"

"Besides the fact that I don't do that surgery, there isn't time. She needs surgery literally within the next few hours in order for her to have any shot. Let me know what happens!"

I hung up the phone with a deep feeling of dread. Holly was one of my very special patients and Mr. Webster was a favorite client. This was not good! Recovery rates from this type of problem are much better now than they were years ago before spinal neurosurgery was routinely done, but time was of the essence. Generally if there is absence of pain sensation that persists for twelve hours or more, the damage is often too great for there to be any real hope of recovery. It sounded like Holly's condition had been fairly long-standing. Her fate would be in the hands of a surgeon who I was sure would be skilled, but whom neither I nor Barney knew. I breathed a deep sigh of concern.

I got a call later in the day from Barney. His voice was sober. Surgery had been done, but the surgeon was very concerned about what he had found. There had been a great deal of compression on the spinal cord, which looked bruised and damaged. Surgery had gone as well as could be expected, but he had not been very optimistic about her chances at regaining function.

I tried to reassure Mr. Webster, reminding him that only time would tell, that I had seen some amazing recoveries that had not been predicted by skilled practitioners. But I felt little comfort speaking the words. Barney was deflated. I could hear the quiver in his voice as he spoke.

"If only I had brought her in three days ago. It's my fault."

But it wasn't his fault that Holly had been unlucky. It wasn't his fault that she had an extraordinarily long back, or that she was overly active for that back.

I next saw Barney about ten days later after he had returned home from Florida when it was time to remove Holly's sutures. He carried her into the room from the lobby somberly. His eyes were not as quick to smile as usual and his gait was rather slow and heavy. He avoided my gaze. I could tell he was fighting tears as he set her onto the table.

"I'm afraid she's not doing real well yet, Doc." His lip quivered and his face flushed even redder than usual. I placed a hand on his shoulder.

"Let's take a look," I said.

If Barney's attitude was somber, Holly's definitely was not. She sat awkwardly on her haunches, her back legs stretched strangely forward with the toes extended. There was no sign of movement in her tail. But from the middle of her back forward, she was the same Holly I had come to love. Her mouth was smiling and happy and she dragged herself quickly to me across the tabletop, yipping excitedly for me to lift her up. I bent down and received the same greeting from her to which I had become accustomed.

"She acts just like nothing ever happened." Barney shook his head. Then he resolutely squared his shoulders, drew himself up to his full height, and looked me in the eye. "But we'll do what we have to now to make her as happy as she can be. I could learn a lot from her. Anyone that can suffer the injury she did, not be able to walk or get around and still be that happy has got a lot of heart. I won't let her down with that kind of attitude."

I carefully evaluated her neurologic status. There was no response to what should have been painful on either of the back legs. The tail hung limp and unfeeling when I squeezed it. The anus sagged loosely with no muscle tone at all. I felt her bladder with my fingers. There was no resistance as I gently squeezed it. Urine flowed freely from her onto the table. In fact, there was no evidence at all that Holly had regained even a shred of spinal cord function below the middle of her back.

"I'm afraid things aren't looking good at this point, Barney." I tried to be upbeat. "But the story's not completely written yet. It sometimes takes a few weeks for function to return. Though the odds are against us, it's not entirely out of the question."

"After looking her over, do you really think so?" He searched my face deeply.

"Honestly, Barney, I'd be very surprised if we got any function back at all the way things look now. You need to start learning how to provide nursing care at home."

"Just tell me what to do."

I went over the things that he could do to help a paraplegic dog. She would need him to squeeze her bladder empty three or four times a day. She would have no control over her bowels and would simply deposit stool around the house at any time—probably the most inopportune ones. She would be immobile except for dragging herself on her bum, so making or buying a little cart with wheels to support her back end would give her more freedom to move around the house for a little while each day.

For some time I saw Barney and Holly weekly to check on her progress. Though her attitude remained bright and sassy, there was no change in her neurologic status. Barney proved to be a very capable and willing nurse, providing her with everything that her condition required. It took a while for him to become proficient with some of the technical parts of her care. But he was a willing and motivated student and dedicated to Holly's comfort.

We had a few challenges to face as she recuperated. Because she didn't evacuate her bladder effectively, she developed a few urinary tract infections. She tended to rub the hair off of her hips and we had to watch these areas carefully in order to avoid bedsores. But, in general, her health remained surprisingly good and, because of the exceptional care that Barney and his wife provided, her life was full and happy.

After a few months, Holly's care became routine for Barney. He was well familiar with what to do, what to watch for, and how to handle the inevitable crises. Though I did not see her as frequently, I still thought of her often and marveled at her good fortune for finding her way into the heart of so gentle and generous a man.

Many people would have been unable or unwilling to have such an expensive surgical procedure done on their pet. Many more would have given up after only a week or two without any signs of recovery. Very few indeed would have committed the time, energy, and diligence to provide the level of care and support that Holly's happiness demanded.

Barney did! And he did it without any hint of resentment or frustration. He did it because his friend needed it; because, despite her disability, her life was full and happy; because his bond with her was no less strong just because her legs were weak.

The power of the love between that little long-backed red dachshund and her tall, red-faced companion was nothing short of inspiring. I became a better veterinarian because she was such a good patient. She and the Websters challenged me to commit my best to all my patients, whose relationships with their owners were no weaker even though their legs were strong.

Holly's Foot

I knew it was bad as soon as I walked into the examination room. Holly seemed as happy as always. She was eager to see me and greeted me with the same enthusiasm for me that she always displayed. But Barney's face was taut and drawn and he greeted me with a strained smile instead of his usual easy one. As I glanced at Holly in Barney's arms there was something else. White tape formed makeshift bandages around both her back feet. And there was a strange odor in the air that I couldn't quite identify.

"Hello, Barney," I greeted him. "Good to see you today. What's going on?"

"Holly's doing something strange, Doc." It was just like Barney to minimize a problem. "The other day I noticed she was licking at the toes on her back feet. I didn't think anything at all about it. But she did it more and more. This morning I got up and found something awful. She's chewed on her feet. Why in the world would she do that?"

Though I had heard of this sort of thing before, I had never seen it.

"No one knows for sure why paraplegic dogs begin to chew on their feet. It may just be a compulsive behavior, but since they don't have any feeling there anymore, some will go on to do damage to themselves. Let's take a look."

I gently began to unwrap the layers of tape and gauze Barney had applied to one of Holly's feet. A sour smell wafted up to my nose as I did so, the source of the unidentified odor. For most patients it is quite painful when bandages that have dried onto a wound are removed. But Holly obviously didn't notice. When I removed the last layer of gauze from the foot, I involuntarily drew a quick, horrified breath.

Holly had chewed her toes off! They were simply gone. No pads; no toes; nothing. From well above where her foot pads should have been, the shattered ends of her metatarsal bones protruded grotesquely. The surrounding muscles, tendons, and connective tissues hung loosely in shreds around the bones. I was horrified.

I looked up sharply at Barney whose ruddy face hung weakly down, not daring to meet my gaze. I saw a tear fall on the table. For a few moments I was utterly speechless. Then I directed my stunned words to my patient.

"Oh, Holly . . . what have you done?"

Her exuberant response was totally incongruous to the gruesome sight before me. She looked up at me with smiling face and lolling tongue and yipped excitedly as if proud of her ingenuity. But with the bandage now off, her attention quickly went to the exposed tissues and she began to lick vigorously at the wound again. I pulled her chin away with difficulty and began to unwrap the other foot.

It was even worse. The damage had been inflicted even higher up on this leg than the first one. Blood oozed menacingly from the open wound. Holly's attempts to get at the foot were compulsive and persistent, prevented only by Barney's holding her head tightly against him. My shoulders slumped in discouragement and defeat. I turned to face Barney, who still kept his face down, his hands absently stroking Holly's face.

"This is not a good development." In tense situations, I often have a real knack for pointing out the obvious. "Because she has no feeling in her rear legs and feet, it doesn't hurt her to chew on her feet like that. So there's no stimulus for her to stop. Paraplegic dogs that develop this compulsive behavior usually continue it. The response to drug therapy for compulsive behaviors has been disappointing. Even amputation above the affected area does not help much as the dogs usually start the behavior again after surgery. These wounds often become infected and nasty and that just makes the situation more dire."

"So there's really nothing left for us to do, is there?"

"Unfortunately, there isn't."

My heart went out to Barney. No pet owner deserves to experience the loss of a beloved pet. But Barney's commitment and devotion to Holly had been legendary. He had provided her every advantage that a paraplegic dog could have. He had assisted her with defecating, with urinating, with walking, with eating. He had purchased her a cart that supported her back end and let her swagger around the house at top speed. He had treated her bedsores and urinary tract infections. But this development was unbeatable. And Barney knew that he could no longer meet her needs.

He gently scolded her through thick eyes with a hoarse, choked voice.

"Well, Holly. You've really done it this time."

He broke down, holding his friend up to his face. She turned and licked lovingly at his tears. It was a scene too dismal and too beautiful to watch; one brave and noble canine heart comforting a broken human one. I averted my face to brush a tear from my own thick eyes.

Barney's lament didn't last long, however. With an unashamed dab at his streaked cheeks, he turned to me.

"Well, I haven't cared for her all these months like this to quit caring for her now. I've never wanted her to suffer before. And even though she hasn't been able to walk all these months, she's not suffered. She's been happy and playful and courageous and strong. I'll not have her suffer now. We'll just have to do what we have to do. I owe her that much. That's what we're up against, isn't it?"

"I'm afraid so, Barney. She's made our decision inevitable." I stroked her face, neck, and back. "There's nothing harder that we pet lovers have to do. Sometimes the decision is not clear. But in this case, we really have no choice."

I took Holly to the treatment room where I inserted a catheter into her vein and gave her a touch of sedative. Then I gently placed her back in Barney's arms. He held her in his big hands, softly petting her face and whispering private things in her ear as I, with brimming eyes, administered the drug that eased her into eternity. Her head sunk in final sleep and the recognition faded from her eyes. I listened through the stethoscope as the heartbeat slowed, became unsteady, and finally ceased. I looked up at Barney, who studied my face questioningly, and nodded. Holly was gone.

I reached up and gently squeezed Barney's quivering shoulders. He was too overcome to respond. Knowing that privacy is important for many pet owners at this time, I slipped quietly from the room, closing the door behind me. As I walked slowly down the hallway, nursing my own sadness, great disconsolate sobs arose from my friend behind the closed doors. His agony was palpable. I could feel it deep in the center of my chest. I fled for the treatment room, unable to contain my own sadness any longer.

Barney stayed behind that closed door for quite some time remembering, no doubt, Holly at her best. As he held her close, I'm sure he relived those times in the woods when her footsteps were strong and swift, when birds and squirrels fled in panic from her approach. He saw once again those floppy ears flying in the breeze and those short legs extended with each long stride. I know he reviewed all the puppy frustrations—the tinsel pulled off the tree, the furniture scarred from her chewing, the stain on the carpet by the door where she hadn't quite made it, the house-training, the cocked head when startled, the play posture with tail and fanny up, head low, and the front legs extended before her.

But he also remembered, I'm sure, the disabled Holly too with equal fondness and affection. Despite her impairment and the work that it had required of him, those times with Holly had been just as precious for the two of them. Her needs and his ability to satisfy them had imbued another, even deeper, layer of fidelity to their relationship that many of us have never experienced. Throughout all those long months with their challenges and setbacks, the one thing Barney had never felt toward Holly was resentment. No regret shaded his memories of her.

As Barney emerged from the room, he was surprisingly calm and serene, at peace both with the last months and the last few minutes. He shook my hand warmly, locking eyes with me in a look that communicated volumes. Then he bravely strode from the office and climbed into his car. I watched him drive away with a lump still aching in my throat.

Several weeks later, Barney strode briskly through the doors of the waiting room, smiling broadly and carrying something in a paper bag. He looked great in his bright blue coach's shorts and sweatshirt, face beaming red color and bonhomie, eyes twinkling like a conspirator. He bellowed a greeting to the staff and motioned me to an open exam room.

"Barney," I exclaimed with a pump of his arm. "Man, it's good to see you. You look great. How are you doing?"

He ignored my greeting, getting directly to his purpose.

"I've got something to show you," he said, taking a frame out of the bag in his hand and placing it on the table. "My niece is an artist. I didn't know she was doing it, but last weekend, she brought me this. What do you think?"

In the frame was a pencil drawing of a miniature dachshund that perfectly captured the personality and image of Holly. The eyes were bright and seemed to search my face for a sign that I might just want to play catch. The ears were alert and ready. She was sitting in a pose so typical of Holly that I almost expected her to jump from the picture, crawl across the table, and greet me in her unique way. It was perfect.

Looking at it Barney's eyes too were once again bright and

eager. I marveled at the power of the bond between a pet and its loving owner. A bond so strong that it has the power to bring smiles and happiness even when the bond has been broken by parting; even when the bond is just one remembered in the perfect likeness of a pencil drawing.

Spirit

"Hello, Dr. Coston."

Barney's voice was so abrupt over the telephone that it took me off guard. It wasn't like him to be this way and it worried me.

"I'm bringing a dog in this afternoon. He's in awful shape. Get him back to health as best you can. Do whatever you need to do. I'll pick him up again at some point, but it will probably be a few weeks."

"Um . . . okay, Barney." I could tell that he really didn't want to go into much detail about the situation. "What's his name?"

"Spirit." There was no smile in Barney's voice.

"Do you know about how old he is?"

"I think he's about thirteen years old."

"Is there anything else?"

"No. Just take care of him. Don't bother calling me about procedures. Neuter him, clean his teeth. Whatever he needs, just do it."

"We'll take care of him as best we can, Mr. Webster. Is there anything else I can do for you?"

"Thanks, but not now. Please don't ask me for any more details. I'll explain later. I've got to go now."

A few hours later Mr. Webster came in the front door with a

nondescript mongrel of medium size. He didn't say a word; just signed the admission forms, turned without comment and left, not daring to meet my questioning gaze. I didn't know what the story was, but I was sure Barney would tell me when he could. In the meantime, the best way I could help was to see to this dog.

I turned my attention to Spirit. It struck me immediately that the name was a misnomer. This dog had little spirit in him. He looked awful! He stood before me with no apparent interest in his surroundings. What little fur he had was brown and dull. From his shoulders back, the coat was mostly gone, exposing reddened, thickened, and angry skin with scabbed and oozing sores. The skin was oily and moist and smelled odd. Scurrying from one flaky patch of hair to another were hundreds of fleas. The skin condition extended down his legs all the way to his feet. His nails were overgrown, some of them curling under, diverting his toes into uncomfortable contortions. Large crusty calluses capped his elbows, and as I watched he turned and chewed at these for a moment before turning his attention to biting at the base of his limp tail, the hair of which was tangled and knotted from his incessant chewing. His ears, which reminded me somewhat of a cocker spaniel's, hung disinterestedly down, and every now and then he shook them cautiously. Each time he did, he whimpered softly and stopped, giving in to the pain. The hair below his ears was knotted and crusted with the discharge that had dried there from the oozing infection in the ears. Even without looking at them, I knew from the putrid odor that emanated from them that they were infected.

"Poor Spirit!" I sighed.

He looked up at me quietly, wagging his tail a few times. My work was cut out for me with this case. I first drew some blood for tests that would evaluate the things I could not see externally: liver function, kidney disease, electrolyte abnormalities, thyroid function. A bacterial culture of the infected ears was collected so I could direct appropriate therapy at the offending organisms. An ear swab was evaluated microscopically, which demonstrated both bacterial and fungal organisms in the ears. Skin swabs and scrapes were done next to evaluate the degree and extent of the skin disease. By the end of these tests, I had a pretty good idea what was needed. I quickly decided on a treatment plan.

Then the real work began. I directed my staff to bathe Spirit with medicated shampoos both to kill the fleas and to subdue the irritation in the skin. Special rinses were used to prolong the beneficial effects of the bath. Next the ears were attended to. We cleaned them as best we could with disinfectants, but Spirit's pain was too great for us to complete the job. Anesthesia would be required for that. Antibacterial and antifungal ointments were started that would kill the organisms and reduce the pain. Oral antibiotics and anti-inflammatory drugs were also initiated.

I was surprised and pleased the next day to find that Spirit's blood work was fairly normal. For such an old dog in such poor condition, this was at least one piece of good news. The tests did indicate that Spirit's thyroid gland was not producing enough hormone, so supplemental hormone therapy was begun. With otherwise normal organ function, I scheduled surgery to neuter him and to clean his teeth and ears the next day.

All the while, I continued to ponder the mysterious circumstances that had placed Spirit under my care. Clearly, something awful and momentous had occurred—something too heavy and too sad for Barney to verbalize to me. At least not yet. The contrast between his usual upbeat and optimistic personality and the tenor of his voice that day made the mystery even deeper. Spirit certainly wasn't Barney's dog. I knew too well the level of care he routinely afforded his pets, and this was not it. He would never have allowed his dog to get into this kind of shape. My guess was that something had happened to a close friend of his and he was helping in this way to ease the difficulty for that person.

Spirit underwent his surgery very well. Neutering is a relatively simple procedure taking a few minutes at most, and soon it was over. While Spirit was asleep, I took advantage of the anesthesia to thoroughly clean and flush his ears and carefully scale and polish his teeth. Many of the teeth, with their infected roots and looseness, could not be salvaged, and had to be extracted. Sacrificing them would not adversely affect his ability to eat and would, instead, remove a source of constant pain and potential infection to distant organs. He would be much better off without them.

Over the next several weeks, a new Spirit began to emerge. I marveled at his progress. With treatment for his allergy and infection, his skin had taken on a new glow. No longer did it crawl with fleas and drip with oily discharge. The skin that had so recently been red and angry was now quiet. His chewing had almost completely stopped. If you looked closely, you could even tell that new hair was beginning to emerge from much healthier follicles.

Though his ears were still a bit uncomfortable, they no longer oozed smelly discharge. Each day they improved to the point where he now solicited us to rub them. While he hated having his ears cleaned, I think he came to understand that our efforts were helping them hurt less. As we rubbed in the cleansers each day, he would lean into our hands, groaning all the while with mixed pain and pleasure. Progressively, it seemed, there was less pain and more pleasure. Where before he reeked with halitosis, his breath now was sweet, his teeth clean and sparkling white. Spirit was truly a different dog.

As his health improved, so did his attitude. Slowly he began once again to deserve his name. He became more aware of and interested in his environment, exploring with a new interest every corner of the hospital and greeting each staff member. Though folded over, his ears were much more erect than before and reacted now to every sound.

Tellingly, he also found his voice. Spirit didn't exactly have a stage voice, though he seldom missed an opportunity to perform. He came out of his kennel baying excitedly like a hound on scent, his little mouth rounded as if saying, "Ooo," his dark nose tilted up precariously. This song increased in intensity if you made the mistake of calling his name. And it crescendoed amazingly if I joined in the singing—the two of us swooning at full voice in unison.

"Ooo-woo-woo, Ooo-woo-woo."

Then he would smile appreciatively and jump up on my leg. Who knows for sure what the lyrics meant, but I'm fairly confident it was a happy song, one of gratitude and contentment. Spirit was getting his spirit back.

Every week or two, Mr. Webster would call to check on Spirit's progress. It was good to be able to report improvement each week. As time went on, I could detect in Barney a little lifting of the heavy cloud over him as well.

Eventually, it must have been six or eight weeks after Spirit joined us, Barney made an appointment to pick him up and go over his care. I was eager to discover the answer to the mystery, and yet cringed with a dark foreboding. I had heard rumors of tragedy, but passed them off as mere gossip. So it was with guarded anticipation that I finally escorted Mr. Webster into an examination room.

"Spirit's doing really well. His skin is better now. His hair is even beginning to grow back. His ears are in control now and no longer painful. I cleaned his teeth, and neutered him. He's got a whole new lease on life. And he's starting to really show himself too. He's a happy boy!"

I went into detail on the care Spirit would need in order to keep his improvement progressing. I covered the medications I was sending home with him and wrote out a schedule for him to follow. Then I paused and looked Barney in the eye.

"You have really been in our thoughts over the last several weeks, Barney. I'm still not sure what the situation is, but I presume it must have been an awful blow to you."

Mr. Webster's lips quivered and there was a long pause.

"I want to thank you for getting Spirit into shape for me. I also want to thank you for demanding no explanation from me. You deserved one, but I wasn't really able to talk about it until now." His voice broke momentarily. "Maybe not even now."

I waited for him to regain his composure.

"Spirit belonged to my son, Tracy. Tracy lived here in town, but we didn't see him all that much. So it wasn't that unusual for us not to hear from him for a day or two. But after a few days with no word, I had a bad feeling and went over to his house. He didn't answer the door. I could hear Spirit in the house barking, but Tracy didn't come to the door. I called the police and they broke in."

Again Barney broke down. But he didn't need to finish the story. I had figured it out. Barney had lost his son. It was even worse than I had imagined.

"I've never much liked Spirit. He's just an old mutt. He's never shown a single redeeming quality. But Tracy sure loved him. I know you wouldn't think so the way he looked when I brought him in here, but he did. He and I never had the same approach to pet care. Now, though, Spirit is the last thing of Tracy that I have. Even though he's an old codger, I'm going to keep him going and keep him as healthy as I can. It's my last gift to Tracy."

With that, Barney smiled bravely through moist eyes and took the end of Spirit's leash.

"Come on, old boy, let's go home."

Dr. Prudence

The Virginia Veterinary Medical Association is the professional organization guarding the interests of the veterinarians within the commonwealth. The majority of vets in the state are dues-paying members of the group either by choice or because their dues are covered by their employers. Such was the case for me for the first four years I was a member. When I left Waynesboro and opened the practice in Woodstock, I continued my membership even though at the time the dues were an expense I could ill afford. Still, more as a professional obligation than anything else, I sent off a check for the dues to the VVMA each year.

It was not until about six or seven years after I opened my doors in Woodstock that I truly began to appreciate the benefits of VVMA membership. This was not because I suddenly needed my organization's support. It was because I was recruited to participate in their activities. One slow afternoon, I was contacted by a local colleague who was slated to become the vice-president of the VVMA the following year. He had sat on the board of directors for several years and had been nominated to start the leadership track: vice-president one year, president the next, then immediate past president. It was a three-year commitment to leadership of the association, which would leave his seat on the board of directors vacant. I was, perhaps, the third or fourth person from our region he had contacted, the others displaying perhaps more mental alacrity in excuse generation than I.

Since I had just hired a veterinarian, my ability to take a little bit of time away from the practice had just increased significantly, so I agreed to serve a three-year term on the board. That was ten years ago. I am still on the board. The time I have committed to serving my profession in this way has been valuable and rewarding. It has also been an eye-opening experience to observe unpaid and underappreciated doctors take time away from the demands of their practices to work tirelessly for the good of the members, most of whom, like me, have little understanding of and less interest in how much their association does for them.

At least, that is how it was for me. I had no idea that my association was the only group watching the legislative activities in the state that might affect how I operated my practice. I didn't know that it was this group that interfaced with the regulatory board that governed the rules of practice and dispensed discipline and oversight of vets in the commonwealth. Though I saw posters and roadway signs that drew attention to the importance of rabies vaccinations for animals, I didn't realize that it was the VVMA that organized and funded these efforts. Nor did I realize it was the VVMA that sponsored and planned numerous continuing education seminars, coordinated and communicated information with the state's many local veterinary groups, interacted with the national association, advocated our concerns before other professional groups, raised and disbursed thousands of dollars each year to support clinical research on pets that would quickly translate into help for our patients, and formulated opinions and positions on any number of issues for the media and for the pet-owning people of the state.

These things I learned from watching them happen; from participating in these endeavors as a member of the board of directors. And I was proud to be involved in this important work. But the most significant reason I enjoyed my work with the VVMA was the opportunity to rub shoulders with some of the state's best, most successful, and most dedicated veterinarians. The veterinary profession is populated by very independent types. We often work alone or with one or two colleagues and have shamefully little overlap with other doctors, even in the same locale. We are colleagues, of course, but usually we are also competitors, attempting to attract the loyalties of clients in the same geographical area. Working with the VVMA removed these barriers and allowed me to relate to my colleagues not as rivals, but as allies working toward the same worthy goals. This camaraderie was a refreshing and welcomed change; one that has made VVMA functions things I look forward to.

I recall clearly the first board meeting I attended, entering the room of well-dressed and collegial professionals bantering easily among themselves. I have never been gifted or comfortable at mingling with unfamiliar people. I have just enough shyness in me, though few who know me would believe it, that I much prefer to lean against a wall and just watch people. I would be an awful political candidate. So I made my way to the seat in front of my nameplate and sat down, carefully arranging and rearranging my meeting materials in order to look busy. I was engaged with this activity when Dr. Prudence walked in.

I heard him before I saw him, his thunderous voice echoing off the walls of the meeting room long before he breached the threshold, its tones gracious and appealing with an unmistakable southern Virginia drawl. His prodigious presence filled the room wholly, preceding him, as did his easy and honest chuckle that was as quintessential and unpretentious as his accent. I knew he would be a large man. I sensed it from the ambience of his persona. And I could judge it objectively by calculating the angle between myself as I sat spellbound at the table and the point from which the monstrous voice emanated. Thus I was not surprised when a mountain of a man entered the room, the Pikes Peak of humanity.

I watched him work the room like a lobbyist, starting with

those grouped in tight knots by the door. He shook each person's hand, asking about their families, their practices, their associates as if he had known them each personally for years, his voice at once booming and intimate. He made his way around the periphery of the room greeting all with a nod, a handshake, a grin; as if doing so was his crucial role and their fundamental right. Yet he did it with a natural ease, fulfilling this emergent duty as if it was autonomic for him, like breathing. The effect of his attentions on the people was a marvelous thing to observe. Conversations trickled to silence as he approached a group, each person waiting breathlessly for his words to be directed to them. Faces turned expectantly up to him, eagerly reflecting back the bonhomie he exuded; then followed his progress as his aura receded from them. It was a thing of beauty. I watched in awe.

He was perhaps six-feet-four-inches tall, though he seemed much larger than that, standing stock straight as he did with his wall-to-wall shoulders thrown back and chin down. His face was long and clean-shaven with a pleasant smile that put you immediately at ease. Heavy, dark eyebrows shaded piercingly blue eyes. His hair was dark too, but salted with gray around the temples, and cut in a stark, military crew cut, perfectly flat on top and tilting slightly from front to back. I judged him to be in his late fifties, more from his graying hair than from any other hint of age about him. His hands were massive and hinged onto bulging forearms. I cringed to think of the poor heifers whose hinder parts were violated during pregnancy checks by those mitts. He wore a tweed dress jacket with black elbow pads and mantle that extended over his shoulders, arching from each side to a point directed downward in the middle of his back. His trousers, crisp and new dark blue denim, flared over dark and lustrous cowboy boots that came to a stern point at the metal-tipped toe, the heels slanted and undercut. He held in his hand a ten-gallon cowboy hat that undoubtedly got its name from the fact that it could literally hold that much liquid, probably whiskey.

The effect of the man was breathtaking. I could see it spreading over the room like a fog, wrapping us in a gratifying mist like the aroma of your favorite meal. I could feel it descend on me, and oddly, it seemed familiar. Before I could process that thought, he was beside me, extending a huge hand toward me in greeting, his left hand hanging, slung down with the weight of that hat it seemed.

"I'm John Prudence."

"Bruce Coston," I replied, standing. It seemed somehow disrespectful not to.

"No, don't get up. I'm sitting right here beside you." He motioned to the placard in front of the seat next to mine. DR. JOHN PRUDENCE. Pulling out the chair he let himself down onto it, sliding the hat under the seat.

"Where's your practice, Bruce?"

"I have a small animal practice in Woodstock. How about you?"

"My practice is a little old place west of Staunton." He pronounced the town's name like a good western Virginian, the first syllable rhyming with ant. You can always tell that someone is not from the valley when they pronounce it "St-on-ton" like an Englishman or a Yankee. He had also characterized his practice using the colloquial term "little old," but I knew, of course, it was neither.

"Is your practice mixed animal?" I hardly needed to ask.

"Sure is. We have a couple of small animal vets. I do a few dairy herds, but mostly horses."

That was not a surprise to me either. A memory was trying to form itself in my head as we spoke. I had a growing impression that I had met Dr. Prudence before. I was surprised at how speaking with him made me feel like I was fifteen again. Then, with a rush, it struck me.

"You're Dr. Prudence!" I said, way too loudly and with excitement.

He looked down at me with a bemused expression. "That's right, sir. I am."

"You practice in Staunton!"

He looked at me as if I was simply repeating everything he had just said, which I was. "Yes, sir."

"Is your practice called Eastwood?"

"It sure is."

"Did you used to work on the horses at Camp Blue Ridge up Highway 56 by Montebello?"

"You know, I did, years ago. I haven't been way up there for a long time, but I used to go up there probably twenty years ago." Now his mind too seemed to be clawing at dim memories. "Why do you ask?"

"Well, I don't expect you to remember me. But about that time, I spent a few summers as a wrangler in the horse barn at Camp Blue Ridge. I remember you very well." And in an instant I was in my mind fifteen again, watching the vet's truck pull into the fenced corral at the horse barn where I fell in love with Virginia.

It was a dark blue Chevy with a Bowie veterinary box filling the truck's bed, the gleaming white fiberglass, with its organized, medication and veterinary equipment filled drawers and cubbies, exuding professionalism. I remembered being overcome with awe and envy when Dr. Prudence unfolded himself from the driver's seat, his presence then no less commanding than when graced by twenty additional years. He was exactly what I pictured myself becoming, an equine veterinarian shrouded in blue coveralls, imbued with confidence and knowledge, and adorned with a stethoscope draped like an inadvertent afterthought around his neck.

At the time, though that was my dream, I was far from it. At fifteen, I had just finished my sophomore year at a boarding high school in Florida. With horses as my first love, I had landed a summer job at the camp by virtue of my many years as a camper at Camp Kulaqua near Gainesville where Camp Blue Ridge's director had previously worked. He had remembered my single-minded devotion to the horse program as a camper and volunteer and had taken a chance on me as a staff member. I had no real experience with horses other than being a constant loiterer at the barn, persistently offering my assistance like a groupie.

When I was offered a job at his new camp in Virginia, I had been flattered beyond description. I had rushed out and bought a few essential items that I was sure would immediately identify me as a horse expert. I had purchased a five-inch pocketknife with three sharp blades that felt strange in the pocket of my new boot-cut jeans. What self-respecting cowboy could mount up without a pocketknife? I had found a beautiful pair of sixty-dollar cowboy boots with upturned, though not stridently pointed toes. Every wrangler must wear boots. You just walk differently in boots somehow, your toes pointed forward and your knees set at a different angle. I'm not really sure what it is, but it's real. I can still feel it now when I pull on my rarely worn boots.

But any old wannabe could don a pair of boots and throw a knife into his pocket. They don't make you a cowboy any more than putting on an apron makes you a chef. What I was sure would set me apart were my gloves. I was proud of them beyond explanation. With all the care of a dueler selecting his weapon, I had located a pair of soft calfskin leather gloves in a pale tan color with a drawstring on the back of the wrists to tighten the thin leather around my hands in preparation for the intricate work of manning the reins. I was sure they were a necessity for me, not only in marking me as an expert in the eyes of all who saw me, but also for the prevention of nasty rope burns inflicted by the pulling of rank and rebellious yearlings. Why it didn't occur to me that at a camp, where the highest priority for a horse would be its pluggish dependability, there would be no rank or rebellious horses, let alone yearlings, I don't know. But the gloves seemed an obviously essential purchase, and I wore them around the house before I left for Virginia just to break them in.

Dr. Prudence had been called to the camp for the most routine of veterinary calls. He was to vaccinate the herd of thirty horses and administer their routine deworming medications. This task involved tubing the horses, an arcane process whereby several ounces of a strong-smelling liquid were introduced directly into the stomachs of the animals by way of a plastic tube inserted through their noses and into their gullets. Even the most docile of horses would exhibit surprise at such a violation of their personal spaces. And often, this procedure resulted in mini-rodeos, so insulted were the thousand-pound beasts. So as I strode forward to greet Dr. Prudence, I pulled on my pristine leather gloves, working my fingers carefully in the tips.

He turned from pulling his equipment from the veterinary box on his truck and thrust out his hand, a puzzled look overtaking his face as he made contact with my glove. "Hey there, I'm Dr. Prudence. How many do we have to work with today?"

"There are thirty horses. I can help in any way you need. And I've got another wrangler here too that's at your disposal. Just tell us what to do." I hoped it was not entirely too obvious to him that I idolized him. But truth be told, I wanted desperately to make a good impression on Dr. Prudence. I wanted him to recognize in me a kindred spirit, one endowed with the inherent qualities that would make me a respected colleague.

"Well, let's bring 'em in to the aisle of the barn one at a time and I'll do 'em. Let's start with the good ones first and leave the rangy ones for later."

We had already confined the entire herd in the stalls of the barn. So it was a simple matter to snap a lead rope onto the halters of the horses and lead them from their stalls to where Dr. Prudence had arranged his work space on one end of the barn closest to his truck. I watched almost reverently as he expertly slapped needles into the thighs of the horses, depositing the vaccines into the muscles almost before the horses had time to react. With awe, I watched how he effortlessly slipped the tube into a nostril, advancing it down the esophagus, the horse's eyes rimmed with white and surprise. When he learned that I wanted to be an equine vet, he showed me how to identify the tip of the tube as it descended down the left side of the neck and explained how important it was to see this in order to know that it was not going into the trachea instead.

I held tightly onto the lead ropes as he worked, ready for any unexpected reaction of the horses, proud of the protection and statement my gloves provided. With each horse, my respect for the man and his boundless knowledge grew. He would point out subtle defects of confirmation that would affect the horse's ability to perform well in any setting other than at a camp. Or he would bring to my attention the twitch of an ear or the stamp of a foot that were unerring and insightful cues to the horse's temperament. He read each horse's personality, tailoring his approach to that horse's mood. He drew me out, joking in ways that made me feel comfortable and affirmed. And with each horse, I noticed that Dr. Prudence seemed to be evaluating me as well, sizing me up in a kind of bemused fashion. As I led each horse back to its stall, I was sure Dr. Prudence's eyes followed me, impressed by my skill with the horses and encouraged that the future of veterinary medicine would be secure in hands like mine.

As I led the fifth horse up to his work area, he turned to me seriously.

"Can I ask you a question?" he asked.

Here it is, I thought. He's recognized my potential. "Shoot," I responded expectantly.

"What you got them gloves for?"

My mind teetered on the brink of disaster. The balloon that was my ego began to rapidly deflate, its sides buckling and collapsing in on itself, emitting what I was sure was an audible whoosh. My lips fumbled for a response. I mumbled something through clenched teeth about how they would protect my hands from rope burns if any of the horses jerked their head away while he worked on them. I said it while carefully avoiding his gaze, but I could feel his eyes searching my face, which I knew was a jumble of embarrassment. I could feel my ears heating up like radiators and the color climbing my face, a high tide of redness cresting now on my cheeks, now climbing to my forehead. The silence that followed seemed interminable, interrupted only by my increasingly rapid and noisy breathing. I wondered what Dr. Prudence was thinking of me now, afraid that I knew. Seeking an answer to this question, my eyes involuntarily rose to his face. He met my gaze, a twinkle in his eye that was either good-natured ribbing or outright mockery, I couldn't distinguish which.

"Hand protection, eh? That's probably a good idea. Maybe I should get me some of those." I could detect no sarcasm in the remark. But absence of overt satire did little to relieve my embarrassment.

I grasped the rope tightly, my knuckles whitening invisibly beneath the soft leather and my mouth a thin, pale line. It seemed to take forever for Dr. Prudence to inject two vaccines and pour eight ounces of fluid into the funnel he attached to the hose that emerged from the horse's nose. I could hear it gurgle as it swirled down the tube ever faster as he held the funnel high over his head; though it may well have been my own stomach churning noisily. I couldn't tell, and frankly, I didn't care. All I wanted to do was lead the horse away and allow myself a little private time to let the brilliant crimson on my face ebb away and my heartbeat to slow. Finally, the fluid level in the funnel disappeared and Dr. Prudence pulled the four feet of tubing slowly from the horse's nose, kinking the opposite end as he did so to keep from sloshing fluid into the trachea as the tube came up.

I turned on my heels and nearly ran away, the horse smacking his lips still with surprise and indignation, snorting and blowing the remaining fumes from his nose, his neck extended from the pull on the rope, and having to trot to keep up with me. As I strode toward the horse's stall, I unceremoniously tugged first one, then the other glove from my hands, tossing them roughly onto a bench that bordered the aisleway. One of them fell to the dirt floor, a small puff of dust rising with the impact. I didn't bother to pick it up.

Jake was the horse in the next stall. Jake would be perfect, I thought. He was black with an overly long nose and ears set high on his poll, mulelike. Though quite tall, he was old and tired and plugged along beside me almost asleep at the wheel, his lower lip sagging limply with the jolt of each plodding step.

He was the perfect camp horse, lacking so much initiative that he was guaranteed not to frighten the campers as he slogged along on trail rides, navigating as much by the feel on his forehead of the horse's rump in front of him as by sight. Handling Jake would give me a few more minutes of recovery time to nurse my injured ego unimpeded by any extraneous effort on my part managing the patient.

Jake stopped of his own accord when we reached Dr. Prudence, his head hanging low, uninterested in the events around him. I held the lead rope a foot or so from the snap on the bottom of his halter, the other end of the rope looped lazily around my other hand. Jake hardly blinked when the needles were driven rapidly into the muscles on the back of his thighs, one hoof chocked up at the heel and resting haphazardly on the toe. Only a swipe of the tail, a single feeble brush as if at a pesky horsefly, let us know that he had even felt them.

When Dr. Prudence raised Jake's head and started to introduce the deworming tube into his nose, however, an amazing transformation occurred in that horse. Before I realized what was happening, Jake's eyes were wide and his nostrils were flaring. With acceleration that I didn't believe he possessed, Jake jerked his head up and back, rearing onto his back legs and wheeling away from us in an instant. I felt the nylon of the rope heating up as it whisked through my bare hands, both of which sent a panicked shout of searing pain to my startled brain. I could feel the blistering of my unsuspecting hands starting immediately.

Then, because I had done what any rookie horse person knows never to do and had looped the bight of the rope around my hand, I was jerked up two or more feet off the ground as Jake turned on his heels like a cutting horse and headed down the center of the barn, me dangling like a bobber on the end of the lead rope. It was only after a couple of amazingly long strides that I could plant both my feet and bring any pressure to bear on Jake's head. This twirled him around again, but did not stop him from bounding in backward hops farther away from the perpetrator. I hung on gamely, both hands gripping feverishly at the taut line, leaning back with both feet planted vainly in front of me as if barefooting behind a ski boat, yelling as calmly as I could things that I hoped would steady the apparently demon-ridden maverick.

Finally Jake decided he had put enough distance between himself and the vet, and, like a transformer, he suddenly became once again the picture of boredom, though this conversion had absolutely nothing to do with my efforts. I dropped the lead rope to the ground and bent over double, compressing my agonizing palms between my knees and grimacing with pain. I thought I smelled the acrid whiff of combustion on my hands as I raised them to inspect the damage. A long red stripe adorned each one from side to side, following the creases on my palms at just the spots where flexing my fingers sent jabbing stings of pain up my arms. I ran down the aisle, past Dr. Prudence who was standing with mouth agape at the spectacle, and plunged my hands deeply into the water trough where I'm sure there was a fizz of sound as the heated palms touched the coolness of the water. It was all I could do to hold back the dam of tears that threatened to break over the spillway of my eyelids as I caught my breath.

Dr. Prudence, I realized with regret, was making his way over to the water trough, his face clouded with concern.

"You all right, young man?" he said. "What in the world happened?"

"Rope burns," I screeched through clenched teeth. "I'll be fine. Just give me a minute."

"By golly, that happened quick," he said, his mouth breaking into a smile. "Whatever happened to those gloves of yours? They sure would have saved your hands, no doubt."

It's funny how time flows on like a stream, always going forward, yet folding back on itself like the seven bends of the Shenandoah River. People who had only a cameo appearance in events long ago, that touched us briefly leaving only a transient impact, come back later to play a much larger role. Chance events that are but a flitting memory, ones we look back on with a smile, roll back on themselves in the fabric of time, grab a random thread from that fabric, and splice themselves into today's textile. The surprising results render unexpected patterns in the weave, patterns we could not have foreseen but that bring serendipitous richness and vividness to the cloth. Here I was retelling the tale to the very same Dr. Prudence, both of us able now to look back on twenty years of flowing time. He sat beside me, his shoulders shaking with mirth that eventually broke out into loud peals of laughter and finally melted into silence again as he continued to laugh, great tears streaming down his face. As the story concluded, he leaned over to me and clapped a huge thump on my back with his mighty hand, his head still thrown back joyfully. When he regained enough control to once again speak, he addressed me between gasping breaths.

"You're all right, Bruce, you know that?" And twenty years later, I was Dr. Prudence's respected colleague.

The Proposal

"Would you be willing to join me for lunch some time?"

It was Barney Webster on the phone and now, a few months after his son had passed away, he was beginning to get the optimism back in his voice.

"I have an idea I'd like to bounce off of you."

I glanced at my appointment book, pleased to see an opening during lunchtime the following day.

"How about tomorrow?"

The next day, a brilliantly clear and cold day in January, Barney picked me up at the office. He drove a luxury sport utility vehicle of immense proportions. I settled into the leather upholstery like a cat on a feather pillow and noted with surprise the warmth that met my posterior.

"These seats are heated!" I exclaimed.

Barney smiled a proud, proprietary smile, without a hint of the self-conscious embarrassment I would probably have felt if I drove such a luxurious car.

"I like this truck a lot," he said. "It's as nice as sitting in a Caddy, but it's not quite so showy. Do you like Italian food? There's a new little Italian restaurant downtown that I thought I'd take you to."

"That sounds great," I responded. "I have been thinking I'd like to try it."

I settled into the rich leather and gazed around the interior of the vehicle, noting with altogether too much envy the polished wood accents on the dash and armrests.

The drive was short. Downtown is a relative concept in such a small community. Though our town is the county seat and boasts the oldest continuously used courthouse in the East, a euphemism for saying that it badly needs renovation, the entire downtown corridor comprises a total of about five blocks.

Squeezed between the offices of the town's optometrist and podiatrist was Antonio's new Italian bistro. It was a small establishment with a few tables scattered randomly in a dimly lit interior. Each table was draped with a tablecloth sporting the colors of the Italian flag on top of which was a glass plate. In front of each chair, on top of the glass, was carefully placed a paper place mat, decorated with a map of Italy.

Barney strode into the restaurant like a New York mob boss, waving at the proprietor familiarly and breezing to the table that was clearly his preferred spot in the dining room. Antonio, the restaurateur, came immediately to the table carrying two glasses of water, the obligatory towel thrown carelessly over his shoulder.

"Meester Vebster!" he crowed loudly in his deep Italian accent, an irresistible draw for people in the Shenandoah Valley. "Soo goo-ood to see jou again! Vould jou lika de usual?"

"Yes, I would, Antonio. But my friend here probably needs some time to look over the menu."

"Of course, Meester Vebster." Antonio dabbed absently at a water spot on the table with his towel. "I bring jou von."

He was back in an instant and placed a menu in my hand, then waited expectantly with his pen on his order pad. He clearly didn't want to make his best customer wait unnecessarily. I quickly scanned the menu and ordered a pasta dish.

"Oh, jes, goo-ood choice, my friend," Antonio crooned as if I had just made the decision that would restore world peace. Then he turned abruptly on his heel and headed to the kitchen. Barney watched him go.

"He's a prince of a guy," Barney said appreciatively. "And he makes some good food. I'm doing my part to make sure he stays open."

My curiosity could wait no longer.

"So what is this idea you have, Barney?"

"Well, I'll tell you." Barney paused and took a long drink from the glass of water on the table. "You know old Spirit."

His eyes misted and there was a long pause. I knew any thoughts of Spirit invariably brought up thoughts of Tracy, his son. I waited respectfully for him to collect his thoughts.

"Well, like I told you before, I really didn't like Spirit at all when Tracy had him. I thought he was just a useless old mongrel. I brought him to you and got him fixed up just for Tracy. But in the six months I've had him now my whole attitude toward old Spirit has changed. He has been the best dog I've ever had. He always comes with me on my walks. He stays with me every step I take. He never complains or pushes me. He's the best dog I've ever had, bar none."

His eyes wandered somewhere over my left shoulder, then far away in time, no doubt recounting all the dogs he'd had over the years. I thought of Holly and the deep bond she and Barney had enjoyed. It made me realize how significant a statement about Spirit Barney had just made. With a laugh he was back again with a playful nod.

"You remember Holly, I know. And you know how much I loved her. But she was nowhere near as smart and perceptive as Spirit is. She was just a bitty thing, but she was so yappy and flighty, I never knew exactly where she was going to be. And I was just as likely to kick her or step on her as I was to step on the carpet. She was always under my feet. Not Spirit! He's as settled as a little old man, except with better manners. He's come to mean everything to me. I love that old dog."

And then he leaned down with both elbows on the table and fixed me with steady eyes.

›st put him down when Tracy died."

ought of it left him shaken and he shuddered visibly.

adn't given him a chance, I would have missed the best ever have! And I've been thinking about that a lot over the ... month or two."

Antonio interrupted our discussion carrying our meals, laying them on the table without the characteristic banter, sensing that Barney and I were deep in discussion. Barney drifted again into circumspection as if myself, Antonio, the meal, the quiet and dark restaurant were not there. I sipped my water thoughtfully, realizing that silence was better than interjection at this point. Presently, Antonio left and Barney continued.

"There must be a lot of dogs out there, cats too—though I'm not really a cat person—that would be the best pet anyone ever had if they just had the chance. Is that something you run into at times in your practice?"

I almost laughed. "Regularly, Barney!"

And it was true. At least two or three times a month, someone would have to make the excruciating decision to let a pet go because they simply couldn't afford the treatment required. These were decisions that were emotional and painful, made by people who dearly loved their pets, but had to decide between its medications and their own, between treating it properly or paying their rent or buying clothes for their kids. It is a grim reality for every veterinarian, one that grates and chafes, but one with which we are all accustomed.

"You like my SUV, don't you?"

I nodded, confused by the turn in the conversation.

"Well, I do too. But I'm almost seventy years old now. I've been richly blessed. I live in a beautiful spot on the river; probably the most beautiful site in the valley. I have every single toy I'll ever want, much less need. I can't find anything else to spend my money on."

This, of course, was not a problem with which I could relate, but I nodded encouragingly for him to continue.

"I need to find something else to do with my money and

Spirit gave me an idea. I want to help other dogs like Spirit have the chance they need. And I thought you might be able to help me formulate something like that. My first thought was to set up a recuperation and adoption facility, but I'm not sure I have the energy for that over the long term. Any ideas?"

I thought for a minute, stunned, but not really surprised by Barney's kindness.

"Have you thought about making some kind of donation to the state's veterinary school to fund some research project or piece of medical equipment? That's along a little bit different vein, but in the long run, could help a lot of animals."

"That's not really what I have in mind. That's good stuff and everything, but what I really want to do is to help individual animals to get better."

"Okay, how about this? Maybe the most frustrating problem I come across in practice is having to put an animal down that has been injured or gotten sick, but has a good prognosis if only the owner was able to afford the costs of treating the acute problem. One thing you could consider would be a fund that would provide assistance to those types of cases for owners who hate the thought of euthanasia, but have no other place to turn for their injured or ill pet. That way you could help individual pets just like Spirit and individual families."

Barney's face lit up noticeably. "That's more what I had in mind. I really like that idea. And that wouldn't require as much physical labor caring for the dogs and managing the adoption process. It has real possibilities!"

As we talked in more detail about the fund and the logistical concerns about setting up and managing it, I turned an Italian place mat over and jotted some notes down. We knocked around ideas about eligibility, availability, promotions, paperwork, and administration. Within just a few minutes we had a tentative outline of how such a fund might work and how it might be started. Barney planned to contact his attorney to begin the legal process of forming a foundation.

For my part, I would take my notes from the place mat, put

them in proper form for usage and eligibility guidelines, and design the needed forms and paperwork for participating veterinarians. Barney's thought was to honor his son with the fund and we immediately began referring to it as the Tracy Webster Memorial Foundation.

Many more meetings followed the initial planning session at Antonio's bistro to iron out the details of the foundation. At every step I remained amazed at Barney's enthusiasm and eagerness to help the animals. Of course it would help the families of the pets as well, but it was always the animals that motivated Barney. Several times during the formation of the foundation, animals came in that would be ideal candidates for assistance. Each time, Barney reluctantly declined to start disbursing funds until all the legalities were completed.

Initially, the Tracy Webster Memorial Foundation was to be made available to veterinarians who were members of the local veterinary association. This would allow us to start out slowly and give us easy access and communication with the participating doctors. With about forty veterinarians in our association, this meant that their clients were to be the first recipients of Mr. Webster's generosity. Each veterinarian would have access to two thousand dollars a year.

I was amazed to learn that Barney planned to fund the foundation in the first year to the tune of about one hundred and twenty-five thousand dollars, with similar amounts to follow in successive years. This level of funding was completely foreign to my mind, but I envisioned with excitement the impact such benevolence could have for my patients and clients.

Within just a few short months, blindingly fast for any legal process, the Tracy Webster Memorial Foundation was a legal entity ready to begin operations. I scheduled some time at our next local veterinary association meeting to present the concept to the veterinarians who attended. Coincidentally, the meeting was scheduled for a night almost exactly one year after Tracy's death. Barney was too overwhelmed emotionally to be able to speak to the association at that time, so he asked me to make the presentation. As a result, I had the honor and distinct privilege of presenting to my colleagues the concept of the Tracy Webster Memorial Foundation.

Their response was astonished enthusiasm. Few could believe the extent of Mr. Webster's care and concern for the patients we treat. All were thankful and vocal in their gratitude. The room hummed with surprise and appreciation as I outlined the guidelines of the foundation. They waited for the catch, the hook that so often accompanies benevolence. But there was none. When I finished my presentation and answered the inevitable questions of clarification, I glanced down at Barney, sitting with folded arms in his chair. His face was down, but I could see a gentle smile and make out the moist trail of a tear making its way from the corner of his eyes down his cheeks. Spirit, I'm sure, would be pleased—in a completely oblivious sort of way. Tracy, on the other hand, would have been totally overwhelmed.

A Rocky Start

"Dr. Coston, something is really wrong with Buddy!"

I recognized Mr. O'Reilly's voice immediately. It sounded strained, well beyond the typical wheezing and grunting of his ever-present heart disease. I could tell he was worried.

"For the last two days, he's hasn't eaten anything. And he keeps trying to vomit. He's really sick, Dr. Coston."

"What does he bring up when he vomits?" I asked.

"That's the thing I don't get," Mr. O'Reilly said between wheezes. "It's mostly whitish to yellowish foam. But every now and then he brings up some gravel."

"Gravel?" I repeated incredulously.

"Yeah, just like the stuff in my driveway. I don't know why in the world he'd eat gravel."

I certainly didn't either. I've removed an amazing array of detritus from the stomachs and intestinal tracts of dogs and cats before. These have included panty hose, tennis balls, diamond rings, fish hooks, coins, socks, baked potatoes still in tinfoil, shoe leather, fishing line, and the odd toy (children's or pet's). But on only a few occasions did they include geologic specimens.

"I think you better bring Buddy in," I said. "Let's just give him a good going-over to make sure everything's okay."

A couple of hours later, Mr. O'Reilly and Buddy dragged into the waiting room. As always, Mr. O'Reilly looked pallid and ashen as he heaved and wheezed into the office. He plunked down into one of the chairs in the waiting room, leaned ponderously on his cane, and breathed heavily as he caught his breath. The color returned slowly to his face. We were used to these entrances from Mr. O'Reilly now, though they still worried us each time.

We were not, however, used to seeing Buddy in this condition. Buddy was a seven-year-old border collie of questionable pedigree who, like everyone in the O'Reilly household, carried too much sheer bulk. In general, despite this familial propensity to corpulence, Buddy had been a healthy patient in the years I had been seeing him. He weighed in at a generous seventy-five or eighty pounds, wore the black-and-white uniform of his breed and was an enthusiastic and ingratiatingly good-natured dog in every respect.

But today, Buddy was definitely not himself. He ambled into the office in a passing imitation of his owner, slow and uncomfortable. His head and tail hung down to about the same level, just off the floor. There was none of the usual exuberance to his greeting when I called his name—just an ambivalent and truncated wiggle to the end of his white-tipped tail. He didn't even raise his head.

In the exam room he grunted painfully when I lifted him onto the table. He looked at me shortly, saliva dripping from his lips from the nausea that was so obvious. I quickly evaluated his status. His heart was rapid and thready; his breaths came in short, guttural pants; his tummy was tight and tense with discomfort. Clearly, Buddy needed help—and fast.

I sent him back to the treatment area with my technician and gave her instructions to collect blood for testing, place an intravenous catheter for fluid administration and get X-rays of his painful belly. Then I turned my attention to Mr. O'Reilly sitting on the corner seat in the exam room, face drawn with concern.

"Buddy looks pretty uncomfortable, Mr. O'Reilly. I'm afraid

he's got an intestinal obstruction that will need immediate attention. The technicians are collecting some more information for me so I'll know for sure, but chances are, he's going to need surgery to get him through this."

"Oh, but Dr. Coston, He's so old already. Do you really think he can stand it?"

"Let's not count him out too soon, Mr. O'Reilly," I responded. "He's only seven now. With good care and some luck, he's got many years left. If you can wait just a few minutes, I'll have results of these tests back and we'll talk about what needs to be done."

As I left Mr. O'Reilly in the exam room, I saw him bow his head. Whether he was just working to calm his nerves and catch his breath or was casting up a prayer for his friend was not obvious. But his anxiety certainly was.

The blood work came back as expected for a dog that had been vomiting repeatedly for a couple of days—some electrolyte abnormalities and evidence of dehydration, but nothing too alarming. When I slipped the X-rays onto the view box, however, I nearly doubled over in pain myself. His stomach and pylorus, the outflow tract of the stomach, were completely packed with hundreds of smallish stones. No wonder Buddy had vomited gravel! It looked as if Mr. O'Reilly's entire driveway had been scooped up, dumped into Buddy's stomach, and tamped down with a ramrod. A few pieces of the gravel had actually made it past the dam of rocks in the pylorus and were strung out in a line within the intestines.

I took the X-rays and went back to the room where I had left Mr. O'Reilly. He was in much the same position as when I left him, head bowed, one hand on his knee and the other leaning heavily on his cane. He didn't look up when I came in.

"You know, Dr. Coston, this is the same room I was in when Cephus was sick. You probably don't remember that, do you?"

I did, very clearly in fact.

"I've been sitting here thinking about that. And I've got the same feeling now that I had then." There was a long pause. "I'm going to lose Buddy too, aren't I?"

"Not if I can help it, Mr. O'Reilly," I responded with grim determination. "Let me show you what we've got here."

I placed the films up on the view box. Mr. O'Reilly raised his head for the first time and looked at them. The rocks were so obviously the problem that even with his uninitiated eye, he made the diagnosis before I could explain. He dropped his head again, placing his forehead on the back of the hand that rested on his cane.

"Oh, dear. Buddy's all blocked up with rocks."

"Yes, he certainly is. And in order to get those out and get his intestines working again, we've got to go in after them."

"Isn't there any other way?"

"No, there isn't."

"That's going to be an expensive treatment, I know. I don't think I'm going to be able to afford it, Dr. Coston. It's just like Cephus all over again." His head shook in resignation.

"It will be expensive, Mr. O'Reilly. But let's worry about that later. The important thing right now is to get those rocks out of him so he can feel better. But before we begin, I need your authorization. Will you let me try?"

"Dr. Coston, you know I want you to help him. But I just don't know how I'll be able to pay for it. Would you let me pay a little bit at a time until it's paid off?"

"I'm sure we can work something out that will work for you, but we just have to get started."

I pushed a clipboard at him with an authorization form. He took it and slowly scrawled his shaky signature on the line at the bottom, handing it back to me with trembling fingers.

"Good. I'm going to get started right away. I'll call you as soon as I'm done," I said over my shoulder as I headed out of the exam room door.

Within just a few minutes I was scrubbed and gowned and stood over the surgery table with scalpel in hand. I made a quick incision in the skin and with a few rapid snips of my scissors had gone through the underlying fat—of which there was plenty—and the muscular body wall. Time was of the essence. I reached into his abdomen and pulled his stomach to the surface. It was like pulling on a bean bag as the rocks bumped and grated against one another in the bulging organ.

I made an incision in the stomach wall and, with a sterile spoon, began to scoop out spoonful after spoonful of gravel from Buddy's stomach. Finally, after what seemed an eternity, I had removed as many of the pebbles as I could from the stomach. But my job was not yet done. Because the stones trailed from the stomach and pylorus down into the small intestine, I had to make three or four incisions into the gastrointestinal tract to remove all the gravel he had ingested. There were even a few stones that had already made it into the colon. Since these were nearly out the back door, they would pose no problem. I left them to find their own way out.

After closing each incision carefully to avoid contamination, I repeatedly flushed the abdominal cavity with warm saline. Then I pulled the edges of the abdominal muscles together with strong sutures and finally closed the skin with a neat row of stitches. Finally, after two and a half hours of tedious operating, I pushed myself away from the table and stretched my tired back muscles.

I had done everything I could for Buddy. Now it was up to him to bounce back from this insult. But I had a good feeling about his odds as I dialed Mr. O'Reilly's number.

"We're all done with surgery, Mr. O'Reilly." I sighed involuntarily.

"You sound tired."

"Well, I am, I guess. But things went very well and I expect Buddy to make a complete recovery. We're not totally out of the woods yet, of course. He was really very sick and he's gone through a major operation; but he's a strong dog and I think he'll come out the other side okay."

"That's great! I'm so happy. I can't thank you enough."

Mr. O'Reilly's voice had indeed lightened noticeably at the news.

"When can I see him?"

"Well, he's pretty much out of it with the anesthetics and the pain medications. And I expect he'll be that way this evening and tonight. But tomorrow he should be brighter and ready for some visitors," I replied optimistically. "It still might take him two or three days before he's ready to come home. He's got a lot of recuperation ahead of him. And we'll just have to take it a day at a time."

"Oh, I know. And I wouldn't want him to come home a minute sooner than he should. Again, Dr. Coston, thank you for all you've done."

I knew in my heart he meant it. I knew it without him saying so. I even knew instinctively the degree of his gratitude, because Mr. O'Reilly is blessed with the Gift. His heart is so large and caring, so soft and filled with devotion for his pets that it is shouted in a thousand little ways each time he comes in—from the unconscious ways he caresses his companions to the attention he pays to my every suggestion; from the financial sacrifices he endures for their care to the pinched-faced apprehension he exhibits when they are ill. Even the overindulgence of their appetites and their unapologetic girth speak of his love for them, though we continue to work on that one. So I knew that my care for his friend was appreciated beyond his ability to express it.

It is, in fact, this knowing, this unspoken and unspeakable cognizance, that is my motivation still, after so many years, to extend, for just a few more golden days or months or years, the time my clients have to spend with their beloved companions.

The next day Mr. O'Reilly came in to visit his friend. He was clearly relieved with Buddy's improvement from the previous day. He sat beside his friend's cage and proffered fingers full of dog food, an offering that Buddy took disinterestedly, more as a favor to Mr. O'Reilly than because he really wanted to eat. Even that was an improvement that pleased us greatly. But there was something about Mr. O'Reilly's demeanor that seemed incongruous with Buddy's steady recuperation. Finally, he took me aside.

"Dr. Coston," he said furtively, "I'm really glad Buddy's feeling better and all. But there's something that's been bothering me since the surgery that I need to discuss with you."

I nodded, thinking I knew what was disturbing him.

"Well, two things, really." He looked from side to side, checking to see that our conversation was not overheard. "I'm pretty sure this is all my fault."

"How's that, Mr. O'Reilly?"

"Well, I've been thinking and thinking about why Buddy would eat gravel from the driveway."

This was a question that had bothered me as well. I nodded my head.

"I figured it out. A few days ago, I poured a bunch of bacon grease from my frying pan out on the driveway gravel to get rid of it."

Realization dawned on me. "Oh, no wonder. I've been trying to figure that out myself. Well, that would explain it then."

"So it's all my fault. I did this to Buddy." Mr. O'Reilly hung his head in shame and remorse.

"Well, yeah, you put the grease out there, but who would have imagined Buddy would think it was the rocks that smelled so good?" I laughed. "No, Mr. O'Reilly, don't beat yourself up over this. Buddy ate the rocks all by himself, you didn't force him to. It's just an honest mistake by both of you. I imagine Buddy is feeling pretty embarrassed by all this too."

This seemed to cheer Mr. O'Reilly up considerably and he chatted for a few minutes about Buddy's confusion and his history of making silly mistakes. Then he stuttered inexplicably again.

"You said there were two things bothering you, Mr. O'Reilly. What is the other one?"

"It's about the bill, Dr. Coston. I know you've saved Buddy's life. I also know it's going to be expensive. You told me we could work something out, but I'm just worried about how I can do it." He looked up at me with concern. "I'm not complaining about the expense, you understand. And as long as you can accept a little at a time, I'll be okay. I just can't afford all of it right now."

"We can work something out, I'm sure," I reassured him. "I don't even have the bill finished yet. Let's worry about that later, okay?"

"It may take me a year or longer, you know," he said.

"It will work out all right," I repeated. "I know it will. Let's just focus on Buddy's recovery now. We'll worry about all that later."

Buddy took a few days to bounce back from his gluttonous affair with the driveway. Age always adds a few extra days of recuperation to a patient, I've learned. But with time, his attitude brightened, his appetite returned, and his step regained its bounce. Four days after surgery, Buddy was ready to go home.

I called Barney Webster and explained the situation to him. Since the inception of the Tracy Webster Memorial Foundation just a few weeks prior, we had been waiting for the perfect case so we could initiate it. Barney was eager to launch the foundation and thought Buddy's case was just the one to be the first patient assisted.

Mr. O'Reilly was sitting on the steps behind the office building, watching Buddy nose around the yard when I approached him. He didn't notice my arrival, his attention was so focused on Buddy's new lease on life.

"Oh, Dr. Coston," he said with excitement. "Look at him. He feels so good now! He's almost back to himself!"

"He sure is. I think he's ready to go home now."

"That's just great! I can hardly believe it. When he came in I never believed he would look this good just a few days later."

"We're really glad he's done so well. He's a fighter!" I turned and looked Mr. O'Reilly in the eye. "Now we need to talk about the bill."

"I know, I know. I promise—"

"Wait a minute and just listen," I interrupted him. "There is a foundation that has been established recently that will provide assistance in cases like Buddy's. They have agreed to help. They're going to pay about three-fourths of the bill. Your portion is just over two hundred dollars."

Mr. O'Reilly's mouth dropped open in astonishment and he said nothing. I hurried on.

"You can take a few months to pay off your portion if you need to. You can work out the details with the office manager."

There was no response from Mr. O'Reilly for quite some time. He looked up at me with a face full of questions, his mouth still hanging open. Finally he stammered haltingly.

"What is this? You mean . . . ? I can't believe it."

Then he lowered his head slowly, putting his forehead on his hands as they rested on his cane. His shoulders began slowly to shake. Then I heard quiet, muffled crying as tears began to sneak down his pale cheeks. Soon he was unashamedly sobbing, heaving his shoulders in an emotional exhibition of unadulterated gratitude. A tight knot was developing in my throat too. The only response I could muster was a choked smile, but tears were welling in my eyes as well. I wished Barney were here.

Inside again, I went right to the phone and called Barney. In great detail I relayed the story of Buddy's recovery and Mr. O'Reilly's grateful response to the assistance the foundation had provided. Between my comments I could occasionally hear a grunt of approval or a chuckle. I left nothing out, finishing with a description of my encounter with Mr. O'Reilly on the stairs with Buddy nosing around, trying to lick the tears from his cheeks.

There was a long silence on the phone, then I heard Barney choke up briefly.

"Thanks for calling," he was able to blurt out finally before hanging up abruptly.

I hung up the phone with a satisfied sigh. In the course of just a few short minutes I had been able to make two elderly men weep like children. I was pleased.

And that was the start to the Tracy Webster Memorial Foundation. A rocky start, to be sure, but one that I will long recall with fond and cherished memories of two old men and one old dog. Every month now new memories are forged, just as poignant and powerful, by the kindness and generosity of Mr. Webster and in proud tribute to Tracy and to Spirit. How fitting that, with the formation of the foundation, Mr. O'Reilly's story had come full circle—from Cephus to Buddy.

Two weeks later Mr. O'Reilly brought Buddy in for his recheck examination. This time, Buddy strained against the leash, pulling Mr. O'Reilly up the handicapped ramp quicker than the elderly gentleman really wanted to go. With a happy face, he eagerly pawed at the door, signaling in no uncertain terms that Mr. O'Reilly was to open it for him. He had made friends here that he was eager to greet again, it was clear.

Mr. O'Reilly too seemed better than usual, not huffing quite so much and with a little more color in his cheeks. In his hand, he carried a little brown, stuffed dog with a large light-colored snout and shaggy eyebrows shading sad, drooping basset hound eyes. When he made his way to the front desk, he set the little dog on the countertop with a grin. It sat there almost glumly on its little fanny, only eight or ten inches in height, its legs thrust forward and off the ground. On its left paw was a small, bright red patch of cloth that said PRESS TO PLAY. I looked up at Mr. O'Reilly, who was beaming like a child with a surprise.

"What's this?" I asked.

"That is Arf Arf," he replied, still smiling broadly. "Press on his hand there." He pointed to the red patch.

I squeezed the little red patch and the dog came alive. Tinny music and children's voices sang out "*How much is that doggie in the window? (arf! arf!) I do hope that doggie's for sale.*" The little dog's shoulders bounced to the rhythm, his head bobbing in time and his whole body swaying and rocking on his little round bottom.

"You gave me my dog back. Buddy's as good as new! Just look at him."

It was true. Buddy looked great, licking excitedly at the faces of the technicians who, having bonded with their patient during his stay, surrounded him like a returning hero. He apparently held no grudge against them for the hardships they had inflicted on him during his hospitalization.

"So I'm giving you a dog too. That's Arf Arf."

Mr. O'Reilly laughed and again squeezed the red patch, nodding his head in time to the tune and singing along with the words. When the rendition finished, he laughed again.

"I've always been a sucker for that song. Many's the time I've brought a dog home that needed some good old TLC. If it hadn't been for the tender loving care you all gave Buddy here two weeks ago, I wouldn't have brought him home again. So how much is that Buddy in the window?" He laughed quietly again as he looked down at him fondly. "More than I can afford, I assure you. But worth every single penny!"

Arf Arf sits beside me on a shelf by my desk even now as I write this. I have, in fact, pressed the little red patch several times as I write to spark my muses. It's been a few years now since Buddy's encounter with the rocks. In fact, Buddy's gone now, resting peacefully beside his friend, Cephus. But he lives on in my memory as just one of the many times I've been blessed with the opportunity to intervene between my patients and eternity, to steal from fate just a little more precious time.

My mind reviewed these memories as I absently press the red patch on Arf Arf's left paw. The song rings out again: *"How much is that doggie in the window? (arf! arf!) I do hope that doggie's for sale."* How much indeed! Not very much, really, for all that pets give in return. Not just dogs, of course, but all my patients of every persuasion from cats to ferrets and birds and rabbits. All of them I've observed to be invaluable companions and irreplaceable friends. Whatever the sum, it's certainly a small price to pay for years of undeserved allegiance and utter devotion from a confidant who understands every nuance of emotion and is always there with uncompromising loyalty and encouragement. Worth every penny as Buddy's dad would say.

And so they are, Mr. O'Reilly. So they are.